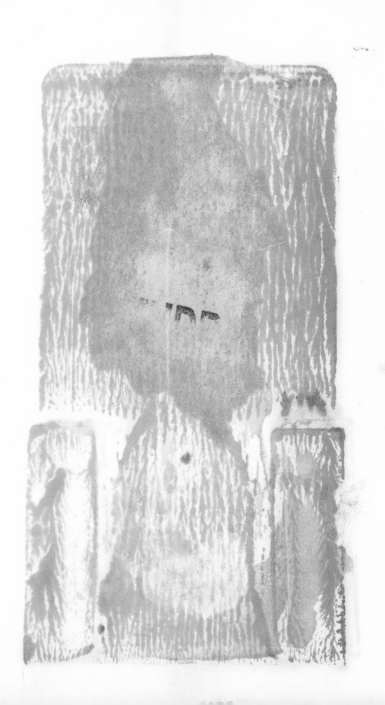

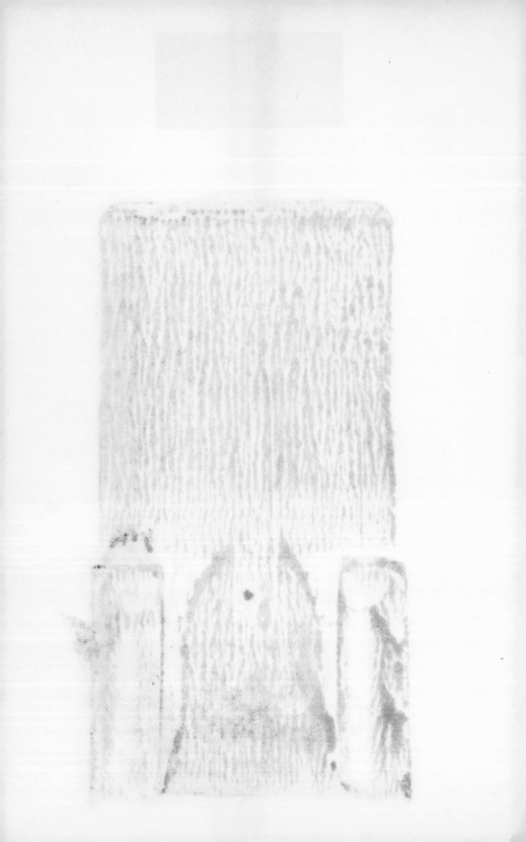

# THE BIAS OF
# COMMUNICATION

# HAROLD A. INNIS

# THE BIAS OF COMMUNICATION

*Introduction by*
*MARSHALL McLUHAN*

UNIVERSITY OF TORONTO PRESS

To

G. S. G.

J. B. B.

M. G.

# CONTENTS

# INTRODUCTION
## Marshall McLuhan

For anyone acquainted with poetry since Baudelaire and with painting since Cézanne, the later world of Harold A. Innis is quite readily intelligible. He brought their kinds of contemporary awareness of the electric age to organize the data of the historian and the social scientist. Without having studied modern art and poetry, he yet discovered how to arrange his insights in patterns that nearly resemble the art forms of our time. Innis presents his insights in a mosaic structure of seemingly unrelated and disproportioned sentences and aphorisms. Such is page 108, for example, with its scholarly footnote that will certainly bear looking into. Anybody who has looked up the reference material that Innis cites so frequently, will be struck by the skill with which he has extracted exciting facts from dull expositions. He explored his source material with a "geiger counter," as it were. In turn, he presents his finds in a pattern of insights that are not packaged for the consumer palate. He expects the reader to make discovery after discovery that he himself had missed. His view of the departmentalized specialisms of our Universities as ignoble monopolies of knowledge is expressed on page 194: "Finally we must keep in mind the limited role of Universities and recall the comment that 'the whole external history of science is a history of the resistance of academies and Universities to the progress of knowledge.' "

One can say of Innis what Bertrand Russell said of Einstein on the first page of his *A B C of Relativity* (1925): "Many of the new ideas can be expressed in non-mathematical language, but they are none the less difficult on that account. What is demanded is a change in our imaginative picture of the world." The "later Innis" who dominates *The Bias of Communication* had set out on a quest for the causes of change. The "early Innis" of *The Fur Trade in Canada* had conformed a good deal to the conventional patterns of merely reporting and narrating change. Only at the conclusion of the fur trade study did he venture to interlace or link complex events in a way that reveals the causal processes of change. His insight that the American Revolution was in large part due to a clash between the interests of the settlers on one hand and the interests of the fur traders on the other is the sort of vision that becomes typical of the later Innis. He changed his procedure from working with a "point of view" to that of the generating of insights by the method of "interface," as it is named in chemistry. "Interface" refers to the interaction of substances in a kind of mutual irritation. In art and poetry this is precisely the technique of "symbolism" (Greek "symballein"—to throw together) with its paratactic procedure of juxtaposing without connectives. It is the natural form of conversation or dialogue rather than of written discourse. In writing, the tendency is to isolate an aspect of some matter and to direct steady attention upon that aspect. In dialogue there is an equally natural interplay of multiple aspects of any matter. This interplay of aspects can generate insights or discovery. By contrast, a point of view is merely a way of *looking at* something. But an insight is the sudden awareness of a complex process of interaction. An insight is a contact with the life of forms. Students of computer programming have had to learn how to approach all knowledge structurally. In order to transfer any kind of knowledge to tapes it is necessary to understand the form of that knowledge. This has led to the discovery of the basic difference between classified knowledge and pattern recognition. It is a helpful distinction to keep in mind when reading Innis since he is above all a recognizer of patterns. Dr. Kenneth Sayre explains the matter as follows in his *The Modelling of Mind* (University of Notre Dame Press, 1963), p. 17: "Classification is a *process,* something which takes up one's time, which one might do reluctantly, unwillingly, or enthusiastically, which can be done with more or less success, done very well or very poorly. Recognition, in sharp contrast, is not time-consuming. A person may spend a long while looking before recognition occurs, but when it occurs it is "instantaneous." When recognition occurs, it is not an act which would be said to be performed either reluctantly or enthusiastically, compliantly or under protest. Moreover, the notion of recognition being unsuccessful, or having been done very poorly, seems to make no sense at all."

In this book Innis has much to say about the oral as opposed to the written methods of approaching the learning process. In the paper titled "A Critical Review" he explains: "My bias is with the oral tradition, particularly as reflected in Greek civilization, and with the necessity of recapturing something of its spirit." (p. 190) E. A. Havelock, a former colleague of Innis, has recently devoted an entire study to the clash of the old oral and the new written culture of Greece. His *Preface to Plato* (Harvard, 1963) would have delighted Innis, and there are very many sentences in Innis which should become the subject of such full investigations.

I am pleased to think of my own book *The Gutenberg Galaxy* (University of Toronto Press, 1962) as a footnote to the observations of Innis on the subject of the psychic and social consequences, first of writing and then of printing. Flattered by the attention that Innis had directed to some work of mine, I turned for the first time to his work. It was my good fortune to begin with the first essay in this book: "Minerva's Owl." How exciting it was to encounter a writer whose every phrase invited prolonged meditation and exploration: "Alexandria broke the link between science and philosophy. The library was an imperial instrument to offset the influence of Egyptian priesthood." (p. 10)

Innis takes much time to read if he is read on his own terms. That he deserves to be read on his own terms becomes obvious as soon as that experiment is tried even once. So read, he takes time but he also saves time. Each sentence is a compressed monograph. He includes a small library on each page, and often incorporates a small library of references on the same page in addition. If the business of the teacher is to save the student's time, Innis is one of the greatest teachers on record. The two sentences just quoted imply and invite an awareness of the specific structural forms of science and philosophy as well as of the structural nature and functions of empires, libraries, and priesthoods. Most writers are occupied in providing accounts of the contents of philosophy, science, libraries, empires, and religions. Innis invites us instead to consider the formalities of power exerted by these structures in their mutual interaction. He approaches each of these forms of organized power as exercising a particular kind of force upon each of the other components in the complex. All of the components exist by virtue of processes going on within each and among them all. Just what "science" or "philosophy" was at this time will be manifested by what each does to the other in their encounter in the social and historic process. And so with the other components. They explain themselves by their behaviour in a historic action. Innis had hit upon the means of using history as the physicist uses the cloud chamber. By bouncing the unknown form against known forms, he discovered the nature of the new or little known form.

This use of history as a scientific laboratory, as a set of controlled conditions within which to study the life and nature of forms, is very far removed from the conventional narrative of a Toynbee. Toynbee is like the announcer of a sporting event. He tells a good deal about what is happening. His tone of earnest concern indicates to the reader or listener that the events have some significance. In the same situation Innis would have observed that the form of the sporting event was an interesting model of perception, giving us an immediate image of the motives and patterns of the society that had invented this corporate extension of itself. He would then explain that his role of announcer, like that of the audience at the sporting event, was part of the structure of the game, having a distorting bias of perception and amplification that gave the game in question a great deal of political and commercial force.

As soon as the reader grasps that Innis is concerned with the unique power of each form to alter the action of other forms it encounters, he will be able to proceed as Innis did. He can begin to observe and estimate the action and counteraction of forms past and present. He will discover that Innis never repeats himself, but that he never ceases to test the action of oral forms of knowledge and social organization in different social contexts. Innis tests the oral form as it reacts in many different written cultures, just as he tests the effects of time-structured institutions in their varieties of contact with space-oriented societies.

It would be a mistake to suppose that Innis has garnered most of the available insights from any given historical test that he happens to run. In the same way, he is quite capable of inaccurate observation during the running of his tests of the interactions of social forms, though this in no way impairs the validity of his way of testing the structural properties of social forms. For example, he notes that: "The Greeks took over the alphabet and made it a flexible instrument suited to the demands of a flexible oral tradition by the creation of words." (p. 7) The alphabet is a technology of visual fragmentation and specialism, and it led the Greeks quickly to the discovery of classifiable data. Havelock clarifies this at length in his *Preface to Plato.* As long as the oral culture was not overpowered by the technological extension of the visual power in the alphabet, there was a very rich cultural result from the interplay of the oral and written forms. The revival of oral culture in our own electric age now exists in a similar fecund relation with the still powerful written and visual culture. We are in our century "winding the tape backwards." The Greeks went from oral to written even as we are moving from written to oral. They "ended" in a desert of classified data even as we could "end" in a new tribal encyclopedia of auditory incantation.

Innis sometimes mistook the interplay of written and oral forms, ascribing to the written form itself what was a hybrid product of its interaction with oral culture: "The alphabet borrowed from the Phoenicians was given vowels and adapted to the demands of speech. The ear replaced the eye. With the spread of writing the oral tradition developed fresh powers of resistance evident in the flowering of Greek culture in the sixth and fifth centuries." (p. 136) Had Innis made a more intense analysis of the visual modalities inherent in the phonetic alphabet, or a more thorough study of the dynamics of oral forms, he would have avoided some of these slips. But the method he discovered remains. He had discovered a means of using historical situations as a lab in which to test the character of technology in the shaping of cultures.

Innis taught us how to use the bias of culture and communication as an instrument of research. By directing attention to the bias or distorting power of the dominant imagery and technology of any culture, he showed us how to understand cultures. Many scholars had made us aware of the "difficulty of assessing the quality of a culture of which we are a part or of assessing the quality of a culture of which we are not a part." (p. 132) Innis was perhaps the first to make of this vulnerable fact of all scholarly outlook the prime opportunity for research and discovery. Peter F. Drucker in *Managing For Results* (Harper and Row, 1964) has shown how in any human organization or situation 90 per cent of the events are caused by 10 per cent. Most human attention is allocated to the 90 per cent area which is the area of problems. The 10 per cent area is the area of irritation and also of opportunity. It was the genius of Harold Innis that refused to be distracted by the 90 per cent area of problems. He went straight to the 10 per cent core of opportunity and sought insight into the causes that underlay the whole situation. For example, he writes: "We are perhaps too much a part of the civilization which followed the printing industry to be able to detect its characteristics. Education in the words of Laski became the art of teaching men to be deceived by the printed word." (p. 139)

Once Innis had ascertained the dominant technology of a culture he could be sure that this was the cause and shaping force of the entire structure. He could also be sure that this dominant form and all its causal powers were necessarily masked from the attention of that culture by a psychic mechanism of "protective inhibition" as it were. At a stroke he had solved two major problems that are forever beyond the power of the "nose-counters" and of statistical researchers. First, he knew what the pattern of any culture had to be, both psychically and socially, as soon as he had identified its major technological achievements. Second, he knew exactly what the members of that culture would be ignorant of in their daily lives. What has been called "the nemesis of creativity" is precisely a blindness to the effects of one's most significant form of invention.

A good example of this technological blindness in Innis himself was his mistake in regarding radio and electric technology as a further extension of the patterns of mechanical technology: "The radio appealed to vast areas, overcame the division between classes in its escape from literacy, and favoured centralization and bureaucracy." (p. 82) Again: "Competition from the new medium, the radio involved an appeal to the ear rather than to the eye and consequently an emphasis on centralization." (p. 188) This is an example of Innis failing to be true to his own method. After many historical demonstrations of the space-binding power of the eye and the time-binding power of the ear, Innis refrains from applying these structural principles to the action of radio. Suddenly, he shifts the ear world of radio into the visual orbit, attributing to radio all the centralizing powers of the eye and of visual culture. Here Innis was misled by the ordinary consensus of his time. Electric light and power, like all electric media, are profoundly decentralizing and separatist in their psychic and social consequences. Had he not been hypnotized by his respect for the pervasive conventional view on this question, Innis could have worked out the new electric pattern of culture quite easily.

What is rare in Innis occurs in his mention of the views of Wyndham Lewis: "Wyndham Lewis has argued that the fashionable mind is the time-denying mind." He is referring to *Time and Western Man* which is devoted to a denunciation of the obsession with time as a religious mystique in the work of Bergson, Alexander, Whitehead, and others. Because of his own deep concern with the values of tradition and temporal continuity, Innis has managed to misread Wyndham Lewis radically. Earlier, in the same essay, "A Plea for Time," he raises an issue that may bear on the occasional miscarriage of his own structural method of analysis. Speaking of the unfortunate effects of the extreme development of print development on our twentieth century culture, he observes: "Communication based on the eye in terms of printing and photography had developed a monopoly which threatened to destroy Western civilization first in war and then in peace." (p. 80) Innis did not like monopolies in any form. He saw that they bred violent reactions: "The disastrous effect of the monopoly of communication based on the eye hastened the development of a competitive type of communication based on the ear, in the radio and in the linking of sound to the cinema and to television. Printed material gave way in effectiveness to the broadcast and to the loud speaker." (p. 81) What Innis has failed to do in this part of his essay is to make a structural analysis of the modalities of the visual and the audible. He is merely assuming that an extension of information in space has a centralizing power regardless of the human faculty that is amplified and extended. But whereas the visual power extended by print does indeed extend the means to organize a spatial continuum, the auditory power extended electrically does in effect abolish space and time alike. Visual technology creates a centre-margin pattern of organization whether by literacy or by industry and a price system. But electric technology is instant and omnipresent and creates multiple centres-without-margins. Visual technology whether by literacy or by industry creates nations as spatially uniform and homogeneous and connected. But electric technology creates not the nation but the tribe—not the superficial association of equals but the cohesive depth pattern of the totally involved kinship groups. Visual technologies, whether based on papyrus or paper, foster fragmentation and specialism, armies, and empires. Electric technology favours not the fragmentary but the integral, not the mechanical but the organic. It had not occurred to Innis that electricity is in effect an extension of the nervous system as a kind of global membrane. As an economic historian he had such a rich experience of the technological extensions of the bodily powers that it is not surprising that he failed to note the character of this most recent and surprising of human extensions.

There is one department in which Innis never fails, and in which the flavour of Inniscence is never lost—his humour. Humour is of the essence of his aphoristic association of incongruities. His technique of discovery by the juxtaposition of forms lends itself everywhere to a series of dramatic surprises. On page 77 in the midst of considering the revolt of the American colonies and nineteenth century wars he suddenly observes a parallel with the press wars of Hearst and Pulitzer as related to the emergence of the comic strip. He is unrivalled in his power to discover choice items in contemporary history to illuminate grave matters of archaeology. Referring to the neglect of the horse as a factor in military history, he recalls that "E. J. Dillon remarked concerning a mounted policeman that he was always surprised by the look of intelligence on the horse's face." (p. 95) The mosaic structure of insights employed in the work of the later Innis is never far removed from the comic irony of an Abraham Lincoln. Innis found that his technique of insight engendered a perpetual entertainment of surprises and of intellectual comedy.

To record the intellectual influences that shaped the work of Innis would be a large, if rewarding, task. His studies at the University of Chicago after the First World War occurred at a most favourable time. The work of Emile Durkheim, Max Weber, and John Dewey had fecundated a new group of economic and social studies that flowered in the writings of Thorstein Veblen, George Herbert Mead, and Robert Ezra Park. These men created an atmosphere at Chicago in the 1920's that attracted and inspired many able students. Most of these men had, like Innis, spent their youth in small towns. The speedy growth of the metropolis after the first war presented an inexhaustible subject for these sociologists, and much of their work was directed to urban study and analysis, using the small town as a basis for comparison and contrast. Innis tended to follow another pattern, though, as we shall see, he was deeply in debt to Robert Ezra Park. Durkheim, the late nineteenth century founder of analytic sociology, dealt with whole populations. The Chicago school dealt with local communities. Innis is European rather than American in his choice of the larger themes. From Park, however, he learned how to identify the control mechanisms by which a heterogeneous community yet manages to arrange its affairs with some degree of uniformity. Perhaps Innis was aided in this choice by his familiarity with the staple economy of Canada. A semi-industrialized country, rich in major resources like wheat, lumber, minerals, fur, fish, and wood pulp has a peculiar economic and social life compared to a more diversified and developed economy. Innis seized the opportunity to deal with this unique pattern of a staple economy and was not led to follow the popular pattern of urban studies that was being pursued by the exciting and productive Chicago group. I suggest that Innis made the further transition from the history of staples to the history of the media of communication quite naturally. Media are major resources like economic staples. In fact, without railways, the staples of wheat and lumber can scarcely be said to exist. Without the press and the magazine, wood pulp could not exist as a staple either.

In May, 1940, the *Canadian Journal of Economics and Political Science* published an article by Robert Park entitled "Physics and Society" (reprinted in *Society* by Robert Ezra Park (Free Press of Glencoe, 1955), pp. 301–21). Park began by citing Walter Bagehot to the effect that society is a social organism maintained by a social process. The theme of his essay is recapitulated this way: "I have gone into some detail in my description of the role and function of communication because it is so obviously fundamental to the social process, and because extensions and improvements which the physical sciences have made to the means of communications are so vital to the existence of society and particularly to that more rationally organized form of society we call civilization." (*Society*, p. 314)

The ideas of Park seem to have appealed more to the mind of Harold Innis than to any other student of Robert Park. Anybody can hear the Innis note in such observations by Park as the following: "Technological devices have naturally changed men's habits and in doing so, they have necessarily modified the structure and functions of society." (p. 308) Again: "From this point of view it seems that every technical device, from the wheelbarrow to the aeroplane, in so far as it provided a new and more effective means of locomotion, has, or should have, marked an epoch in society. This is so far true as most other important changes in the means of transportation and communication. It is said likewise that every civilization carries in itself the seeds of its own destruction. Such seeds are likely to be the technical devices that introduce a new social order and usher out an old." (*Society*, pp. 309–10) In the same year as his "Physics and Society" article, Park published "News as a Form of Knowledge": "I have indicated the role which news plays in the world of politics in so far as it provides the basis for the discussions in which public opinion is formed. The news plays quite as important a role in the world of economic relations, since the price of commodities, including money and securities, as registered in the world market and in every local market dependent upon it, is based on the news." (p. 86)

These ideas were not lost on Harold Innis. Indeed, Innis developed them much further than Park did, and should be considered as the most eminent of the Chicago group headed by Robert Park.

# PREFACE

THIS volume includes revisions of papers published elsewhere. They are brought together for purposes of accessibility and to support in more detailed fashion the thesis developed in *Empire and Communications* (Oxford, 1950). In a sense they are an attempt to answer an essay question in psychology which the late James Ten Broeke, Professor of Philosophy in McMaster University, was accustomed to set, "Why do we attend to the things to which we attend?" They do not answer the question but are reflections stimulated by a consideration of it. They emphasize the importance of communication in determining "things to which we attend" and suggest also that changes in communication will follow changes in "the things to which we attend."

It is assumed that history is not a seamless web but rather a web of which the warp and the woof are space and time woven in a very uneven fashion and producing distorted patterns. With the bias of an economist I may have extended the theory of monopoly to undue limits, but it is a part of the task of the social scientist to test the limits of his tools and to indicate their possibilities, particularly at a period when he is tempted to discard them entirely. Similarly an extension of cyclical theory may seem to have been carried too far but the neglect of the field of communication in studies of cycles warranted a consideration of the extent to which monopolies of knowledge collapse and extraneous material is lost, to be followed by the prospect of an emphasis on a fresh medium of communication and on a fresh approach. Moreover, the papers are concerned primarily with the political approach and reflect an Anglo-Saxon obsession. They are restricted to consideration of two dimensions of political organizations, on the one hand the length of time over which the organization persists, and on the other hand the territorial space brought within its control, and are perhaps in themselves a product of the instability which they attempt to describe as characteristic of a period in which time has been torn into fragments. At best they are an attempt to enhance an awareness of the disaster which may follow a belief in the obvious. The letter killeth and the concern has been with the diverse means by which different types of letters bring about their deadly results.

Papers have appeared in the *Canadian Journal of Economics and Political Science,* the *Proceedings* of the Royal Society of Canada, the *Manitoba Arts Review* and the *Proceedings* of the Sixth Conference of the Universities of the British Commonwealth, 1948, to all of which I express my indebtedness and my gratitude. The University of New Brunswick printed one of the papers, presented on the occasion of its hundred and fiftieth anniversary, and has been good enough to permit its republication. I should like also to thank the editorial staff of the University of Toronto Press and in particular Miss Francess Halpenny for her relentless interest in accuracy in details. They cannot be held responsible for "faults escaped." It would be ungracious to omit a reference to the members of the staff of the Library of the University of Toronto, nor must I forget because it is so easy to take them for granted, the teaching staff of the University and in particular of the Department of Political Economy. I must avoid tedious references to numerous others who have assisted in many ways but I cannot refrain from mentioning Mr. A. A. Shea.

H. A. I.

# THE BIAS OF
# COMMUNICATION

# MINERVA'S OWL[1]

"MINERVA'S OWL begins its flight only in the gathering dusk . . ."
Hegel wrote in reference to the crystallization of culture achieved in
major classical writings in the period that saw the decline and fall
of Grecian civilization. The richness of that culture, its uniqueness,
and its influence on the history of the West suggest that the flight
began not only for the dusk of Grecian civilization but also for the
civilization of the West.

I have attempted to suggest that Western civilization has been
profoundly influenced by communication and that marked changes
in communications have had important implications. Briefly this
address is divided into the following periods in relation to media of
communication: clay, the stylus, and cuneiform script from the
beginnings of civilization in Mesopotamia; papyrus, the brush, and
hieroglyphics and hieratic to the Graeco-Roman period, and the
reed pen and the alphabet to the retreat of the Empire from the
west; parchment and the pen to the tenth century or the dark ages;
and overlapping with paper, the latter becoming more important
with the invention of printing; paper and the brush in China, and
paper and the pen in Europe before the invention of printing or the
Renaissance; paper and the printing press under handicraft methods
to the beginning of the nineteenth century, or from the Reformation
to the French Revolution; paper produced by machinery and the
application of power to the printing press since the beginning of the
nineteenth century to paper manufactured from wood in the second
half of the century; celluloid in the growth of the cinema; and finally
the radio in the second quarter of the present century. In each
period I have attempted to trace the implications of the media of
communication for the character of knowledge and to suggest that a

[1]Presidential Address to the Royal Society of Canada, 1947.

monopoly or an oligopoly of knowledge is built up to the point that equilibrium is disturbed.

An oral tradition[2] implies freshness and elasticity but students of anthropology have pointed to the binding character of custom in primitive cultures. A complex system of writing becomes the possession of a special class and tends to support aristocracies. A simple flexible system of writing admits of adaptation to the vernacular but slowness of adaptation facilitates monopolies of knowledge and hierarchies. Reading in contrast with writing implies a passive recognition of the power of writing. Inventions in communication compel realignments in the monopoly or the oligopoly of knowledge. A monopoly of knowledge incidental to specialized skill in writing which weakens contact with the vernacular will eventually be broken down by force. In the words of Hume: "As force is always on the side of the governed, the governors have nothing to support them but opinion. It is, therefore, on opinion that government is founded; and this maxim extends to the most despotic and the most military governments as well as to the most free and most popular." The relation of monopolies of knowledge to organized force is evident in the political and military histories of civilization. An interest in learning assumes a stable society in which organized force is sufficiently powerful to provide sustained protection. Concentration on learning implies a written tradition and introduces monopolistic elements in culture which are followed by rigidities and involve lack of contact with the oral tradition and the vernacular. "Perhaps in a very real sense, a great institution is the tomb of the founder." "Most organizations appear as bodies founded for the painless extinction of ideas of the founders." "To the founder of a school, everything may be forgiven, except his school."[3] This change is accompanied by a weakening of the relations between organized force and the vernacular and collapse in the face of technological change which has taken place in marginal regions which have escaped the influence of a monopoly of knowledge. On the capture of Athens by the Goths in 267 A.D. they are reported to have said, "Let us leave the Greeks these books for they make them so effeminate and unwarlike."

[2]"Communications and Archaeology," *Canadian Journal of Economics and Political Science,* XVII, May, 1951, 237-40.
[3]Albert Guérard, *Literature and Society* (Boston, 1935), p. 286.

With a weakening of protection of organized force, scholars put forth greater efforts and in a sense the flowering of the culture comes before its collapse. Minerva's owl begins its flight in the gathering dusk not only from classical Greece but in turn from Alexandria, from Rome, from Constantinople, from the republican cities of Italy, from France, from Holland, and from Germany. It has been said of the Byzantine Empire that "on the eve of her definite ruin, all Hellas was reassembling her intellectual energy to throw a last splendid glow."[4] ". . . the perishing Empire of the fourteenth and fifteenth centuries, especially the city of Constantinople, was a centre of ardent culture, both intellectual and artistic."[5] In the regions to which Minerva's owl takes flight the success of organized force may permit a new enthusiasm and an intense flowering of culture incidental to the migration of scholars engaged in Herculean efforts in a declining civilization to a new area with possibilities of protection. The success of organized force is dependent on an effective combination of the oral tradition and the vernacular in public opinion with technology and science. An organized public opinion following the success of force becomes receptive to cultural importation.

Burckhardt has stated: "It may be, too, that those great works of art had to perish in order that later art might create in freedom. For instance, if, in the fifteenth century, vast numbers of well-preserved Greek sculptures and paintings had been discovered, Leonardo, Raphael, Titian and Correggio would not have done their work, while they could, in their own way, sustain the comparison with what had been inherited from Rome. And if, after the middle of the eighteenth century, in the enthusiastic revival of philological and antiquarian studies, the lost Greek lyric poets had suddenly been rediscovered, they might well have blighted the full flowering of German poetry. It is true that, after some decades, the mass of rediscovered ancient poetry would have become assimilated with it, but the decisive moment of bloom, which never returns in its full prime, would have been irretrievably past. But enough had survived in the fifteenth century for art, and in the eighteenth for poetry, to be

[4]Cited by A. A. Vasiliev, *History of the Byzantine Empire,* II, "University of Wisconsin Studies in the Social Sciences and History," no. 14 (Madison, 1929), p. 401.
[5]*Ibid,* p. 400.

stimulated and not stifled."[6] David Hume wrote that "when the arts and sciences come to perfection in any state, from that moment they naturally, or rather necessarily decline, and seldom or never revive in that nation, where they formerly flourished. . . . Perhaps it may not be for the advantage of any nation to have the arts imported from their neighbours in too great perfection. This extinguishes emulation and sinks the ardour of the generous youth."[7]

Dependence on clay in the valleys of the Euphrates and the Tigris involved a special technique in writing and a special type of instrument, the reed stylus. Cuneiform writing on clay involved an elaborate skill, intensive training, and concentration of durable records. The temples with their priesthoods became the centres of cities. Invasions of force based on new techniques chiefly centring around the horse, first in the chariot and later in cavalry, brought the union of city states, but a culture based on intensive training in writing rendered centralized control unstable and gave organized religion an enormous influence. Law emerged to restrain the influence of force and of religion. The influence of religion in the Babylonian and Assyrian empires was evident also in the development of astronomy, astrology, and a belief in fate, in the seven-day week, and in our sexagesimal time system. Successful imperial organization came with the dominance of force represented by the Pharaoh in Egypt though the Egyptian Empire depended on cuneiform for its communications. It was followed by the Assyrian, the Persian, the Alexandrian, and the Roman empires.

While political organization of oriental empires followed the Egyptian model, religious organization was powerfully influenced by Babylonia as was evident in the traditions of the Hebrews in the marginal territory of Palestine. With access to more convenient media such as parchment and papyrus and to a more efficient alphabet the Hebrew prophets gave a stimulus to the oral and the written tradition which persisted in the scriptures, the Jewish, Christian, and Mohammedan religions. Written scriptures assumed greater accessibility and escaped from the burdens of the temples of Babylonian and Assyrian empires.

[6]Jacob Burckhardt, *Force and Freedom* (New York, 1943), pp. 368-9.
[7]David Hume, *Essays, Moral, Political and Literary*, ed. T. H. Green and T. H. Grose (London, 1875), I, 195-6.

The Egyptians with an abundance of papyrus and the use of the brush had worked out an elaborate system of writing and the Babylonians with dependence on clay and the stylus had developed an economical system of writing. Semitic peoples borrowed the Sumerian system of writing but retained their language and in turn improved the system of writing through contacts with the Egyptians. The Phoenicians as a marginal Semitic people with an interest in communication and trade on the Mediterranean improved the alphabet to the point that separate consonants were isolated in relation to sounds. The Greeks took over the alphabet and made it a flexible instrument suited to the demands of a flexible oral tradition by the creation of words. The flowering of the oral tradition was seen in provision for public recitations in the Panathenaea of the *Iliad* and the *Odyssey* and in the birth of tragedy after 500 B.C.

An intense and sustained interest in Greek civilization by a wide range of scholars has pointed to numerous factors leading to its cultural flowering. Ionian culture reflected the contact of a vigorous race with the earlier rich Minoan civilization and the emergence of a potent oral tradition. This tradition absorbed and improved the instruments of a written tradition built up on the opposite side of the Mediterranean. Toynbee has emphasized the limitations of migration across bodies of water and the significance of those limitations to cultural borrowing.

In the written tradition the improved alphabet made possible the expression of fine distinctions and light shades of meaning. Opening of Egyptian ports to the Greeks in 670 B.C. and establishment of Naucratis about 650 B.C. made papyrus more accessible. The burst of Greek lyric poetry in the seventh century has been attributed to the spread of cheap papyrus. Werner Jaeger has shown the significance of prose to law and the city state. The flexibility of law shown in the major reforms centring around the names of Draco, Solon, and Cleisthenes was possible before a written tradition had become firmly entrenched. Written codes not only implied uniformity, justice, and a belief in laws but also an element of rigidity and necessity for revolution and drastic change. No effective device was developed to facilitate the constant shifting power and as in present-day Russia ostracism was essential. Laws weakened the interest in punishment in another world for those who escaped justice in this. Solon reflected the demands of an oral tradition for flexibility by providing for the constitution of judicial courts from the people, and Cleisthenes gave the whole body of citizens a decisive part in the conduct of human affairs. Political science became the highest of the practical sciences. Political freedom was accompanied by economical freedom particularly with the spread in the use of coins after 700 B.C. To quote Mirabeau: "The two greatest inventions of the human mind are writing and money—the common language of intelligence and the common language of self-interest."

Encroachment from the centralized empires of the east through the Persians led to the flight of Ionians, who had inherited to the fullest degree the legacies of earlier civilizations, from Miletus, and to an interest in science and philosophy in Athens. Ionians developed the great idea of the universal rule of law, separated science from theology, and rescued Greece from the tyranny of religion. The self was detached from the external object. With this came limitations reinforced by an interest in music and geometry which implied concern with form and measure, proportion and number in which relations between things in themselves were neglected. But in spite of this neglect an appeal to atomism and science had been made and through this Europeans worked themselves out of the formal patterns of the Orient. The Ionian alphabet was adopted in Athens in 404-3 B.C. suggesting the demands of the city for greater standardization in writing. Prose was brought to perfection by the middle of the fourth century and Plato sponsored its supremacy by ruling out the poets and by his own writing. When Athens became the centre of the federation in 454 B.C. the way was opened to greater flexibility in law notably through the contributions of orators to the improvement of prose from 420 to 320 B.C. By 430 a reading public had emerged in Athens and Herodotus turned his recitations into book form. The spread of writing checked the growth of myth and made the Greeks sceptical of their gods. Hecataeus of Miletus could say, "I write as I deem true, for the traditions of the Greeks seem to me manifold and laughable" and Xenophanes that "if horses or oxen had heads and could draw or make statues, horses would represent forms of the gods like horses, oxen like oxen." Rapid expansion in the variety and volume of secular literature became a check to organized priesthood and ritual.

Socrates protested against the materialistic drift of physical science and shifted from a search for beginnings to a search for ends. Concentrating on human life he discovered the soul. Absolute autocracy of the soul implied self-rule. Virtue is knowledge. "No one errs willingly." After the fall of Athens and the death of Socrates, Plato turned from the state. Socrates had been profoundly influenced by the advance of medical science but Plato gave little attention to experimental science. Collapse of the city state and of religion attached to the city state was followed by conscious individualism. The results were evident in complexity, diversity, and perfection in a wide range of cultural achievements. The significance of the oral tradition was shown in the position of the assembly, the rise of democracy, the drama, the dialogues of Plato, and the speeches including the funeral speech of Pericles in the writings of Thucydides. Hegel wrote regarding Pericles: "Of all that is great for humanity the greatest thing is to dominate the wills of men who have wills of their own." The Greeks produced the one entirely original literature of Europe. The epic and the lyric supported the drama. Democracy brought the comedy of Aristophanes. Poetics and the drama had a collective purgative effect on society but with decline of the stage, oratory and rhetoric reflected the influence of an individual.

The oral tradition emphasized memory and training. We have no history of conversation or of the oral tradition except as they are revealed darkly through the written or the printed word. The drama reflected the power of the oral tradition but its flowering for only a short period in Greece and in England illustrates its difficulties. A simplified and flexible alphabet and the spread of writing and reading emphasized logic and consequently general agreement. The spread of writing widened the base by which the screening of ability could take place. The feudal hierarchy of Greece was weakened by an emphasis on writing which became a type of intelligence test. A writing age was essentially an egoistic age. Absorption of energies in mastering the technique of writing left little possibility for considering implications of the technique.

Richness of the oral tradition made for a flexible civilization but not a civilization which could be disciplined to the point of effective political unity. The city state proved inadequate in the field of international affairs. Consequently it yielded to force in the hands of the Macedonians though the genius of Greek civilization was again evident in the masterly conquests of Alexander. The heavy infantry of Greece and the navy were no match for the light infantry and cavalry which struck from the rear. The first of the great sledgehammer blows of technology in which force and the vernacular hammered monopolies of knowledge into malleable form had been delivered. The Alexandrian Empire and the Hellenistic kingdoms favoured the organization of Alexandria as the cultural centre of the Mediterranean.

Aristotle bridged the gap between the city state and the Alexandrian Empire. He rejected the dualism of Plato and affirmed the absolute monarchy of the mind. He marked the change "from the oral instruction to the habit of reading." The immortal inconclusiveness of Plato was no longer possible with the emphasis on writing. It has been said that taught law is tough law; so taught philosophy is tough philosophy. The mixture of the oral and the written traditions in the writings of Plato enabled him to dominate the history of the West. Aristotle's interest in aesthetics reflected a change which brought the dilettante, taste, respectability, collectomania, and large libraries. As an imperial centre Alexandria emphasized the written tradition in libraries and museums. The scholar became concerned with the conservation and clarification of the treasures of a civilization which had passed. Minerva's owl was in full flight. Other imperial centres such as Pergamum (197-159 B.C.) became rivals in the development of libraries and in the use of parchment rather than papyrus. The period had arrived when a great book was regarded as a great evil. Books were written for those who had read all existing books and were scarcely intelligible to those who had not. Literature was divorced from life. In the words of Gilbert Murray, Homer in the Alexandrian period came under "the fatal glamour of false knowledge diffused by the printed text." Alexandria broke the link between science and philosophy. The library was an imperial instrument to offset the influence of Egyptian priesthood. Greek advances in mathematics were consolidated and the work of Aristotle as the great biologist extended.

Writing with a simplified alphabet checked the power of custom of an oral tradition but implied a decline in the power of expression and the creation of grooves which determined the channels of thought of readers and later writers. The cumbersome character of the papyrus roll and its lack of durability facilitated revision and restricted the influence of writing at least until libraries were organized under an imperial system. Greece had the advantage of a strong oral tradition and concentration on a single language. With the strong patriarchal structure of European peoples she resisted the power on the one hand of the Babylonian priesthood and goddesses and on the other of the Egyptian monarchy as reflected in the pyramids.

As the Greeks had absorbed an earlier culture and adapted it to their language so the Latins absorbed Etruscan culture. The absorptive capacity of language was significant in the history of Greece, Rome, and England. The contact of language with an earlier developed culture without its complete submergence implied an escape from the more subtle aspects of that culture. It facilitated the rise of philosophy and science in Greece in contrast with religion. The civilization of Greece emphasized unity of approach but Rome absorbed rhetoric and excluded science. In the East, Persian and Arabic literature excluded the influence of Greek literature but absorbed science. Pervasiveness of language becomes a powerful factor in the mobilization of force particularly as a vehicle for the diffusion of opinion among all classes. Language exposed to major incursions became more flexible, facilitated movement between classes, favoured the diffusion of technology, and made for rapid adjustment.

Roman force supported the extension of the Republic to Carthage and Corinth in 146 B.C. and was followed in turn by the Hellenistic cultural invasion of Rome. Inclusion of Egypt in her possessions widened the gap by which Eastern influences penetrated Rome. Greek literature collected and edited in Alexandria had its impact on Rome. Roman literature was "over-powered by the extremely isolated and internally perfect Greek literature." Greek became a learned language and smothered the possibilities of Latin. Access to supplies of papyrus brought the growth of libraries, and of offices of administration. Hellenistic civilization warped the development of Rome toward an emphasis on force, administration, and law. While Cicero contributed to the perfection of Latin prose he followed the model set up by Isocrates. As the Empire followed the Republic, restrictions were imposed on the senate and on the oral tradition. Disappearance of political activity through censorship meant the increased importance of law and rhetoric. The literature of knowledge was divorced from the literature of form which eventually became panegyric. Oratory and history were subordinated to the state, the theatre was displaced by gladiatorial games. "It was jurisprudence, and jurisprudence only which stood in the place of poetry and history, of philosophy and science."[8] Interest in Greek in Rome halted literature and accentuated the interest in the codification of law.

The spread of militarism implied an emphasis on territorial rather than personal interests. It meant individual self-assertion and the temporary overthrow of customary restraints. Blood relationship and the dominance of the group over the individual were not suited to the military efficiency of the Roman legion. The extent of the Roman Empire in contrast with the city state necessitated written law as a means of restraining the demands of force. The rise of a professional legal class particularly with the decline of the Republic and the senate, and the separation of judicial power from legislative and executive powers, were marked by systematic development of law which weakened the power of *patria potestas*. Force and law weakened the patriarchal system. Family relations were created artificially, a development concerning which Maine wrote that there was "none to which I conceive mankind to be more deeply indebted." Legal obligation was separated from religious duty. The contract was developed from the conveyance and as a pact plus an obligation was, again in the words of Maine, "the most beautiful monument to the sagacity of Roman jurisconsults." Written testimony and written instruments displaced the cumbersome ceremonies of the oral tradition. It has been said of Roman law that the indestructibility of matter is as nothing compared to the indestructibility of mind. While Roman law was flexible in relation to the demands of Mediterranean trade and in the hands of the bar and the lecturers rather than the bench

[8]H. S. Maine, *Ancient Law* (London, 1906), p. 352.

MINERVA'S OWL                                                    13

it began to harden under the influence of Greek scholars and com-
mentators and eventually was subjected to elaborate codes. "It is only
when people begin to want water that they think of making reservoirs,
and it was observed that the laws of Rome were never reduced into
a system till its virtue and taste had perished."⁹ Papyrus and the roll
limited the possibilities of codification of Roman law.

The increasing rigidity of law and the increasing influence of the
East shown in the emergence of the absolute emperor opened the way
to the penetration of Eastern religions. The political animal of Aristotle became the individual of Alexander. Roman architecture,
Roman roads, and Roman law enhanced the attraction, accessibility,
and prestige of Rome. The Alexandrian tradition of science and
learning implied not only a study of the classics of Greece but also a
study and translation of the Hebrew scriptures. Hebraic literature had
arisen among a people who had been trampled over by the armies of
oriental empires and exposed during periods of captivity to the
influence notably of Persian religion with its conceptions of immortality and of the devil. The law and the prophets had been incorporated in holy scriptures. Under the influence of monotheism
writings had become sacred. The written bible assumed monotheism,
doctrine, and priesthood. "No book, no doctrine, no doctrine, no
book" (De Quincey). Pagan cultures lacked the act of thanksgiving
and the act of confession. Greece and Rome as polytheistic cultures
had supported an empire. Bibles were not suited to empires. Greek
philosophy was represented by the teacher and Eastern religions by
the priests and the prophets. "Thus saith the Lord." Zeno the Stoic
had introduced the latter note into Greek philosophy and its influence
was evident in the absorption of Stoicism in Roman law. "The exile
of the Jews and the defeat of Greece brought Christianity and
Stoicism. All great idealisms appear to spring from the soil of
materialistic defeat."¹⁰

The development of the Empire and Roman law reflected the
need for institutions to meet the rise of individualism and cosmo-
politanism which followed the break-down of the polis and the city
state. The Roman Empire opened the way to a rich growth of

⁹Thomas Constable, *Archibald Constable and His Literary Correspondents*
(Edinburgh, 1823), I, 261.
¹⁰R. T. Flewelling, *The Survival of Western Culture* (New York, 1943),
p. 26.

associations and the spread of religious cults. Organized religion
emerged to prevent the sense of unity implied in Greek civilization.
A relatively inflexible alphabet such as Hebrew and limited facilities
for communication narrowed the problem of education to a small
highly-trained group or special class. Its capacities were evident in
the literary achievements of the Old Testament. The dangers became
apparent in the difficulty of maintaining contact with changes in the
oral language. The people spoke Aramaic and Hebrew became a
learned language. Christianity was saved from being a Jewish sect by
the necessity of appealing to the spoken Greek language. "It is written
. . ., but I say unto you." The New Testament was written in col-
loquial Greek.

Christianity exploited the advantages of a new technique and the
use of a new material. Parchment in the codex replaced papyrus in
the roll. The parchment codex was more durable, more compact, and
more easily consulted for reference. The four Gospels and the Acts
could be placed in four distinct rolls or a single codex. Convenience
for reference strengthened the position of the codex in the use of the
scriptures or of codes of law. The codex with durability of parchment
and ease of consultation emphasized size and authority in the book.
Verse and prose which had been read aloud and in company to the
third and fourth centuries declined. Reading without moving of the
lips introduced a taste and style of its own. The ancient world
troubled about sounds, the modern world about thoughts. Egoism
replaced an interest in the group. A gospel corpus of powerful coherent
pamphlets written in the Greek vernacular had emerged as the basis
of the New Testament by 125 A.D. and with the Old Testament con-
stituted a large volume which became a dominant centre of interest
in learning.

Pressure from the barbarians to the north led to a search for a
more secure capital than Rome, to the selection of Constantinople in
330 A.D., and to the fall of Rome in 410 A.D. The court had cut itself
off from the centre of legal development and turned to organized
religion as a new basis of support. Christianity based on the book, the
Old and New Testaments, absorbed or drove out other religions such
as Mithraism and lent itself to co-operation with the state. In the
East the oriental concept of empire developed in Egypt, Babylonia,

Assyria, and Persia was restored. In the West law tempered the influence of Christianity and in the East particularly after the Justinian codes the influence of the absolute emperor. To quote Maine again: "It is precisely because the influence of jurisprudence begins to be powerful that the foundation of Constantinople and the subsequent separation of the western empire from the eastern are epochs in philosophical history." "Of the subjects which have whetted the intellectual appetite of the moderns, there is scarcely one, except physics, which has not been filtered through Roman jurisprudence."[11] Unequal to Greek metaphysical literature the Latin language took it over with little question. The problem of free will and necessity emerged with Roman law.

The Roman Empire failed to master the divisive effects of the Greek and Latin languages. Inability to absorb Greek culture was evident in movement of the capital to Constantinople and the tenacity of Greek language and culture supported the Byzantine Empire to 1453. Greek disappeared in Rome under pressure from the vernacular as did Latin in Constantinople. The alphabet had proved too flexible and too adaptable to language. Language proved tougher than force and the history of the West was in part an adaptation of force to language. The richness of Greek civilization, the balance between religion, law, and emperor which characterized the Byzantine Empire, enabled it to withstand the effects of new developments in the application of force.

William Ridgeway has shown the significance of the crossing of the light Libyan horse with the stocky Asiatic horse in the development of an animal sufficiently strong to carry armed men, and in turn, of the cavalry. Charles Oman has described the defeat of the Emperor Valens at Adrianople in 378 A.D. by heavy Gothic cavalry, the reorganization of the armies of the Byzantine Empire, the defeat of the barbarians following that reorganization, and the movement of the barbarians, successfully resisted in the East, to the conquest of the West. Dependence on roads in the Roman Empire, as in the Persian Empire, facilitated administration and invasion. In the West in the face of barbarian encroachment the hierarchy of the Roman Empire became to an important extent the hierarchy of the church.

[11]Maine, *Ancient Law*, pp. 351-2.

Monarchy in the Eastern empire was paralleled by monarchy in the Western papacy. In the East the position of the emperor and his control over the state were followed by religious division and heresy whereas in the West the position of the papacy was followed by political division.

Ecclesiastical division in the East weakened political power in that heresies reinforced by regionalism brought the loss of Egypt and other parts of the Byzantine Empire to the Mohammedans. With the fanaticism of a new religion based on a book, the Koran, with polygamy, with the opening of new territory to crowded peoples, and with the division of Christendom, Mohammedanism spread to the east and to the west. Defeated at Constantinople in 677 its followers concentrated on the West until they were halted by Charles Martel in 732. Again following Ridgeway, the heavier cross-bred horses of the Franks defeated the lighter cavalry of the Mohammedans. Military pressure from Spain brought the growth of centralization which culminated in Charlemagne and the rise of the German emperors. "Without Islam the Frankish Empire would probably never have existed and Charlemagne, without Mahomet, would be inconceivable" (Pirenne). In 800 the Byzantine Empire was ruled by an empress, Irene, and the emphasis on the male line in the West strengthened the position of Charlemagne, crowned by the papacy. A new empire in the West was followed by the Carolingian renaissance.

The position of the emperor in the East led to a clash with monasticism, the iconoclastic controversy, and separation of the Eastern from the Western church. In the West monasticism with little check accentuated the influence of celibacy and of Latin in the church. In the East monasticism was brought under control but in the West it strengthened its position to the point that political history has been powerfully influenced by the struggle between church and state to the present century. The power of monasticism in the West was enhanced by the monopoly of knowledge which followed the cutting-off of supplies of papyrus from Egypt by the Mohammedans. "The Mediterranean had been a Roman lake; it now became, for the most part, a Muslim lake" (Pirenne). In the East the last of the schools of Athens were closed by Justinian in 529 and new centres of learning were established in Constantinople, but in the West an interest in classical studies was discouraged by the monastic tradition of learning which began in Italy. Monasteries concentrated on the scriptures and the writings of the Fathers. The classics were superseded by the scriptures. The blotting-out of the learning of Spain by the Mohammedans and restricted interest in learning in Europe meant that the most distant area of Europe, namely Ireland, alone remained enthusiastic for knowledge and from here an interest in learning spread backwards to Scotland and England and to Europe. Alcuin was brought from the north of England to strengthen the position of learning under Charlemagne. A renewed interest in learning brought an improvement of writing in the appearance of the Carolingian minuscule. Its efficiency was evident in a spread throughout Europe, in ultimate supremacy over the Beneventan script in the south of Italy, and a supply of models for the modern alphabet.

The spread of learning from the British Isles to the Continent preceded the invasions of the Scandinavians to the north. Pressure from this direction was evident in the emergence of the duchy of Normandy in 911 and the reorganization of European defence. By the eleventh century the invasions of the Vikings and the Magyars had left cavalry and the feudal knights in supremacy. The cultural tenacity of language was shown in the conquest of the conquered, the adoption of the French language in Normandy and eventually of the English language in England by the Normans. Military reorganization in Europe, the ascendancy of the papacy, and the break between the Eastern and the Western church in 1054 were followed by the Crusades, the Norman conquest of Apulia and Sicily after 1061, and of England in 1066, and the driving of the Moors out of Spain. The energies of the West were turned against the Mohammedans in the Holy Land and against the schismatic church of the Byzantine Empire. The capture of Constantinople in 1204 was the beginning of the end of the eastern Roman Empire.

Decline in the use of papyrus particularly after the spread of Mohammedanism necessitated the use of parchment. The codex was suited to the large book whether it was the Roman law or the Hebrew scriptures. In the Byzantine Empire successive codifications of Roman law were undertaken. Caesaropapism and the iconoclastic controversy assumed control over the church by the emperor. In the West the law

of the barbarians was personal and the church emphasized the scriptures and the writings of the Fathers. With the Greeks virtue is knowledge, particularly the knowledge that we know nothing, and with the
Hebrew prophets, perhaps in protest against the monopoly of knowledge held by the scribes of Egypt and Babylonia, knowledge is evil.
The emphasis on the authority of the scriptures and the writings of the
Fathers in the West was supplemented by ceremonial and by alle-
gorical writings. The metre of classical poetry was replaced by accent
and rhyme. Reading assumed submission to authority.

But long before the influence of Grecian culture was being filtered
through Persian and Arabian civilization in the south to Spain, Sicily,
and Europe. The process was hastened by a new medium, namely
paper, from China. The invention of the manufacture of paper from
textiles in China in the early part of the second century A.D., the
adaptation of the brush used in painting to writing, and the manufacture of ink from lamp black marked the beginnings of a written
tradition and a learned class. In the Chinese language the pictograph
survived though most of the characters were phonetic. With a limited
number of words, about 1,500, it was used with extraordinary skill
to serve as a medium for a great diversity of spoken languages. But its
complexity emphasized the importance of a learned class, the limited
influence of public opinion, and the persistence of political and
religious institutions. The importance of Confucianism and the classics
and worship of the written word led to the invention of devices for
accurate reproduction. Neglect of the masses hastened the spread of
Buddhism and the development of a system for rapid reduplication,
particularly of charms. Buddhism spread from India where the oral
tradition of the Brahmins flourished at the expense of the written
tradition and proved singularly adaptable to the demands of an
illiterate population. Printing emerged from the demands of Buddhism
in its appeal to the masses and of Confucianism with its interest in the
classics, the literature of the learned. Complexity of the characters
necessitated the development of block printing and reproduction of
the classics depended on large-scale state support. The first printed
book has been dated 868 A.D. Severe limitations on public opinion
involved a long series of disturbances in the overthrow of dynasties
and in conquest by the Mongols but the tenacity of an oral tradition
gave enormous strength to Chinese institutions and to scholars.

Expansion of Mohammedanism and the capture of Turkestan by the Arabs in 751 were followed by the introduction of paper to the West. It was manufactured in Baghdad and its introduction corresponded with the literary splendour of the reign of Haroun-al-Raschid (786-809). It was used in Egypt by the middle of the ninth century, spread rapidly in the tenth century, declined sharply in the eleventh century, and was produced in Spain in the twelfth century, and in Italy in the thirteenth century. By the end of the fourteenth century the price of paper in Italy had declined to one-sixth the price of parchment. Linen rags were its chief cheap raw material. In the words of Henry Hallam, paper introduced "a revolution . . . of high importance, without which the art of writing would have been much less practised, and the invention of printing less serviceable to mankind. . . ." It "permitted the old costly material by which thought was transmitted to be superseded by a universal substance which was to facilitate the diffusion of the works of human intelligence." With a monopoly of papyrus and paper the Mohammedans supported an interest in libraries and in the transmission of Greek classics, particularly Aristotle and science. Prohibition of images in the Mohammedan religion facilitated an emphasis on learning. From libraries in Spain a knowledge of Aristotle spread to Europe and became important to the works of Albertus Magnus and St. Thomas Aquinas. Arabic numerals, and a knowledge of mathematics and astronomy, of science and medicine found their way through Sicily and Spain to Europe. Writing developed beyond monastic walls and in the twelfth century numerous attacks were made on ecclesiastical corruption. Werner Sombart has emphasized the importance of Arabic numerals to the spread of exact calculations, the growth of business, and the commercial revolution from 1275 to 1325. Cursive handwriting emerged in the thirteenth century. Expansion of commerce favoured the growth of lay schools and closing of the monasteries to secular students increased the importance of cathedral schools and universities. The rural interest of the monasteries was succeeded by the urban interest of the university. Knowledge of architecture imported from Constantinople and adaptation of buildings to northern conditions led to the wave of construction of Gothic cathedrals from 1150 to 1250. With the cathedral came an improvement in various arts such as stained glass and counterpoint music. The University of Paris was started about 1170 and as a master's university its model was followed in later institutions.

The spread of paper from China hastened the growth of commerce in Italy and northern Europe. It supported an increase in writing beyond the bounds of the monasteries. It was a medium for the spread of Greek science through Mohammedan territory and of Arabic numerals and more efficient calculation into Europe. Aristotle became accessible through Arabic and attempts to reconcile his writings with the scriptures were evident in the work of Maimonides and St. Thomas Aquinas. Universities emerged in cathedral centres and supported an interest in the oral tradition, dialectic, and scholasticism. The Byzantine Empire disappeared as a balance between papacy and empire and left them to destroy each other. The papacy became more involved in problems of territorial rights. As a result of the Babylonian captivity in Avignon it incurred the antagonism of England. The papacy was no longer able to check the spread of translations of the scriptures in the vernacular, and the spread of Roman law from the Byzantine Empire strengthened the new monarchies in France and England. Concentration on the vernacular produced a new and powerful literature.

Commercial activity in Italy assumed a renewed interest in law. The barbarian invasions had meant an emphasis on personal law and through this Roman law persisted in a modified form. At the beginning of the twelfth century there emerged at Bologna an intensified interest in the study of Roman law and the student type of university. Weakening of the Byzantine Empire was followed by the struggle between church and empire in the West and the latter seized upon Roman law as a powerful instrument with which to reinforce the position of the emperor. Its influence spread in Italy and in southern France and was evident in the development of canon law in the church. "The worst corruption of the middle ages lay in the transformation of the sacerdotal hierarchy into a hierarchy of lawyers" (Hastings Rashdall). In the words of Frederic Harrison: "The peculiar, indispensable service of Byzantine literature was the preservation of the language, philology, and archaeology of Greece." But it had perhaps no influence in any field greater than in that of Roman law.

The strength of the church in the north where the traditions of Roman municipalities and Roman law were weak was shown in the University of Paris. In France and particularly in England the weakness of the written tradition favoured the position of custom and the common law. Law was found, not made, and the implications were evident in the jury system, the King's Court, common law, and parliament. In England, law and religion were not fortified by universities since these were not located at the capital or in cathedral cities. Law and religion were responsive to the demands of an oral tradition. The flexibility of the English language as a result of the invasion of successive languages from Europe made for common law, parliamentary institutions, and trade. In Scotland the universities were typically urban and, located in large cities, became the basis for the rich development in philosophy in the eighteenth century. The variety of types of university and geographical isolation provided the background for the diversity of interest which characterized the intellectual activity of Europe. The increasing strength of the vernaculars weakened the position of the University of Paris. The Franciscans in Oxford revived an interest in Plato in contrast with the Dominican interest in Aristotle in Paris. The councils of the church became ineffectual and the monarchy of the papacy became more absolute. The supremacy of celibacy favoured the concentration of power in Rome, prevented the establishment of ecclesiastical dynasties, and facilitated constant appeal to intellectual capacity. Concentration of power in Rome hastened the development of the Gallican church.

In Europe the rise of commerce, of cities, and of universities brought conflict between monasticism and the secular clergy, and between the church and the state particularly in the control over education. Introduction of paper and the spread of writing hastened the growth of the vernacular and the decline of Latin. Control of the church was inadequate to check the oral tradition, and the spread of heresies which followed the growth of trade and the weakening of the Byzantine Empire. But the church undertook its first counter-reformation. In a letter of 1199 Innocent III frowned on translations of the scriptures, writing that "the secret mysteries of the faith ought not therefore to be explained to all men in all places." Translation and lay reading of the New Testament by the Waldensians, and the

22      THE BIAS OF COMMUNICATION

rise of romantic poetry in Provence probably under the influence of
the Mohammedans and the Byzantine Empire, were ruthlessly stamped
out. Establishment of new orders, the Dominicans and the Franciscans,
and of the Inquisition was designed to check the spread of heresy
incidental to the emergence of translations in the vernacular and of
oral discussions in universities. The new courts of Europe were
strengthened by the lawyers and writers in the vernacular. Dante
wrote that "a man's proper vernacular is nearest unto him as much as
it is more closely united to him, for it is singly and alone in his mind
before any other." "Since we do not find that anyone before us has
treated of the science of the Vulgar Tongue, while, in fact, we see
that this tongue is highly necessary for all, inasmuch as not only men,
but even women and children strive, in so far as Nature allows them,
to acquire it . . . we will endeavour by the aid of the Wisdom which
breathes from Heaven to be of service to the speech of the common
people."[12] The power of the vernacular was evident in the growth of
nationalism and the rise of universities particularly in Germany.
Wycliffe's translation of the Lollard Bible and his influence on Huss
in Bohemia pointed to the breaking of the power of the church on the
outer fringes of Europe. Opposed to the influence of the University of
Paris and its interest in councils the papacy favoured the establishment
of universities in Germany and in Spain. The republican cities of
Italy, particularly Venice and Florence, prospered with the decline of
Byzantine commerce and the Hohenstaufen court. The migration of
Greek scholars from the East contributed to an intense interest in
classical civilization. Florence became a second Athens in its concern
for letters and the arts. Learning had been banked down in the
Byzantine Empire and broke out into new flames in the Italian
Renaissance. The vitality of the classics of Greece which reflected the
power of civilization based on an oral tradition gradually weakened
the monopoly of knowledge held by the church. "Nothing moves in
the modern world that is not Greek in its origin" (Maine).

As the prejudice against paper as a product of Jews and Arabs
had been broken down with the spread of commerce the position of
parchment as a medium for the scriptures and the classics was

[12]Dante in *De vulgari eloquentia;* cited in Vernon Hall, Jr., *Renaissance
Literary Criticism* (New York, 1945), pp. 16-17.

enhanced. The product of the copyist and the miniaturist increased in value. The monopoly of the manuscript and its high value intensified an interest in the development of a technique of reproduction in areas in which the copyist had limited control, namely in Germany. The use of oil in painting and its extension to ink, the development of an alloy which could be melted at low temperatures and remained consistent in size with changes in temperature, the growth of skill in cutting punches, the invention of an adjustable type mould, and the adaptation of the press were brought into a unified system as a basis for printing. Production of a large volume such as the Bible assumed concentration of capital on a substantial scale and a continued output of books. Limited transportation facilities and a limited market for books hastened the migration of printers particularly to Italy, a region with abundant supplies of paper, a commodity adapted to the printing press. Migration to new markets compelled the adoption of new types. The Gothic black-letter type which characterized German printing was replaced by the Roman type in Italy. Resistance of copyists delayed the spread of printing in France, but the delay possibly facilitated artistic development in French type. The demands of the press for manuscripts and the necessity of creating new markets favoured extension to the production of the classics in Greek, the use of more compact type for smaller portable volumes in italic, and the emphasis on the vernacular. The technique of printing crossed the water of the English Channel and Caxton with a concern for the market concentrated on English and avoided the depressed market for books in the classical languages.

An enormous increase in production and variety of books and incessant search for markets hastened the rise of the publisher, an emphasis on commerce at the expense of the printer, and a neglect of craftsmanship. As the supply of manuscripts in parchment which had been built up over centuries had been made available by printing, writers in the vernacular were gradually trained to produce material. But they were scarcely competent to produce large books and were compelled to write controversial pamphlets which could be produced quickly and carried over wide areas, and had a rapid turnover. The publisher was concerned with profits. The flexibility of the European alphabet and the limited number of distinct characters, capable of innumerable combinations, facilitated the development of numerous printing plants and the mobilization of a market for a commodity which could be adapted to a variety of consumers. Knowledge was not only diversified, it was designed by the publisher to widen its own market notably in the use of advertising.

The monopoly position of the Bible and the Latin language in the church was destroyed by the press and in its place there developed a widespread market for the Bible in the vernacular and a concern with its literal interpretation. To quote Jefferson, "The printers can never leave us in a state of perfect rest and union of opinion." In the words of Victor Hugo the book destroyed the "ancient Gothic genius, that sun which sets behind the gigantic press of Mayence." Architecture which for six thousand years had been "the great handwriting of the human race" was no longer supreme. It was significant that printing spread most rapidly in those regions in Europe in which the cathedral was not dominant and in which political division was most conspicuous—in Italy and in Germany. In Italy, with its access to Constantinople, emphasis had been given to the classics; in Germany emphasis was given first to bulky theological volumes and in turn, with the shift of the industry to Leipzig, to the small polemical publications which characterized the writings of Luther and his successors of the Reformation and to the Bible in High German dialect. "The growth and surprising progress of this bold sect [Lutherans] may justly in part be ascribed to the late invention of printing and revival of learning." "The books of Luther and his sectaries, full of vehemence, declamation and rude eloquence were propagated more quickly and in greater numbers." (Hume.) "One of the first effects of printing was to make proud men look upon learning as disgraced by being brought within reach of the common people" (Southey).

As in the paper revolution the church was compelled to mobilize its resources in counter-attack, notably in the Council of Trent and the establishment of the Jesuit order. In Italy the power of law and of the church and division among the republics checked the spread of the Reformation and produced Machiavelli. He wrote: "We Italians then owe to the church of Rome and to her priests our having become irreligious and bad; but we owe her a still greater debt, and that will be the cause of our ruin namely, that the church has kept and still keeps our country divided." In France the restricted influence of Greek and the supremacy of Latin favoured an outburst of literary activity in the vernacular in Montaigne and Rabelais. With the suppression of Protestantism Estienne and Calvin fled to Geneva and by the end of the sixteenth century the great scholars of France left for Holland. In Germany political division laid the basis for the bitter religious wars of the seventeenth century. The arguments of William of Occam and of Wycliffe had gained in England with the decline of Italian financiers. Weakness of the church, of monasticism, and of the universities enabled the crown to break with the papacy. The rise of the printing industry had its implication in technological unemployment shown in part in the decline of monasticism.

The failure of the Counter-Reformation reflected the influence of force. The growth of industrialism, the interest in science and mathematics, and the rise of cities had their effects in the use of gunpowder and artillery. The application of artillery in destroying the defences of Constantinople in 1453 was spectacular evidence of the decline of cavalry and systems of defence which had characterized feudalism. The instruments of attack became more powerful than those of defence and decentralization began to give way to centralization. The limitations of cavalry had been evident in the mountainous region of Switzerland and the low country of the Netherlands and in the success of movements toward independence in those regions. The military genius of Cromwell and of Gustavus Adolphus in using new instruments of warfare guaranteed the position of Protestantism in England and Germany.

A revolution in finance accompanied change in the character of force. In Italy independent republics had continued the traditions of Rome in the emphasis on municipal institutions. The importance of defence in construction of city walls necessitated development of municipal credit and responsibility of citizens for the debt of a corporate entity. In the struggle of the Netherlands against Spain the principle was extended and the republic became an instrument of credit. In England the ultimate supremacy of parliament in 1689 meant further elaboration, and recognition of the role of public debts was shown in the establishment of the Bank of England in 1694. Extension of the principle of corporate entity from Roman law eventually clashed with the traditions of common law in the revolt of the American colonies in the eighteenth century. The growth of public credit increased the importance of information, of organized news services, and of opinion. Organized exchanges emerged in Antwerp, in Amsterdam, and in London. The importance of opinion in relation to finance accentuated the significance of the vernacular.

The effects of the Counter-Reformation in France were shown in the suppression of printing, the massacre of St. Bartholomew in 1572, and finally in the revocation of the Edict of Nantes in 1685. Suppression of printing in response to ecclesiastical demands was accompanied by an interest in the increased production and export of paper by the state. As a result of this conflict between restriction of consumption and increase of production and exports, cheaper supplies were available in the Netherlands, Geneva, and countries in which printing remained free. From these marginal areas printed material was smuggled back into France. Freedom of the press in marginal free countries was supported by repression in France. In the eighteenth century evasion of censorship was shown in the preparation and printing of the *Encyclopaedia,* and the writings of Voltaire and Rousseau.

Abolition of the monasteries and celibacy in the Church of England, the reform of education in the first half of the sixteenth century, and censorship of the press in the second half of the century had their effects in the flowering of the drama in the plays of Shakespeare. Weakening of the monarchy under the Stuarts was accompanied by the publication of the King James version of the Bible and the prose of Milton and the sharp decline of the theatre. The impact of the Bible was shown in the separation of church and state as enunciated by the Puritans. It recognized the clash between the written and the oral tradition, the latter persisting in parliament and the common law, and the former in the scriptures. In the Restoration Dryden supported the interest of the court and after the revolution of 1689 and the lapse of the Licensing Act in 1694 the demands of political parties were met by the writings of Addison, Steele, Swift, Defoe, and others. Suspension of printing had brought news-letters and discussion in the coffee-houses. Revival of the classics by Dryden and Pope was the prelude to financial independence of Pope, Johnson, and Goldsmith. The restrictive measures of Walpole and the increasing importance of advertising as a source of revenue for newspapers directed the interest of writers to compilations, children's books, and novels, and the interest of readers to the circulating library. The position of the church with the supremacy of parliament and constitutional monarchy favoured the growth of deism on the one hand and of Methodism on the other.

In the colonies books were imported on a large scale from England and Europe by booksellers and the colonial printer turned his attention to newspapers. In the eighteenth century the energetic writing in London papers before their suppression by Walpole and after the success of Wilkes and others in securing the right to publish parliamentary debates served as an example to colonial journalists. The printing industry crossed the water of the Atlantic Ocean and changed its character. The prominent role of the newspaper in the American Revolution was recognized in the first article of the Bill of Rights. The movement towards restriction of the press by taxes in the latter part of the eighteenth century and the early part of the nineteenth century in England was paralleled by an insistence on freedom of the press in the United States. The results were shown in the rapid expansion in exports of rags from Italy to the United States.

From the invention of printing to the beginning of the nineteenth century the manufacture of paper and the production of the printed word were handicraft processes. The invention of the paper machine and the introduction of the mechanical press involved a revolution in the extension of communication facilities. In England taxes on paper and advertising favoured the monopoly of *The Times* to the middle of the century and removal of these taxes by 1861 was followed by a rapid increase in the number of newspapers and in their circulation and in the demand for raw material. In the United States the demands of large numbers of newspapers hastened the introduction of the fast press, the spread of advertising, inventions such as the telegraph and the cable and the linotype, and a rapid shift from rags to wood as a source of raw material. English authors such as Dickens emphasized the importance of sentimentalism and sensationalism in part through the demands of a new reading class and of an American market. "Dickens introduces children into his stories that he may kill them to slow music" (J. M. Barrie). American authors with lack of copyright protection turned to journalism. Artemus Ward stated that "Shakespeare wrote good plays but he wouldn't have succeeded as the Washington correspondent of a New York daily newspaper. He lacked the reckisit fancy and imagination." Extension of the newspaper in the United States had its implications for Great Britain in the rise of the new journalism particularly after the South African War. Hearst, Pulitzer, Scripps, Northcliffe, and Beaverbrook became dominant figures. In the United States the political ambitions of journalists were checked by competition, in England by nomination to the House of Lords, in Canada by an LL.D. In the twentieth century the power of English journalists was evident in restrictions imposed on the radio through government ownership while limitations of the power of American journalists in the United States were indicated by the effective use of radio by Franklin Delano Roosevelt.

In Anglo-Saxon countries the impact of technological advances on the frontier in the course of which Hearst and Pulitzer from San Francisco and St. Louis introduced revolutionary changes in New York and J. G. Bennett, Jr. and Whitelaw Reid hastened revolutionary changes in Great Britain and Europe, involved an irregular interest on the part of governments in communication and education. Extension of the franchise and the problems of military organization with its demands for technical knowledge and trained men contributed to the improvement of postal facilities and the extension of compulsory education. In Europe the dominance of the book meant less rapid extension of newspapers and restriction in such countries as Germany, Italy, and Russia, and personal and political journalism in France. The varied rate of development of communication facilities has accentuated difficulties of understanding. Improvements in communication, like the Irish bull of the bridge which separated the two countries, make for increased difficulties of understanding. The cable compelled contraction of language and facilitated a rapid widening between the English and American languages. In the vast realm of fiction in the Anglo-Saxon world, the influence of the newspaper and such recent developments as the cinema and the radio has been evident in the best seller and the creation of special classes of readers with little prospect of communication between them. Publishers demand great names and great books particularly if no copyright is involved. The large-scale mechanization of knowledge is characterized by imperfect competition and the active creation of monopolies in language which prevent understanding and hasten appeals to force.

I have tried to show that, in the words of Mark Pattison, "Writers are apt to flatter themselves that they are not, like the men of action, the slaves of circumstance. They think they can write what and when they choose. But it is not so. Whatever we may think and scheme, as soon as we seek to produce our thoughts or schemes to our fellow-men, we are involved in the same necessities of compromise, the same grooves of motion, the same liabilities to failure or half-measures, as we are in life and action."[13] The effect of the discovery of printing was evident in the savage religious wars of the sixteenth and seventeenth centuries. Application of power to communication industries hastened the consolidation of vernaculars, the rise of nationalism, revolution, and new outbreaks of savagery in the twentieth century. Previous to the invention of printing the importance of Latin and the drain on intellectual energies of a dual language had been evident in the problems of scholastic philosophy. After the invention of printing, interest in the classics in Italy and France and in the Bible in Protestant countries divided the Western world. Hebraism and Hellenism proved difficult to reconcile as did Aristotle and Plato. Roman law and the classics in Italy and the cathedrals in France checked the influence of the Bible and in France emphasized an interest in literature. In Germany the influence of the Bible strengthened the power of the state and favoured the growth of music and letters independent of political life. In England division between the crown, parliament, law, the universities, and trade checked the dominance of single interests, but favoured mediocrity except in finance and trade. In England monasticism contributed to the delay in education and printing which strengthened the position of the vernacular to the point that violence broke out in destruction of the monasteries in the sixteenth century, civil war in the seventeenth century, and the American Revolution in the eighteenth century.

In the free countries of Europe revival of the classics and the demands of printing on logic had their effects in the powerful impact

[13]Mark Pattison, *Isaac Casaubon (1559-1614)* (London, 1875), p. 383.

of mathematics on philosophy in Descartes and on political science in Hobbes. The application of power to the communication industries after 1800 hastened the spread of compulsory education and the rise of the newspaper, and intensified interest in vernaculars, in nationalism, and in romanticism. Mechanized communication divided reason and emotion and emphasized the latter. Printing marked the first stage in the spread of the Industrial Revolution. "The influence of passion over any assembly of men increases in proportion to their numbers more than the influence of reason" (J. Scarlett). It became concerned increasingly with the problem of distribution of goods, and with advertising. Its limitations became evident in the decline of the book to the level of prestige advertising, in the substitution of architecture in the skyscraper, the cathedral of commerce, and in simplified spelling and semantics. Ernst Cassirer, a German refugee scholar, has described the word-coiners as masters of the art of political propaganda. *Nazi-Deutsch,* a glossary of contemporary German usage, included a long list of words which he found it impossible to render adequately into English. As a result of the new words coined to support the Hitler-fascist myth he no longer understood the German language.

Since its flight from Constantinople Minerva's owl has found a resting-place only at brief intervals in the West. It has flown from Italy to France, the Netherlands, Germany and after the French Revolution back to France and England and finally to the United States. These hurried and uncertain flights have left it little energy and have left it open to attack from numerous enemies. In the words of the Parnassus Plays:

> Let schollers bee as thriftie as they maye
> They will be poore ere their last dying daye;
> Learning and povertie will ever kisse.

Or, as Johnson put it:

> There mark what ills the scholar's life assail,—
> Toil, envy, want, the patron, and the jail.

The Industrial Revolution and mechanized knowledge have all but destroyed the scholar's influence. Force is no longer concerned with his protection and is actively engaged in schemes for his destruction. Enormous improvements in communication have made understanding more difficult. Even science, mathematics, and music as the last refuge of the Western mind have come under the spell of the mechanized vernacular. Commercialism has required the creation of new monopolies in language and new difficulties in understanding. Even the class struggle, the struggle between language groups, has been made a monopoly of language. When the Communist Manifesto proclaimed, "Workers of the world unite, you have nothing to lose but your chains!" in those words it forged new chains.

I have attempted to show that sudden extensions of communication are reflected in cultural disturbances. The use of clay favoured a dominant role for the temples with an emphasis on priesthood and religion. Libraries were built up in Babylon and Nineveh to strengthen the power of monarchy. Papyrus favoured the development of political organization in Egypt. Papyrus and a simplified form of writing in the alphabet supported the growth of democratic organization, literature, and philosophy in Greece. Following Alexander empires returned with centres at Alexandria and elsewhere and libraries continued as sources of strength to monarchies. Rome extended the political organization of Greece in its emphasis on law and eventually on empire. Establishment of a new capital at Constantinople was followed by imperial organization on the oriental model particularly after official recognition of Christianity. Improvement of scripts and wider dissemination of knowledge enabled the Jews to survive by emphasis on the scriptures and the book. In turn Christianity exploited the advantages of parchment and the codex in the Bible. With access to paper the Mohammedans at Baghdad and later in Spain and Sicily provided a medium for the transmission of Greek science to the Western world. Greek science and paper with encouragement of writing in the vernacular provided the wedge between the temporal and the spiritual power and destroyed the Holy Roman Empire. The decline of Constantinople meant a stimulus to Greek literature and philosophy as the decline of Mohammedanism had meant a stimulus to science. Printing brought renewed emphasis on the book and the rise of the Reformation. In turn new methods of communication weakened the worship of the book and opened the way for new ideologies. Monopolies or oligopolies of knowledge have been built up in relation to the demands of force chiefly on the defensive, but improved technology has strengthened the position of force on the offensive and compelled realignments favouring the vernacular. Cultural disturbances are accompanied by periods in which force occupies an important place and are followed by periods of quiescence in which law establishes order. The disturbances of the Macedonian and Roman wars were followed by the growth of Roman law, the end of the barbarian invasions by the revival of Roman law, the end of the religious wars by the development of international law under Grotius, and the end of the present wars of ideology by a search for a new basis of international law.

Perhaps we might end by a plea for consideration of the role of the oral tradition as a basis for a revival of effective vital discussion and in this for an appreciation on the part of universities of the fact that teachers and students are still living and human. In the words of Justice Holmes, "To have doubted one's own first principles is the mark of a civilized man," but the same wise man in *Abrams* v. *United States* stated that "the best test of truth is the power of thought to get itself accepted in the competition of the market" without appreciating that monopoly and oligopoly appear in this as in other markets.

# THE BIAS OF COMMUNICATION[1]

THE APPEARANCE of a wide range of cultural phenomena at different periods in the history of Western civilization has been described by Professor A. L. Kroeber in *Configurations of Cultural Growth* (Berkeley, 1946). He makes suggestive comments at various points to explain the relative strength or weakness of cultural elements but refrains from extended discussion. I do not propose to do more than add a footnote to these comments and in this to discuss the possible significance of communication to the rise and decline of cultural traits. A medium of communication has an important influence on the dissemination of knowledge over space and over time and it becomes necessary to study its characteristics in order to appraise its influence in its cultural setting. According to its characteristics it may be better suited to the dissemination of knowledge over time than over space, particularly if the medium is heavy and durable and not suited to transportation, or to the dissemination of knowledge over space than over time, particularly if the medium is light and easily transported. The relative emphasis on time or space will imply a bias of significance to the culture in which it is imbedded.

Immediately we venture on this inquiry we are compelled to recognize the bias of the period in which we work. An interest in the bias of other civilizations may in itself suggest a bias of our own. Our knowledge of other civilizations depends in large part on the character of the media used by each civilization in so far as it is capable of being preserved or of being made accessible by discovery as in the case of the results of archaeological expeditions.[2] Writing on clay and on stone has been preserved more effectively than that on papyrus. Since durable commodities emphasize time and continuity, studies of

[1] A paper presented at the University of Michigan on April 18, 1949.
[2] See the complaint that archaeologists have been unduly concerned with objects of art. S. Clarke and R. Engelbach, *Ancient Egyptian Masonry, the Building Craft* (London, 1930), p. vi.

civilization such as Toynbee's tend to have a bias toward religion and to show a neglect of problems of space, notably administration and law. The bias of modern civilization incidental to the newspaper and the radio will presume a perspective in consideration of civilizations dominated by other media. We can do little more than urge that we must be continually alert to the implications of this bias and perhaps hope that consideration of the implications of other media to various civilizations may enable us to see more clearly the bias of our own. In any case we may become a little more humble as to the characteristics of our civilization. We can perhaps assume that the use of a medium of communication over a long period will to some extent determine the character of knowledge to be communicated and suggest that its pervasive influence will eventually create a civilization in which life and flexibility will become exceedingly difficult to maintain and that the advantages of a new medium will become such as to lead to the emergence of a new civilization.

Egyptian civilization appears to have been powerfully influenced by the character of the Nile. Utilization of its periodic floods depended on the unified control of an absolute authority. It has been claimed that the discovery of the sidereal year as early as 4241 B.C. made it possible to work out a calendar avoiding the difficulties of a year dependent on the moon. The discovery and the adoption of a calendar with the certainty of dates for religious festivals facilitated the establishment of an absolute monarchy and the imposition of the authority of Osiris and Ra, the Nile and the Sun, on upper Egypt. Success of the monarchy in acquiring control over Egypt in terms of space necessitated a concern with problems of continuity or time. The idea of immortality strengthened the position of the monarch. Mummification and construction of the pyramids as devices for emphasizing control over time were accompanied by the development of the art of pictorial representation as part of the funerary ritual and by the emergence of writing. The spoken word, by which the orders of the monarch were given, in itself possessed creative efficiency which in turn was perpetuated in the written word in the tomb. Pictorial decorations became hieroglyphic script. Writing gradually developed toward phoneticism and by the time of Menes (about 3315 B.C.) many picture signs had a purely phonetic value and were regularly spelled out. Autocratic monarchy developed by divine right culminated in the pyramids of about 2850 B.C. Private property disappeared and all arable land became the king's domain.

The monopoly of knowledge centring around stone and hiero-glyphics was exposed to competition from papyrus as a new and more efficient medium. Royal authority began to decline after about 2540 B.C. and its decline was possibly coincident with the discovery of the solar year by the priestly class as a device to overcome the deficiencies of the sidereal year in which a day was gained each year. The king was lowered from the status of the Great God to the son of Ra. The chief priest of the Ra cult was exalted to the rank of chief god and Heliopolis became the centre of priestly power. Oligarchy succeeded an absolute monarchy. After about 2000 B.C. the masses were admitted to religious rites and immortality and to political rights. The gates of heaven and the jaws of hell were opened and a "most powerful instrument for the domination over men's unruly wills" devised.[3] The increasing use of papyrus and the brush was accompanied by the development of the hieratic character and the emergence of the profession of scribes. Writing and thought were secularized. Admin-istration was extended following the spread of writing and reading. The social revolution involved in a shift from the use of stone to the use of papyrus and the increased importance of the priestly class imposed enormous strains on Egyptian civilization and left it exposed to the inroads of invaders equipped with effective weapons of attack. The Hyksos or Shepherd Kings captured and held Egypt from 1660 to 1580 B.C. The strength of Egyptian cultural elements facilitated reorganization, and mobilization of resources was directed to expul-sion of the invaders. The introduction of the horse and light four-spoked chariots enabled Egyptian rulers not only to expel the Hyksos but also to conquer vast new territories and to build an empire.

An extension of political organization to include peoples of different races and religions reflecting a temporary solution of problems of space in government compelled the king to attempt a solution of problems of continuity. Worship of the solar disc was designed to provide an imperial religion which would overrule dis-tinctions between Egyptians and foreigners. Failure to overcome the

[3]V. Gordon Childe, *What Happened in History* (New York, 1946), p. 150.

hostility of the entrenched priestly class in Egypt was followed by imperial decline and eventually by the subjugation of Egypt by the Assyrians and the Persians. A monopoly of knowledge supported by a difficult script resisted demands for change and brought the Egyptian Empire to an end. With abundant supplies of papyrus and the conservative influence of religion on writing, pictographic writing was maintained and the emergence of consonantal signs was largely a result of the introduction of foreign names and words. The spoken word tended to drift away from the written word in spite of the efforts of Ikhnaton to bring them into closer accord.

In contrast with the civilization of the Nile that of the Euphrates and the Tigris lacked the necessity of unity and was characterized in its early development by a number of small theocratic city states in which the chief priest of the temple was direct representative of the god. Rivers were subject to irregular and incalculable flooding. The growth of city states assumed continuity in time and the development of writing and reading by which the complex systems of accounting could be made intelligible to individuals and to their successors.

Alluvial clay as the medium for writing had implications for Sumerian civilization in the difficulties of transport and the tendency to encourage the development of a decentralized society. The difficulties of writing on moist clay led to the disappearance of pictographs and the emergence of conventional signs or formal patterns of cuneiform. The stylus was developed in relation to the demands of clay. With a language which was largely monosyllabic, signs were introduced to meet the demands of economy and the necessity of uniformity to establish communication between scattered cities. The administration of temple properties and trade implied an emphasis on mathematics in the early development of writing and in turn an emphasis on abstractions.

Accumulation of wealth in temple organizations involved rivalry, warfare between city states, the emergence of a military leader and an army. The problems of control over space in contrast to the success with which problems of time were met in a religious organization necessitated centralization in the hands of a king. Control over large stretches of territory meant delegation of authority and an emphasis on law as a means of offsetting religious jealousies. To the same end

THE BIAS OF COMMUNICATION

old capitals were destroyed and new capitals were built to strengthen the prestige of the king, and the deities of conquered cities were arranged in hierarchies under the deity of the conqueror. The difficulties of political organization were evident in the ultimate break-down of Sumerian empires and in the success of Semitic invaders, as the advantages of cultural organization were evident in the tenacity of Sumerian institutions under alien rule. Semitic invaders rearranged the position of the chief gods of city states.

The eventual success of Semitic peoples was marked by the ascendancy of Babylon as a new capital and by the reforms of Hammurabi. The centralized power of a monarchy favoured the architecture of palaces, and the use of stone in sculpture and as a medium of writing, particularly of laws designed to establish uniformity over vast empires. The language of the conquerors could not be united to that of the conquered but the signs of the latter were used by the former. The Semitic language was made official by Hammurabi. The spoken word was Semitic but the written word was in the non-Semitic forms of the Sumerians. The conventionalization of written language was hastened by the demands of the conquerors. "The basis of the Sumerian system of writing was word-values, while that of the Accadian method was syllable-values."[4] Sumerian became a fossilized sacred language of priests. Hammurabi developed the territorial state with a centralized system of administration, a common collection of written laws, a common capital, and a common calendar. Trade over a vast territory was facilitated by the use of fixed standards of weights and measures. Mathematics was developed in the use of the sexagesimal system with its enormous advantages in the handling of fractions, advantages still exploited in the currency system of Great Britain, and in the twenty-four hour system which has persisted in the reckoning of time.

A centralized system of administration persisted with modification under peoples speaking Aryan languages. Equipped with more efficient instruments of warfare, particularly the horse and the chariot, the invaders captured and dominated Babylon from about 1740 B.C. to the end of the thirteenth century. Political organizations in northern

[4]See G. R. Driver, *Semitic Writing from Pictograph to Alphabet* (London, 1948), p. 59.

regions without an abundant supply of writing material such as clay
were built up but were unable to find an effective solution to problems
of time. The Hittites worked out a highly organized central administration with a strong imperial capital and a system of radiating
communications but were unable to capture Babylon in their attack
about 1150 B.C. The Assyrians succeeded in disrupting the Hittite
federation and eventually dominated the Aramaeans by the use of
heavier horses which made possible the introduction of cavalry, and
the use of iron which had been developed by the Hittites. Their
imperial organization was based on the establishment of provincial
governments placed under governors who exacted tribute. Babylonia
was captured in 729 B.C. and the religious pantheon subjected to
rearrangement under Ashur as the Assyrian god. The power of
Babylonian religion and culture was apparent in the difficulties of
governing Babylon evident in its destruction in 689 B.C. and in the
attempt to develop the prestige of the capital at Nineveh by the building of a library of Sumerian documents. Egypt was invaded and
made an Assyrian province in 674 B.C. but the task of governing two
powerful and divergent religious centres proved insuperable, and
Nineveh was destroyed in 612 B.C.

Expansion of the Assyrian Empire was accompanied by the subjugation of peoples of different languages, races, and cultures, the
destruction of Aramaean city states, and the practice of deportation
on a large scale to stamp out narrow local cultures. As a result of
these measures trade increased greatly. In the twelfth century the
camel was domesticated and caravan trade was extended. An enlarged
empire facilitated the growth of trade and industry. In turn these
developments assumed a more efficient system of writing shown in
the increasing dominance of Aramaic.

Monopolies of knowledge to an important extent dominated by
priestly organization and protected by complex types of script such as
the cuneiform and the hieroglyphic checked the growth of political
organization. Escape from these monopolies came from the fringes
of Babylonian and Egyptian civilizations in which new languages
among primitive peoples demanded simplicity. Semitic peoples in
contact with Egypt before 1500 B.C. apparently invented an alphabet
in Palestine and perfected it on the Phoenician coast. Access to

supplies of papyrus from Egypt and acquaintance with the reed pen enabled marginal peoples to borrow the simplest signs of the Egyptian system and to abandon its complexities. Invasion of the Hyksos apparently created a barrier between the south and the north of Arabia and led to a divergence between Aramaic and Phoenician writing. Aramaic script developed in relation to the demands of an extensive land trade for a concise conventional alphabet and possibly in relation to the use of parchment. The Phoenician script developed as a result of the demands of an extensive maritime trade for an alphabet in relation to the use of papyrus. Sounds of human speech were analysed into primary elements represented by twenty-two consonants.

A flexible alphabet favoured the growth of trade, development of the trading cities of the Phoenicians, and the emergence of smaller nations dependent on distinct languages. Hebrew was probably spoken in Palestine after 1200 B.C. The oral tradition was written down and the sacred character of writing emphasized by the Egyptians was reflected in the writing of the Hebrews. The importance of sculpture to large-scale political and religious organizations was shown in the prohibition of images by the Hebrews. The written letter replaced the graven image. Concentration on the abstract in writing opened the way for an advance from blood relationship to universal ethical standards, to the influence of the prophets in opposition to the absolute power of kings, and to an emphasis on monotheism. Laws were collected and written down in codes. Literature such as is presented in the Old Testament took root and flourished. Destruction of local sanctuaries by Sennacherib was followed by an emphasis on Jerusalem as the single sanctuary after 621 B.C.[5] After the fall of the Assyrian Empire the Babylonians extended their control and captured Jerusalem in 586 B.C.

With the advantage of new instruments of war such as the long bow and the long pike and of an improved alphabet, the Persians rapidly built up an empire to take the place of the empire of the Assyrians. As a result of support from the priests Cyrus became king of Babylon in 536 B.C. Cambyses added Egypt to the Empire in

[5]J. M. P. Smith, *The Origin and History of Hebrew Law* (Chicago, 1931), p. 55.

525 B.C. The problems of the Assyrians in dominating two divergent religious centres were inherited by the Persians. They were solved in part by a policy of toleration in which subject peoples were allowed to keep their gods and their religions. The Jews were released from captivity in Babylonia in 539 B.C. and Judah became the centre of an effective religious organization. The Persians developed an elaborate administration based on a system of roads and the use of horses to maintain communication by post with the capital. Satrapies were created and three officials, a satrap, a military governor, and a secretary of state, each acting independently of the other and directly responsible to the capital, were appointed. But centralization of power in the hands of the king quickly brought to the fore the problem of administrative capacity and of continuity or the problem of time. Difficulties increased with the tenacious religious centres of Babylonia, Egypt, and Jerusalem and with peoples such as the Greeks located on the fringe of the Empire. The introduction of new tactics of warfare enabled Alexander to overthrow the Empire in the decisive battles of 333 B.C. and 331 B.C. Oriental empires succeeded in organizing vast areas and in solving territorial problems but failed to find a solution to problems of continuity and of time. The empires of Assyria and Persia emphasized control over space but were unable to solve the problems of time in the face of the monopolies of religion in Babylonia and Egypt.

The Phoenician Semitic consonantal alphabet was taken over by the Greeks on the north shore of the Mediterranean. Unlike the peoples of Aryan speech in Asia Minor the Greeks escaped the full effect of contact with the civilizations of Egypt and Babylonia. The necessity of crossing water enabled the Greeks to select cultural traits of significance to themselves and to reject others. Without a script they had built up a strong oral tradition centring about the courts of conquering people from the north. The Homeric poems were the work of generations of reciters and minstrels and reflected the demands of generations of audiences to whom they were recited. This powerful oral tradition bent the consonantal alphabet to its demands and used five of the twenty-four letters as vowels. As vowels were equal in value to consonants they were used in each written word. The written language was made into an instrument responsive to the demands of the oral tradition. Introduction of the alphabet meant a concern with sound rather than with sight or with the ear rather than the eye. Empires had been built up on communication based on sight in contrast with Greek political organization which emphasized oral discussion. Greece escaped the problem of worship of the written word which had embarrassed oriental empires. The delay in the introduction of writing until possibly as late as the beginning of the seventh century, the difficulties of securing large and regular supplies of papyrus from Egypt, and the limitations of stone as a medium combined to protect the oral tradition. No energy was lost in learning a second language and monopolies of knowledge could not be built around a complex script.

The significance of the oral tradition and its vitality in Greek civilization became evident in its influence on the later history of the West. Its power has been such that it becomes impossible for modern Europeans who have participated in the heritage to approach it from an objective point of view. The impact of writing and printing on modern civilization increases the difficulties of understanding a civilization based on the oral tradition. We can perhaps remain content in quoting Renan, "Progress will eternally consist in developing what Greece conceived."

The power of the oral tradition was evident in the Homeric poems and in the adaptability of the hexameter to a wide variety of content. Hesiod's poetry was in sharp contrast with that of Homer. It facilitated the break of the individual from the minstrel tradition. The demands for greater sensitivity were met by the development of elegiac and iambic poetry. With accessibility to papyrus from Egypt in the late seventh and sixth centuries and the use of the lyre as a musical instrument, the position of professional minstrels was weakened. Lyric poetry developed on an impressive scale.

Not only did the strength of the oral tradition bend the alphabet to suit its needs, it also adapted other contributions of earlier civilizations. In the Homeric poems the gods became anthropomorphic deities. The supernatural was replaced by a concern with nature and science. The Ionian philosopher was able to reject the implications of the word as implying a creative act. "And God said" of the Hebrews ceased to be the symbol of creation. The contributions of the Chaldeans after the introduction of an exact system of chronology in 747 B.C. which facilitated a study of the periodic character of celestial phenomena were apparently used by Thales of Miletus to predict the eclipse of May 28, 585 B.C. The Olympian tradition which assumed fixed limits to the power of gods and men emphasized spatial concepts and in turn geometry. The science of nature dominated by geometry involved a concern with the internal properties of things rather than their relations with other things.

A concern with geometry and spatial relations was reinforced by the place of land and the search for land in colonization in Greek life. The results were evident in the evils which followed attempts to monopolize land. The growth of written laws in the colonies and in Athens in the seventh century threatened to impose a heavy load on debtors. But the power of the oral tradition was evident in the effectiveness of a search for means by which freedom might be achieved. It was possible to give individuals such as Draco, Solon, and Cleisthenes power to set up machinery adapted to continuous adjustment. Solon in the tradition of Ionian philosophy sought for universal truths and expressed the conviction that violation of justice involved disruption of the life of the community. The individual became responsible for his actions and the root of authority was destroyed. The rights of creditors engraved on ward stones erected on property were destroyed and the enslavement of labour as a disruptive force avoided. Solon discovered the secret of democracy in "the constitution of the judicial courts out of the whole people" (Bury).

Solon's reforms reflected the increasing significance of trade in contrast to land but their inadequacy became evident in the rise of a commercial class and in turn of tyrants in the sixth century. The Apollonian religion and Ionian philosophy were offset by encouragement of the worship of Dionysus. The tyrants encouraged the arts and in 537 B.C. assembled a collection of oracles to offset the prestige of the temple of Delphi. Increased trade and a concern with money suggested the limitations of an interest in geometry and spatial relations and the necessity of an interest in arithmetic and time. The philosophy of spatial externality involved discreteness and neglected the importance of continuity. The religion of Dionysus was probably modified by the influence of Mithraism from the East and by the Orphic revival. In turn Pythagoras developed a philosophy of numbers rather than geometry. As a result of these refinements a reconciliation between the Dionysian religion and the Apollonic became possible and the road was opened leading to the overthrow of the tyrants and the reforms of Cleisthenes. Solon had been largely concerned with problems incidental to the importance of land, space, and geometry and Cleisthenes was concerned with problems incidental to the importance of trade, time, and arithmetic. He rescued control over time from the nobles and introduced a solar calendar which governed a definite system of rotation in elections to the councils. The family state was replaced by the city state.

The effectiveness of the oral tradition in the development of the state became evident in the success with which the Greeks checked the expansion of the Persian Empire and in the cultural flowering of Athens in the fifth century. A powerful stimulus was given to philosophical speculation by the arrival of Ionian refugees from Miletus. The Dionysiac ritual and the choral lyric as perfected by Pindar provided the background for the development of the drama[6] under Aeschylus, Sophocles, and Euripides. In the second half of the fifth century writing began to make its encroachments on the oral tradition. Nietzsche has pointed to the significance of music, in which the joy of annihilation of the individual was understood, to tragedy. Disappearance of the spirit of music was followed by the decline of tragedy.[7] An increase in laws reflected an interest in prose. Literature in prose increased rapidly after the beginning of the Peloponnesian War. Plays were widely read in the time of Euripides. By the end of the fifth century the *boustrophedon* style had been abandoned and changed to writing from left to right. The Ionic alphabet was adopted in Athens with the codification and republication of the laws in 403-2 B.C.[8]

An increase in writing in Athens created divergences in the Greek community and accentuated differences particularly with Sparta. The

[6]J. E. Harrison, *Prolegomena to the Study of Greek Religion* (Cambridge, 1908), p. 568.
[7]F. Nietzsche, *The Birth of Tragedy from the Spirit of Music* (Edinburgh, 1923), pp. 120-7.
[8]W. S. Ferguson, *The Treasures of Athena* (Cambridge, Mass., 1923), p. 178.

Athenian Empire proved unable to meet the strains imposed by diverging cultures. Athenian courts were unable to escape charges of favouritism to democratic states. Interstate co-operation imposed demands which could not be met. The end came with the outbreak of war and the defeat of Athens.

In the fourth century Plato attempted to save the remnants of Greek culture in the style of the Socratic dialogues which in the words of Aristotle stood half way between prose and poetry. In the seventh epistle he wrote, "no intelligent man will ever be so bold as to put into language those things which his reason has contemplated, especially not into a form that is unalterable—which must be the case with what is expressed in written symbols." The interest of Aristotle in science was reflected in prose. But neither Aristotle nor Plato thought of a library as a necessity to the city state. It was significant that a library was founded by Aristotle in 335 B.C. and a public library started in 330 B.C. The written tradition had brought the vitality of the oral tradition to an end. In the words of Nietzsche, "Everyone being allowed to read ruineth in the long run not only writing but also thinking."

The role of the oral tradition in providing the milieu for the cultural activity of Greece had a profound significance for the history of the West and immediately for the history of Rome. The success with which the problems of time and space were solved had its implications for Roman culture. Greek culture awakened the native forces of Rome. Greek gods and Greek architecture were introduced in the latter part of the sixth century. The struggles for reform in Greece culminating in the work of Draco, Solon, and Cleisthenes were paralleled at a later date in Rome in the decemvirs' code of the Twelve Tables in 451 and 450 B.C. and in the increasing powers of the plebeians culminating in the appointment of the first plebeian pontifex maximus in 253 B.C.

The comparative isolation of Roman culture from Greece in the fifth and fourth centuries was followed by a fresh invasion of Greek influence in which the rich development of Greek culture checked that of Rome and compelled the latter to concentrate on its own capacities notably in law. Flexibility inherent in the oral tradition was evident in the rise of the plebeians, and in constitutional changes,

THE BIAS OF COMMUNICATION 45

in the activity of lawyers, and in the creation of machinery designed to meet the increasing demands for adjustment. In 242 B.C. the position of a second praetor, *peregrinus,* was introduced to reflect the importance of an expanding trade with alien peoples. Formulae were made more flexible in spite of the spread of writing. Praetors issued new edicts at the beginning of their years of office adapted to changing demands. The *patria potestas* was broken down to make way for the individual, and the contract, that "greediest of legal categories," developed. The concept of property was isolated. *Res privata* necessitated a concern with *res publica* and an interest in the legal concept of the state. By the middle of the first century B.C. the influence of writing became evident in the demand for codes. Laws and precedents in the oral tradition had been largely in men's minds to the time of Cicero. In the senate the introduction of an official gazette in 54 B.C. compelled speakers to consider a wide public and created a demand for a matter-of-fact style. Limitation of time for pleas in court in 52 B.C. reinforced the tendency. Latin prose which had developed in relation to the demands of the republic in the speeches of the Gracchi, of Cato, and of Cicero was subjected to the influence of writing.[9] The oral tradition absorbed the philosophy of teachers of Stoicism from the East and law was subjected to the demands of universality. Custom was criticized, the religious and ceremonial character of law was weakened, equality was promoted, harshness mitigated, and the factor of intent emphasized.

The adaptability of Roman law in the oral tradition facilitated the extension of the Roman Empire which followed the success of Roman arms. Wars with Carthage brought Rome into conflict with Hellenistic kingdoms and into contact with Greek culture. The Antigonids who succeeded Alexander in Macedonia gradually changed Greek city states into municipalities but continued difficulties enabled Rome to destroy the Achaean League in 168 B.C. and to dominate Greece and Macedonia. The Ptolemies inherited the problems of political control in Egypt. They created a new capital at Alexandria, a large library, and a new god Serapis to offset the influence of the

[9]"The build of the Roman sentence was but another consequence of Rome's battles which in giving her conquests forced her people as a nation to think administratively" (Spengler).

priestly class at Thebes. The demotic system and the use of the pen were encouraged at the expense of the hieratic system and the brush. As Rome acquired control over Egypt she adopted the policies of the Ptolemies. The Attalids built up a library at Pergamum to offset the prestige of the Ptolemies and, prevented from using papyrus by prohibitions on export, began the use of parchment on a large scale. Friendly relations with Rome were evident in the transfer of the *Magna Mater* in 204 B.C. The Seleucids, inheriting the problems of the Persian Empire of dominating the Persian, Babylonian, and Hebrew religions, attempted to introduce the city state as an instrument of government but failure was evident in the ultimate collapse of the kingdom. Rome fell heir to the unfortunate legacy.

As a result of expansion to the east Rome felt the full effects of Greek cultural achievements. Libraries were brought from Greece. Supplies of papyrus were available from Egypt. A book trade was developed and public and private libraries constructed. The spread of writing brought an interest in the codification of laws. Bureaucratic administration emerged. The Republic was replaced by the Empire. The emperor began to face the problems of empire which had been faced by earlier civilizations and to rely on solutions which had been developed in the East. Emperor worship gradually became more important. The dynastic problem which had menaced the attempts of former absolute monarchs to establish control over time strengthened the position of the army and a bureaucratic administration. New dynasties relied to an increasing extent on the prestige of Greece.

Under the influence of law the individual had been separated from the family. With the increasing rigidity of codes in the Empire the individual turned to Eastern religions. Efforts to exclude alien religions gradually broke down. The scrupulous fear of the gods which according to Polybius kept the Roman Empire together was no longer adequate.[10] Attempts of the nobility to maintain the traditional religion of the state against new tendencies meant leading a class against the masses and conflict with the "religious feelings of those lacking social privilege" (Max Weber).[11] Military campaigns in the

[10]T. R. Glover, *The Conflict of Religions in the Early Roman Empire* (London, 1932), p. 17.
[11]Franz Altheim, *A History of Roman Religion* (London, 1938), p. 330.

east were followed by the spread of Mithraism and in 274 A.D. Aurelian dedicated a shrine to the god *Sol Invictus*. Recognition of an Eastern religion as a basis of political support brought a revival of the hostility of Hellenism and compelled the emperor to accept the support of a religion more acceptable to Greek demands. Unable to provide a link between Greece and Persia since the Greeks refused to accept an absolute emperor Rome was compelled to set up a model similar to that of Persia in Constantinople. In turn the demands of bureaucracy were reflected in the division of the Empire between the Latin West and the Greek East. The Illyrian mountains prevented the establishment of a capital linking the Latin and the Hellenic provinces as the Alps were later to prevent the establishment of a capital uniting the German and Italian divisions of the Holy Roman Empire.[12]

The bureaucratic development of the Roman Empire and success in solving problems of administration over vast areas were dependent on supplies of papyrus. The bias of this medium became apparent in the monopoly of bureaucracy and its inability to find a satisfactory solution to the problems of the third dimension of empires, namely time. A new medium emerged to meet the limitations of papyrus. The handicaps of the fragile papyrus roll were offset by the durable parchment codex. With the latter the Christians were able to make effective use of the large Hebrew scriptures and to build up a corpus of Christian writings. The contributions of Alexandrian scholars in translating the Hebrew scriptures into Greek and the development of a Christian centre of learning at Caesarea after 231 A.D. checked the influence of a Babylonian priesthood, which had been encouraged by the Seleucids to check the influence of Persian religion, and which had been reconciled with Persian religion after the fall of Babylon in 125 A.D. Support of these religions for the Sassanid dynasty after 228 A.D. hindered the spread of the Roman Empire and compelled Constantine to select a new capital in Constantinople in 330 whence he could command the interest of a Christian population. The problem of the Roman Empire in relation to time was solved by the support of religion in the Christian church. The cumulative bias of papyrus in

[12]Vaughan Cornish, *The Great Capitals: An Historical Geography* (London, 1923), p. 140.

relation to bureaucratic administration was offset by an appeal to parchment as a medium for a powerful religious organization. Recognition of Christianity was followed by the drastic suppression of competing pagan cults.

The attempt of emperors to build up Constantinople as the centre of the civilized world especially after the fall of the Western Empire in 476 A.D. by establishing a large library and producing a code of civil law created friction with Rome and with Alexandria. Justinian's *Digest* carried in its prefix a description of law identical with that of Demosthenes, namely, an invention and gift of the gods, the opinion of sensible men, the restitution of things done amiss voluntary and involuntary, and a general compact of a state in accordance with which it is proper that all in that state should live.[13] But geographical separation reinforced differences in religion and exposed the Eastern Empire to the attacks of the Persians and in turn of the Arabs.

The spread of Mohammedanism cut off exports of papyrus to the east and to the west. The substitution of parchment in the West coincided roughly with the rise of the Carolingian dynasty and the decline of the Merovingians. Papyrus was produced in a restricted area and met the demands of a centralized administration whereas parchment as the product of an agricultural economy was suited to a decentralized system. The durability of parchment and the convenience of the codex for reference made it particularly suitable for the large books typical of scriptures and legal works. In turn the difficulties of copying a large book limited the numbers produced. Small libraries with a small number of large books could be established over large areas. Since the material of a civilization dominated by the papyrus roll had to be recopied into the parchment codex, a thorough system of censorship was involved. Pagan writing was neglected and Christian writing emphasized. "Never in the world's history has so vast a literature been so radically given over to destruction."[14] "Whatever knowledge man has acquired outside Holy Writ, if it be harmful it is there condemned; if it be wholesome it is there contained" (St. Augustine).[15] The ban

    13J. L. Myers, *The Political Ideas of the Greeks* (New York, 1927), pp. 308-16.
    14T. K. Osterreich, *Possession Demoniacal and Other, among Primitive Races, in Antiquity, the Middle Ages, and Modern Times* (London, 1930), p. 160.
    15Benjamin Farrington, *Science and Politics in the Ancient World* (London, 1939), p. 46.

on secular learning gave a preponderance to theological studies and made Rome dominant.[16] The monopoly of knowledge centring around parchment emphasized religion at the expense of law.

Parchment as a medium was suited to the spread of monasticism from Egypt throughout western Europe. St. Benedict founded a monastery at Monte Cassino about 520 A.D. and emphasized rules which made the preservation of books a sacred duty. His work followed by that of Cassiodorus gave "a scholarly bent to western monasticism." In spite of these efforts learning declined in Europe. Revival came on the fringes of the West in the independent and self-governing monasteries of Ireland. Missionary zeal led to the establishment of monasteries in Scotland and northern England and early in the seventh century on the Continent. The revival gained impetus with the support of Charlemagne and the migration of Alcuin from York. England and northern France were exposed to Danish raids but European monasteries had acquired transcriptions from English codices and supplemented them with those from Rome. Durable parchment books could be moved over long distances and transferred from regions of danger to regions of safety.

In the Byzantine Empire attempts to check the spread of Mohammedan influence were made by appeals to monophysite influence in the proscription of image worship and in attacks on the drain of monasticism on economic life. Resistance to Mohammedanism in the East strengthened the pressure of Mohammedanism in the West but the dangers were checked by the success of Charles Martel in 732 A.D. The ultimate effects were evident in the division between the East and the West. Encouraged by the success of resistance in the west, the papacy allied itself to the Carolingian line and anathematized the iconoclasts of the East. To recapture the West the Byzantine emperors abandoned the iconoclastic controversy in 775 A.D. In turn Charlemagne forbade the worship of images. The accession of the Empress Irene to the Byzantine throne in 797 enabled Charlemagne and the papacy to regard the throne as vacant under Salic law. Charlemagne was accordingly crowned emperor. The concern of Charlemagne for an efficient administration was reflected in efforts to improve educational institutions under control of the church and in his success in

[16]P. H. Lang, *Music in Western Civilization* (New York, 1941), p. 46.

encouraging the development of an efficient uniform script, the minuscule.[17] His contributions toward the unification of Europe were destroyed by recognition of the Teutonic principle of equal division among the heirs. A nucleus of power emerged in Paris following attempts to check the influence of the Danes and in Germany following attempts to defeat the Magyars. Encroachments of the Holy Roman Empire on the papacy were followed by reforms in the church and the development of a powerful ecclesiastical organization. Parchment became the medium through which a monopoly of knowledge was built up by religion.

This monopoly of knowledge invited the competition of a new medium, namely paper from China. Discovery of the technique of making paper from textiles provided a medium with which the Chinese, by adaptation of the brush for painting to writing, were able to work out an elaborate system of pictographs. A system of four to five thousand characters was used for ordinary needs "enabling those who speak mutually unintelligible idioms to converse together, using the pencil instead of the tongue."[18] Its effectiveness for this purpose meant the abandonment of an attempt to develop an alphabet system.

An elaborate development of writing supported the position of the scholarly class in administration of the empire. In turn a wide gap between a limited governing class and the mass of the people led to the spread of Buddhism from India. The monopoly of knowledge of the Brahmins in India based on the oral tradition and the limitations of communication had led to the spread of Buddhism with its emphasis on writing and its appeal to the lower classes. After Alexander, Buddhism had been encouraged but decline of Macedonian power brought a revival of the power of the Brahmins and migration of Buddhism to China. Access to supplies of paper in China enabled Buddhists to develop block printing on a large scale. Confucianism gained by the influence of the state and the reproduction of the classics. A script which provided a basis for administration in China and emphasized the organization of an empire in terms of space proved inadequate to meet the demands of time and China was

[17]The minuscule was a descendant of papyrus cursive writing which had been submerged by the vellum uncials after the fourth century. See F. G. Kenyon, *The Palaeography of Greek Papyri* (Oxford, 1899), pp. 124-5.

[18]Edward Clodd, *The Story of the Alphabet* (New York, 1913), p. 182.

THE BIAS OF COMMUNICATION

exposed to dynastic problems and to the domination of the Mongols from 1280 to 1368.

The spread of Mohammedanism to the east was followed by introduction to the technique of paper production. After establishment of a capital at Baghdad by the Abbasids paper manufacturing expanded and became the basis for an intense interest in learning. The Nestorians excommunicated from the church had established schools in which Greek and Latin works were translated into Syriac. Closing of the schools in Athens by Justinian in 529 A.D. had been followed by the migration of scholars to Persia. From this background of learning Baghdad became a centre for translators of Greek, Syriac, and Persian works into Arabic.

The prestige of Baghdad provoked a revival of Greek learning in Constantinople and of Latin learning in the West in the ninth century.[19] Revival of Greek learning in Constantinople was followed by the hostility of Rome. Rivalry between the Eastern and the Western church was accompanied by missionary activity and extension of the activities of the Eastern church to Bulgaria. The scriptures were translated into the Slavic vernacular on the one hand in the East, and translations from Latin into the vernacular were discouraged on the other hand in the West. The Cyrillic and the Glagolitic alphabets were invented to represent the sounds of the Slavonic language and to provide the basis for a richer expression.[20] An emphasis on secular learning in Byzantine education widened the breach with Rome and led to final separation of the churches of the East and West in 1054. Decline of the Abbasids was accompanied by activity of the Seljuk Turks and the capture of Jerusalem in 1070. The papacy refused to meet the requests of the Byzantine emperor for assistance and organized the Crusades. Ultimate failure to maintain control over Jerusalem led Crusaders to turn to Constantinople. It became subject to Latin states from 1204 to 1261 when it was recaptured by the Greeks.

Paper production spread from Baghdad to the West. After the capture of Baghdad by the Mongols in 1258, manufacturing was confined to western centres. With its development in Italy in the

[19]Werner Jaeger, *Humanism and Theology* (Milwaukee, Wisc., 1943), p. 24.
[20]D. Diringer, *The Alphabet, a Key to the History of Mankind* (London, n.d.), p. 475.

latter part of the thirteenth century new processes were introduced and a much better quality of paper produced. The art of paper making spread to France in the fourteenth century. Since linen rags were the chief raw material and the large cities provided the chief market for paper, production was determined to an important extent by proximity to cities with access to supplies of water and power. The commercial revolution beginning about 1275 paralleled increasing production of paper. The activity of the commercial cities of Italy weakened the Byzantine Empire. Religious prejudice against a product of Arabic origin was broken down and the monopoly of knowledge held by the monasteries of rural districts was weakened by the growth of cities, cathedrals, and universities.

The effects of the introduction of paper suggested by the rise of Baghdad were evident also in the concern with learning among the Mohammedans in Sicily and Spain. Large libraries were collected in Spain and following the recapture of Moorish cities by the Spaniards their contents in philosophy, mathematics, and medicine were made available to Europe. Acquaintance with the writings of Aristotle led to attempts such as those of St. Thomas Aquinas (1227-74) to reconcile classical with Christian teaching. Aristotle as a creator of formal logic could be absorbed in orthodoxy. Attempts of the church to dominate learning in the universities were paralleled by attempts to check the spread of the scriptures in the vernacular. Persecution of the Waldensians and other heretics and the Albigensian crusades were followed by the creation of new preaching orders, the Dominican and the Franciscan, and the establishment of the Inquisition. Revival of an interest in the study of Roman law in the twelfth century strengthened the position of the emperor but it was offset by the codification of canon law. In spite of this activity the increased use of paper and the growth of trade favoured the development of cities and the position of monarchies. The increasing importance of the vernacular and the rise of lawyers strengthened the position of political at the expense of ecclesiastical organizations. The power of France was evident in the migration of the papacy to Avignon (1308-78) and in the hostility of England. Roman law made little impression in England and the influence of the common law was shown in the jury system and in parliament. Again as a result of the war with France the court encouraged the vernacular. Decline of the monopoly of knowledge based on parchment in which an ecclesiastical organization emphasized control over time followed the competition of paper which supported the growth of trade and of cities, the rise of vernaculars, and the increasing importance of lawyers, and emphasized the concept of space in nationalism.

Monopolies of knowledge controlled by monasteries were followed by monopolies of knowledge controlled by copyist guilds in the large cities. The high price for large books led to attempts to develop a system of reproduction by machine and to the invention of printing in Germany which was on the margin of the area dominated by copyists. The centralized control of France was less adapted to evasion than the numerous political divisions of Germany. The coarse brown parchment of Germany led to an interest in the use of paper. The beauty of Gothic script in manuscript[21] and its adaptability to printing were other factors emphasizing an interest in the invention with its numerous problems of ink, production of uniform type on a large scale, and a press capable of quick operation. Abundance of paper in Italy and political division similar to that of Germany led to the migration of printers to Italian cities and to the development of Roman and italic types. Printing in Paris was delayed until 1469 and in England until even later.

Manuscripts which had accumulated over centuries were reproduced and by the end of the fifteenth century printers became concerned with the possibilities of new markets. Commercialism of the publisher began to displace the craft of the printer. The vernacular offered new authors and new readers. The small book and the pamphlet began to replace the large folios. In England, Caxton avoided the competition of Latin books produced on the Continent and attempted to widen his own market. He wrote in the Prologue to the *Eneydos*: "And that comyn englysshe that is spoken in one shyre varyeth from another. . . . I haue reduced and translated this sayd booke in to our englysshe, not ouer rude ne curyous, but in suche termes as shall be vnderstanden. . . ."[22] In Germany opposition of the German language to scholasticism as it had developed in Paris in the

[21]A. W. Pollard, *Early Illustrated Books* (New York, 1927), pp. 7-8.
[22]Cited G. M. Trevelyan, *English Social History* (New York, 1942), p. 82.

French language implied an emphasis on mystical teaching and the vernacular. The attack on the pride of scholastic philosophy was evident in the words of Thomas à Kempis, "But what is the good of wisdom without the fear of God?"[23] "For lack of training the mind turns to reason" (Henry Adams). German music protected by the Hohenstaufens resisted encroachments from the church. An interest in the vernacular was supplemented by the concern of scholars such as Reuchlin and Erasmus with Hebrew and Greek and led to the translations of Luther and Tyndale of the Bible in German and English. Publication of the scriptures in the vernacular was followed by new interpretations and by the intensive controversies conducted in pamphlets and sheets which ended in the establishment of Protestantism. Biblical literalism became the mother of heresy and of sects.

Printing activity incidental to the Reformation in Germany was accompanied by repressive measures against heretical publications in France. The authority of the University of Paris stood in contrast to the Frankfort Book Fair and the rise of Leipzig as a publishing centre. Printers migrated from France to adjacent countries such as Switzerland and the Netherlands and published books to be smuggled back to France. Learning declined in France in the sixteenth century but the vernacular found fresh support in printers shown in the writings of Montaigne and Rabelais. French became an official language after 1539. Its influence in the Huguenot controversies was evident in the Edict of Nantes of 1598, the first acknowledgment of a Roman Catholic country that heretics should be accorded civil rights. A policy of restrictions on publications paralleled a policy encouraging exports of paper. Countries encouraging a free press were subsidized by French mercantilist policies and the difficulties of restricting the smuggling of prohibited literature were increased. In the Empire repression in Antwerp was followed by the migration of printers such as Plantin to Holland and by an intensive development evident in a large-scale type-founding industry. Printing was accompanied by the production of printed sheets and postal services and by the growth of a financial centre at Antwerp. After the destruction of Antwerp in 1576 Amsterdam increased in importance. The Union of Utrecht in

[23]Jaeger, *Humanism and Theology*, p. 14.

1579 with ample financial resources was able to withstand the demands of the Empire and of France.

In England the absolutism of the Tudors involved suppression of printing but encouragement of the Renaissance and of the Reformation. Abolition of the monasteries and disappearance of clerical celibacy were followed by sweeping educational reforms. The printing press became "a battering-ram to bring abbeys and castles crashing to the ground."[24] Freedom from the Salic law made it possible for women to ascend the throne and to encourage the literature of the court. Restrictions on printing facilitated an interest in the drama and the flowering of the oral tradition in the plays of Shakespeare.

By the end of the sixteenth century the flexibility of the alphabet and printing had contributed to the growth of diverse vernacular literatures and had provided a basis for divisive nationalism in Europe. In the seventeenth century France continued to implement a mercantilist policy in suppression of publications and encouragement of exports of paper. Revocation of the Edict of Nantes in 1685 was followed by migration of skilled paper makers and the growth of paper making in England and Holland. Inefficiency in paper making incidental to state interference in France was paralleled by the introduction of more efficient methods in Holland. Refugees from France such as Pierre Bayle and Descartes developed a critical literature and a philosophy which had repercussions in the later criticism of the eighteenth century. In Holland type founding became an industrial enterprise and publishing activity by such firms as the Elzevirs built up markets throughout Europe. In England suppression of printing contributed to the outbreak of civil war. Increase in numbers of booksellers who encouraged printers as a means of reducing costs of publication led inevitably to the production of seditious literature, to renewed suppression, and finally to the outburst of controversial literature of the civil war.[25] Emphasis on the Bible accompanied restrictions on printing and facilitated an attack on Aristotelianism and scholastic philosophy and contributed to an interest in the moderns, the emergence of science, and deism. The Royal Society

[24]Trevelyan, *English Social History*, p. 58.
[25]H. R. Plomer, *A Short History of English Printing, 1476-1900* (New York, 1927), p. 169.

founded in 1662 was concerned with the advancement of science and the improvement of the English language as a medium for prose. It demanded a "mathematical plainness of language" and rejection of "all amplifications, digressions and swellings of style."[26]

Suppression of printing limited the attention to language which characterized France. Dictionaries were gradually developed but the English language was not adequate to the precision of the law codes of the Continent. Printing and improved communication strengthened a representative system in parliament. Suppression was met by newsletters and the rise of coffee-houses. The absolute power of parliament emerged to offset the absolute power of monarchy and annihilated the claims of common law which persisted in the colonies. It became the basis of public credit. The revolution of 1689 was followed by establishment of the Bank of England in 1694. Again, the revolution brought an end to the Licensing Act in 1694. Immediately large numbers of papers were printed and the first daily appeared in 1701. In the Augustan age, Addison and Steele reconciled "wit and virtue, after a long and disastrous separation, during which wit had been led astray by profligacy and virtue by fanaticism." Limitations of the hand press led to a political war of pamphlets and to the imposition of a stamp tax in 1712. The excessive burden of a tax on a commodity selling at a very low price compelled printers to undertake compendious works such as weeklies and monthlies and Ephraim Chambers's *Universal Dictionary of Arts and Sciences* which appeared in 1728. Restrictions on political writing hastened the development of other types of literature such as the novel and children's books and the establishment of circulating libraries. The Copyright Act of 1710 gave protection to publishers but a legal decision of 1774 denying the right to perpetual copyright under common law destroyed control over publications, encouraged large numbers of small publishers to engage in the production of reprints, supported a large second-hand book trade, and compelled large publishers to concentrate on expensive publications. Scottish writers who had not been hampered by the Grub Street of English writing in the early part of the eighteenth century and who had the support of universities and a background of Roman law concentrated on such philosophical speculations as those

[26]M. M. Lewis, *Language in Society* (London, 1947), p. 38.

produced by Hume and Adam Smith. Scottish publishers exploited the limitations of English publishing.[27] Constable was concerned with publication of the work of Sir Walter Scott and the *Edinburgh Review*.

The decline of political censorship after the fall of Walpole, an increase in the production of paper, escape from the monopoly of Dutch type foundries in the work of Caslon, and increased reliance on advertising following legislation against bill posters were followed by an expansion of newspapers. Resistance of the city of London against the absolute supremacy claimed by parliament supported the activities of Wilkes and Junius in the demand for the right to publish debates. Alderman Oliver, a member of parliament, stated that "whenever King, Lords or Commons assume unlimited power I will oppose that power."[28] The press attacked "the triple union of Crown, Lords and Commons against England." The newspaper article displaced the editorial and the essay in the writings of Junius who chose anonymity as it was "by no means necessary that he should be exposed to the resentment of the worst and most powerful men in the country." In spite of the achievement, taxes and threats of libel suits restricted expansion of newspapers and contributed to an interest in romantic literature. The position of deism which had been strengthened by the problems of the church during the revolution was weakened by the attacks of Hume and the way was opened to romanticism and to the religious revivals of Wesley and Whitefield.

The interest in literature which paralleled suppression of newspapers checked the growth of literature in the colonies and compelled an emphasis on newspapers. In the colonies a demand for printers for the publication of laws of the assemblies was followed by an interest in newspapers and in the post office. Printers were concerned with an agitation against restrictions and followed the arguments imported from England. The enormous burden of the stamp tax in 1765 on a low-priced commodity led to successful demands for repeal. Protests of Wilkes and Junius against the supremacy of parliament were

[27]See L. E. Gates, *Three Studies in Literature* (New York, 1899), pp. 50 ff.; also J. A. Greig, *Francis Jeffrey of the Edinburgh Review* (Edinburgh, 1948). On the influence of Roman law on Adam Smith see the Rt. Hon. Lord Macmillan, *Two Ways of Thinking* (Cambridge, 1934), pp. 28-30.

[28]Michael MacDonagh, *The Reporters' Gallery* (London, n.d.), p. 236.

elaborated in the colonies and the role of the newspapers in the
Revolution was recognized in a bill of rights guaranteeing freedom of
the press. Reliance on the common law implied a refusal to accept
the principle of supremacy of parliament. Inability to find a middle
course between absolute dependence and absolute independence broke
the first empire. The influence of Roman law evident in an absolute
parliament implied a conflict with an emphasis on common law in the
colonies.

In France increasing centralization imposed heavy burdens on
the administrative capacity of the monarchy. The increasing dis-
equilibrium which followed attempts to export paper and to restrict
publications led to increased development of printing in Holland and
Switzerland and to continued smuggling of books into France. Attacks
of French writers on restrictions became more aggressive in the
writings of Voltaire, Diderot, Montesquieu, Rousseau, and others.
The *Encyclopaedia* based on Chambers's work in England became a
storehouse of ammunition directed against the monarchy. With the
outbreak of revolution newspapers became the artillery of ideas.
After the Revolution Napoleon introduced a system of censorship.
Throughout the nineteenth century the long struggle for freedom of
the press was marked by advance culminating in the revolution of
1830, by recession under Louis Napoleon, and by advance under the
republic. Journalists played an active role as politicians with disturb-
ing effects on the political history of France.

Fear of the effects of the French Revolution in England was
evident in the severely repressive taxes on the press.[29] Introduction of
machinery in the manufacture of paper and in the printing press and
restrictions on newspapers led to an emphasis on media concerned
with material other than news. Periodicals, magazines, and books
increased in importance and brought a demand for the reduction of
taxes and cheap postage. The moderation of the French revolution of
1830 preceded the bloodless revolution of the Reform Acts.[30] In the
second half of the century the monopoly of *The Times* protected by

[29]See A. Aspinall, *Politics and the Press, c. 1780-1850* (London, 1949); and
W. H. Wickwar, *The Struggle for the Freedom of the Press, 1819-1832* (London,
1928).

[30]Emery Neff, *A Revolution in European Poetry, 1660-1900* (New York,
1940), p. 110.

taxes disappeared and newspapers increased in number and circulation in London and in the provinces. The monopoly of London strengthened by the railway was destroyed by the invention of the telegraph which encouraged provincial competition after 1868.[31] The success of German education, regarded as responsible for the defeat of Austria in 1866 and of France in 1870, led to the Education Act of 1870 and the creation of a large number of new readers. Newnes and Northcliffe exploited the new market in the new journalism. The monopoly of the circulating library disappeared before the new periodicals, cheap editions of novels, and literary agents.

An emphasis on literature in England in the first half of the nineteenth century incidental to the monopoly of the newspaper protected by taxes on knowledge and absence of copyright legislation in the United States compelled American writers to rely on journalism.[32] Publishers in New York such as Harper after the introduction of the steamship line drew on the vast stores of English literature and made them available to the enormous reading public of the United States.[33] Publishers and paper dealers such as Cyrus W. Field and Company opposed proposals for international copyright in 1852.[34] The emphasis on news which consequently characterized American journalism protected by the Bill of Rights supported the development of technological inventions in the fast press, the stereotype, the linotype, and the substitution of wood for rags. As in England the telegraph destroyed the monopoly of political centres and contributed, in destroying political power, to the outbreak of the Civil War. Technological development had its effects in the new journalism in England and on the Continent. The varying effects of technological change spreading from the United States destroyed the unity of Europe and contributed to the outbreak of the First World War. The British according to Bismarck were unable to participate in the work of the intimate circle of European diplomacy because of responsibility to parliament, and the inability increased with the new

[31] James Samuelson, ed., *The Civilization of Our Day* (London, 1896), p. 277.
[32] E. L. Bradsher, *Mathew Carey, Editor, Author and Publisher: A Study in American Literary Development* (New York, 1912), p. 79; and L. F. Tooker, *The Joys and Tribulations of an Editor* (New York, 1924), pp. 3-10.
[33] J. H. Harper, *The House of Harper* (New York, 1912), p. 89.
[34] *Ibid.*, p. 108.

journalism.[35] The attitude of Bismarck expressed in the remark, "Never believe a statement until you see it contradicted,"[36] was in contrast with Anglo-American journalism. The great pioneers of intellectual life in Germany left a legacy of leadership assumed after about 1832 by the state culminating in a deadening officialdom.[37] Northcliffe in the search for news made unprecedented use of cables and private wires and exploited Paris as a vast and cheap source of journalistic wealth with the result that French influence became more powerful.[38] The diplomatic institutions and techniques of an age of dynastic cabinet politics failed to work in a situation characterized by the press, electrical communications, mass literacy, and universal suffrage.[39] The Treaty of Versailles registered the divisive effects of the printing industry in its emphasis on self-determination. The monopoly of knowledge centring around the printing press brought to an end the obsession with space and the neglect of problems of continuity and time. The newspaper with a monopoly over time was limited in its power over space because of its regional character. Its monopoly was characterized by instability and crises. The radio introduced a new phase in the history of Western civilization by emphasizing centralization and the necessity of a concern with continuity. The bias of communication in paper and the printing industry was destined to be offset by the bias of the radio. Democracy which in the words of Guizot sacrificed the past and the future to the present was destined to be offset by planning and bureaucracy.

[35]J. A. Spender, The Public Life (London, 1925), p. 48.
[36]Harold Spender, The Fire of Life: A Book of Memories (London, n.d.), p. 36.
[37]Viscount Haldane, Selected Addresses and Essays (London, 1928), p. 22.
[38]Max Pemberton, Lord Northcliffe: A Memoir (New York, n.d.), p. 62.
[39]O. J. Hale, Publicity and Diplomacy, with Special Reference to England and Germany, 1890-1914 (New York, 1940), p. 209.

# A PLEA FOR TIME

I MUST PLEAD the bias of my special interest in the title of this paper. Economic historians and indeed all historians assume a time factor and their assumptions reflect the attitude towards time of the period in which they write. History in the modern sense is about four centuries old[1] but the word has taken on meanings which are apt to check a concern with facts other than those of immediate interest and its content is apt to reflect an interest in immediate facts such as is suggested by the words "all history proves." As a result history tends to repeat itself but in the changing accents of the period in which it is written. History is threatened on the one hand by its obsession with the present and on the other by the charge of antiquarianism. Economic history is in a particularly exposed position as is evident in the tendency to separate it from economics or to regard it as a basis of support for economics. "Knowledge of the past is at all times needed only to serve the present and the future, not to enfeeble the present or to tear the roots out of the vigorous powers of life for the future" (Nietzsche). The danger that knowledge of the past[2] may be neglected to the point that it ceases to serve the present and the future—perhaps an undue obsession with the immediate, support my concern about the disappearance of an interest in time.

Perhaps the exposed position of economic history may strengthen the urge to discover a solution of the difficulty, particularly as it becomes imperative to attempt to estimate the significance of the

[1] The use of the letters A.D. and B.C. apparently dates from the eighteenth century. Hellenic rationalism might be said to have persisted for 700 years and to have been obscured for 1,200 years. ". . . the longest period of consecutive time in human history on which we can found inductions is, upon the whole, a period of intellectual and moral darkness." Julien Benda, *The Great Betrayal* (London, 1928), p. 159.

[2] History "threatens to degenerate from a broad survey of great periods and movements of human society into vast and countless accumulations of insignificant facts, sterile knowledge, and frivolous antiquarianism" (Morley in 1878). Emery Neff, *The Poetry of History* (New York, 1947), p. 193.

attitude towards time in an analysis of economic change. The economic historian must consider the role of time or the attitude towards time in periods which he attempts to study, and he may contribute to an escape from antiquarianism, from present-mindedness, and from the bogeys of stagnation and maturity. It is impossible for him to avoid the bias of the period in which he writes but he can point to its dangers by attempting to appraise the character of the time concept.

It has been pointed out that astronomical time is only one of several concepts. Social time, for example, has been described as qualitatively differentiated according to the beliefs and customs common to a group and as not continuous but subject to interruptions of actual dates.[3] It is influenced by language which constrains and fixes prevalent concepts and modes of thought. It has been argued by Marcel Granet that the Chinese are not equipped to note concepts or to present doctrines discursively. The word does not fix a notion with a definite degree of abstraction or generality but evokes an indefinite complex of particular images. It is completely unsuited to formal precision.[4] Neither time nor space is abstractly conceived; time proceeds by cycles and is round; space is square.[5]

The linear concept of time was made effective as a result of humanistic studies in the Renaissance. When Gregory XIII imposed the Julian calendar on the Catholic world in 1582 Joseph Justus Scaliger following his edition of Manilius (1579) published the *De emendatione temporum* and later his *Thesaurus temporum* (1606) "probably the most learned book in the world."[6] With his work he developed an appreciation of the ancient world as a whole and introduced a conception of the unity of history at variance with the attitude of the church. While Scaliger assisted in wresting control over time from the church he contributed to the historical tradition

[3]P. A. Sorokin and R. K. Merton, "Social Time: A Methodological and Functional Analysis," *American Journal of Sociology*, XLII, 1936-7.

[4]"In general, the rigidity of the Japanese planning and the tendency to abandon the object when their plans did not go according to schedule are thought to have been largely due to the cumbersome and imprecise nature of their language, which rendered it extremely difficult to improvise by means of signalled communication" (Winston Churchill).

[5]R. K. Merton, "The Sociology of Knowledge," in *Twentieth Century Sociology*, ed. G. Gurvich and W. E. Moore (New York, 1945), pp. 387-8.

[6]H. W. Garrod, *Scholarship, Its Meaning and Value* (Cambridge, 1946), p. 42.

of philosophy until Descartes with his emphasis on mathematics and his unhistorical temper succeeded in liberating philosophy from history. The ideal of mathematical sciences dominated the seventeenth century. It was not until the Enlightenment that the historical world was conquered and until Herder and romanticism that the primacy of history over philosophy and science was established. Historicism was almost entirely a product of the nineteenth century.[7] In geology the precise date of the earth's formation advanced by Bishop Ussher was destroyed. "The weary series of accommodations of Genesis to geology was beginning."[8] In archaeology a knowledge of earlier civilizations implied a vast extension of time. In the hands of Darwin the historical approach penetrated biology and provided a new dimension of thought for science. In astronomy time was extended to infinity. Laws of real nature became historical laws. Even in mathematics arithmetic escaped from its bondage to geometry and algebra as "the science of pure time or order in progression" (Sir William Hamilton) came into its own.

The effects on history were evident in a recognition of the limitations of the written and the printed record. Mommsen made politics proper the subject-matter of historical knowledge but in the last decades of the nineteenth century the limitations of political historiography were evident. Burckhardt and to some extent Lamprecht approached the study of civilization through fine art. The highest value of art as of all free intellectual activity was to provide release from subservience to the will and from entanglement in the world of particular aims and individual purposes.[9] Taine held that intellectual development was the moving force behind political affairs and that the classical spirit was responsible for the French Revolution.[10] Fustel de Coulanges emphasized the myth[11] as a device for studying periods before writing had developed. Worship of the dead

[7]Ernst Cassirer, *The Problem of Knowledge: Philosophy, Science, and History since Hegel,* trans. W. H. Woglom and C. W. Hendel (New Haven, Conn., 1950), pp. 170-3.
[8]Leslie Stephen, *History of English Thought in the Eighteenth Century* (London, 1876), I, 458.
[9]Cassirer, *The Problem of Knowledge,* p. 277.
[10]*Ibid.,* p. 251.
[11]See H. and H. A. Frankfort, J. A. Wilson, T. Jacobsen, and W. A. Irwin, *The Intellectual Adventure of Ancient Man: An Essay on Speculative Thought in the Ancient Near East* (Chicago, 1946).

was regarded as the inner bond uniting divergent expressions of faith.

I have attempted to show elsewhere[12] that in Western civilization a stable society is dependent on an appreciation of a proper balance between the concepts of space and time. We are concerned with control not only over vast areas of space but also over vast stretches of time. We must appraise civilization in relation to its territory and in relation to its duration. The character of the medium of communication tends to create a bias in civilization favourable to an overemphasis on the time concept or on the space concept and only at rare intervals are the biases offset by the influence of another medium and stability achieved. Dependence on clay in Sumerian civilization was offset by dependence on stone in Babylon and a long period of relative stability followed in the reign of the Kassites. The power of the oral tradition in Greece which checked the bias of a written medium supported a brief period of cultural activity such as has never been equalled. Dependence on the papyrus roll and use of the alphabet in the bureaucracy of the Roman Empire was offset by dependence on parchment codex in the church and a balance was maintained in the Byzantine Empire until 1453. "Church and Army are serving order through the power of discipline and through hierarchical arrangement" (Metternich).[13] On the other hand in the West the bias of the parchment codex became evident in the absolute dominance of the church and supported a monopoly which invited competition from paper as a new medium. After the introduction of paper and the printing press, religious monopoly was followed by monopolies of vernaculars in modern states. A monopoly of time was followed by a monopoly of space. A brief survey of outstanding problems of time will perhaps assist in enabling us to understand more clearly the limitations of our civilization.

The pervasive character of the time concept makes it difficult to appreciate its nature and difficult to suggest its conservative influence. The division of the day into 24 hours, of the hour into 60 minutes, and of the minute into 60 seconds suggests that a sexagesimal system prevailed in which the arrangement was worked out and this

[12]*Empire and Communications* (Oxford, 1950).
[13]Cited by Alfred Vagts, *A History of Militarism* (New York, 1937), p. 16.

carries us immediately into Babylonian history.[14] The influence persists in systems of measurement and more obviously, for example, in Great Britain where the monetary system is sexagesimal. The advantages of the sexagesimal system are evident in calculations which permit evasion of the problem of handling fractions and have been exploited effectively in the development of aviation with its demands for rapid calculation.

In a system of agriculture dependent on irrigation the measurement of time becomes important in predicting periods of floods and the important dates of the year, seed-time and harvest. A concern with time was reflected in the importance of religion and in the choice of days on which festivals might be celebrated. The selection of holy days necessitated devices by which they could be indicated and violation of them could be avoided.[15] Dependence on the moon for the measurement of time meant exposure to irregularities such as have persisted in the means of determining the dates for Easter. Sumerian priesthoods apparently worked out a system for correcting the year by the adjustment of lunar months but the difficulties may have contributed to the success of Semitic kings with an interest in the sun, and enabled them to acquire control over the calendar and to make necessary adjustments of time over the extended territory under their control.[16] With control over time kings began the system of reckoning in terms of their reigns; our present statutes defy Anno Domini and date from the accession of the king in whose reign they are enacted. Control over time by monarchies, on the other hand, in addition to the human limitations of dynastic and military power, was limited by the continuity of priesthoods and the effectiveness of an ecclesiastical hierarchy.

[14]See J. T. Shotwell, "The Discovery of Time," *Journal of Philosophy, Psychology, and Scientific Methods*, 1915, 198-206, 254-316. It is argued that mathematics made the use of time possible. See F. Thureau-Dangin, "Sketch of a History of the Sexagesimal System," *Osiris*, VII. The Sumerian system was developed by crossing the numbers 10 and 6. Babylonian science was weak in geometry whereas the Greek science was strong. The Greeks learned the sexagesimal system through astronomy and discovered the Hindu system with a zero.

[15]J. T. Shotwell, *An Introduction to the History of History* (New York, 1922), pp. 43-4.

[16]The calendar was apparently organized by Marduk and was under the control of the ruler of Mesopotamia. Frankfort *et al.*, *The Intellectual Adventure of Ancient Man*, p. 181.

In Egypt and Babylonia the principal changes in nature were accompanied by appropriate rituals which were part and parcel of cosmic events. Time was a succession of recurring plans each charged with peculiar value and significance.[17] In a sense it was a biological time with a sequence of essentially different phases of life. In Egypt as in Babylonia the importance of the Nile floods and dependence on irrigation were linked with the celebration of religious festivals and the importance of determining an exact date. It is possible that the absolutism of Egyptian dynasties was dependent on the ability of kings to determine the sidereal year in relation to the appearance of the star Sirius. Recognition of the first dynasty by the Egyptians implied a recognition of time as dating from it. The joining of the two lands in Egypt apparently coincided with kingship and implied an emphasis on religious ceremony and ritual. The power of absolute kings over time and space was reflected in the pyramids which remain a standing monument to justify their confidence, in the development of mummification, a tribute to their control over eternity, and in the belief in immortality. The power of the absolute monarchy may have been weakened by the priesthood which discovered the more reliable solar year. Absolutism passed with control over time into the hands of the priesthood and checked expansion over space in the Egyptian Empire.

In Egypt the power of the absolute monarchy reflected in the monumental architecture of the pyramids and in sculpture was offset by the power of the priesthood based on a complex system of writing and the use of papyrus. The emphasis of a civilization on means of extending its duration as in Egypt accompanied by reliance on permanence gives that civilization a prominent position in periods such as the present when time is of little significance. In Babylonia the power of the priesthood was dependent in part on a mastery of complex cuneiform writing on clay tablets, and an increasing power of the monarchy on the creation of new and elaborate capitals emphasizing sculpture and architecture. Relative stability was gradually established over a long period by compromises between political and religious power. In turn the Kassites, the Assyrians, and the Persians recognized the power of the Babylonian priesthood. In Egypt

[17]*Ibid.*, pp. 23-5.

the power of the priesthood checked the possibilities of political development of the monarchy and prevented effective conquest by conquerors such as the Hyksos and later the Assyrians and the Persians. Monopolies of control over time exercised by the priesthoods of Babylonia and Egypt made the problems of political organization in the Assyrian and Persian empires and indeed of later empires insuperable.

The Babylonian priesthood in its concern with time contributed to the study of astrology and astronomy by the introduction of a system of chronology at the era of Nabonassar in 747 B.C. It possibly followed the discovery that every 18 years and 11 days the moon returned almost to the same position in relation to the sun.[18] The discovery of the periodic character of celestial phenomena and the possibility of prediction gave Babylonia an enormous influence on religious cults and led to the domination of fatalism based on scientific knowledge.

The limited possibility of political organizations expanding their control over space incidental to the control of priesthoods in their monopolies of knowledge over time facilitated the development of marginal organizations such as those of the Jews in Palestine. Periods of expansion and retreat in political organization centring on Egypt or Babylonia weakened an emphasis on political organization and strengthened an emphasis on religious organization. The marginal relation to cultures with monopolies of complex systems of writing favoured the development of relatively simple systems of writing such as emerged in the alphabet of the Phoenicians and the Aramaeans. In these marginal cultures religious organization emphasized a system of writing in sharp contrast with those of Egypt and Babylonia, and in compensation for lack of success in political organization with control over space built up an elaborate hierarchy with control over time. The latter emphasized the sacred character of writing and drew on the resources of Egyptian and Babylonian civilizations to an extent obvious to students of the Old Testament. There was "no engrossment in the moment but full recognition that human life is a great stream of which the present is only the realized moment. . . . It was no accident that the supremely religious people

[18]Shotwell, *An Introduction to the History of History*, p. 45.

of all time were likewise our first great historians." (W. A. Irwin.) History emerged with the Hebrews as a result of the concern with time.

Contact of barbarians on the north shore of the Mediterranean with older civilizations was followed by the emergence of Greek civilization. An emphasis on problems of space incidental to a concern with conquest of territory was evident in the Homeric poems developed in the oral tradition. Geometry with its bias toward measurement and space imposed restrictions on a concern with time. The spread of a money economy strengthened an interest in numbers and arithmetic and in turn in mystery religions in conflict with the established Apollonic religion. The flexibility of an oral tradition enabled the Greeks to work out a balance between the demands of concepts of space and time in a city state. In the reforms of Cleisthenes control over time was wrested from religion and placed at the disposal of the state. The results of a balanced society were evident in the defeat of the Persians and the flowering of Greek culture in the fifth century. But such a balance was not long maintained.[19] Cleisthenes created a senatorial year with ten prytanies of 36 or 37 days in each solar year averaging 365¼ days over a period free from cycles and intercalations, but the old civil calendar sanctioned by religious observance continued. The Metonic cycle[20] of 19 years, 30 days in each month, was introduced on June 27 (Julius) 432 B.C. and became a norm for the accurate measurement of time. A change was made to a new senatorial year probably in the year of anarchy 404-3. When democracy was re-established the senatorial year was made to conform to the civil year. The Callippic cycle was introduced in the first summer solstice June 27-8, 330 B.C. with 30 days to each month and every sixty-fourth day dropped.

The spread of writing in the latter part of the fifth and in the fourth centuries accentuated strains which destroyed Greek civiliza-

---

[19]A new concern with time was evident in Herodotus who presented a history "that neither the deeds of men may fade from memory by lapse of time, nor the mighty and marvellous works wrought partly by the Hellenes, partly by the Barbarians, may lose their renown." See also Thucydides' reasons for writing history.

[20]See J. K. Fotheringham, "The Metonic and Callippic Cycles," *Monthly Notices of the Royal Astronomical Society*, LXXXIV, 384; also B. D. Meritt, *The Athenian Calendar in the Fifth Century* (Cambridge, Mass., 1928), pp. 72, 102, 122, 126.

tion. Following the collapse of Greece and the success of Alexander, the East was divided in the Hellenistic kingdoms. In Egypt in a new capital at Alexandria the Ptolemies attempted to offset the influence of the priesthood at Thebes and of Babylonian science by the creation of a new religion and the encouragement of research in libraries and museums. Aristotelian influence was evident in the concern with science and in developments in astronomy. The names of the planets and constellations remain as testimonials to the interest of antiquity in astronomy. Leap year was introduced in 239 or 238 B.C. but was later abandoned until taken up by the Romans.

After the conquest of Egypt by the Romans Julius Caesar employed Sosigenes, an Egyptian astronomer, to work out an accurate calendar and it is probably significant that the new calendar recognized the festivals of Isis and contributed to the spread of Egyptian and other religions in the Empire. Exploitation of the irregular measurement of time for political purposes[21] and demands for regularity and the power of Julius Caesar in enforcing the new calendar led to a change from the beginning of the new year on March 1 to January 1 in 46 B.C., or 708 years from the date of the foundation of Rome, and to a year of 365¼ days. A fixed date of reckoning, that of the founding of the city, reflected the interest of Rome in the unique character of a single day or hour and the belief that continuity was a sequence of single moments. An emphasis on specific single acts at a unique time contributed to the growth of Roman law notably in contracts in which time is of the essence. Alternate odd months were given 31 days and even months 30 days excepting February which had 29 days but 30 days every fourth year. The month following that named for Caesar, July, was called Augustus and was given the same number of days. A day was taken from February and given to August. September and November were

[21]The calendar was controlled by the college of pontifices. Of 192 days in a year on which people could be called together only 150 were left after ruling out days falling on market days, the last day of the Roman eight-day week, and days of seasonal games. An intercalary month was inserted in February every two years to bring the linear year into harmony with the solar year but in the early second century B.C. the pontifices obtained the right to insert it at will. The magisterial year for purposes of litigation, public contracts, and the like was changed according to their interests. These abuses were brought to an end by Caesar and the days added to the year by him as *dies fasti* were possibly intended as meeting days. See L. R. Taylor, *Party Politics in the Age of Caesar* (Berkeley, Calif., 1949), pp. 79-80.

reduced to 30 days and October and December increased to 31 days to avoid three months in succession with 31 days.

A powerful bureaucracy at Rome and at Constantinople maintained control over time. Toward the end of the third century a 15-year cycle was introduced for tax purposes and after 312 A.D. the Egyptian date of indiction was changed from August 29 to September 1, the beginning of the Byzantine year. As a result of the influence of astronomy each day became sacred to a planet and the liturgy of the mysteries of Mithra contributed to the substitution of the seven-day week for the Roman eight days about the time of Augustus. December 25 as the date of the birth of the sun in the worship of Mithra was replaced by Christmas Day between 354 and 360 A.D.[22] Easter probably took the place of festivals celebrating Attis at the vernal equinox.[23] The Christians used March 1 as the beginning of the year following the Mosaic ordinance as to the Passover.

Following the collapse of the Empire in the West the church supported the system of dating events from the supposed year of the birth of Christ. The concern of religion for the domination of time evident in stories of the flood designed to show that a past had been wiped out and that a new era began, in the beginnings of Egyptian time, in the history of Greece and Rome continued in the Christian era. St. Cyril was reputed to have drawn up a table of 95 years (five cycles of 19 years each) to be based on the accession of Diocletian in 284 A.D. The base was changed to the Incarnation and the table introduced into the calendar of the West by Dionysius Exiguus in 525 A.D. St. Wilfrid secured adoption of the system to celebrate Easter on or after March 15 at Whitby in 664 A.D. in opposition to the Celtic system which allowed the celebration of Easter on the 14th and calculated the moon on a cycle of 84 years. From the time of Bede, in England the year was reckoned from the Incarnation. The system was carried by missionaries to the eastern regions of the Franks and the Incarnation became the official date in 839. Under the influence of Otto the Great it was adopted in the papal chancery

[22]Franz Cumont, *Astrology and Religion among the Greeks and Romans* (New York, 1912), pp. 162-5.
[23]J. G. Frazer, *Adonis, Attis, Osiris: Studies in the History of Oriental Religion* (London, 1906), p. 200.

in 963.[24] Use of the imperial year and indiction had apparently begun in the papal chancery in 537 and had become general practice in 550. They were never used after 781 A.D.[25] Charles the Great visited Rome in that year and under Hadrian the Frankish practice of using a double form of dating documents was used, the pontifical year replacing the regnal of the emperor at Constantinople.

By at least the last quarter of the ninth century Frankish emperors reckoned from Christmas Day as the beginning of the New Year. Religious movements stimulating devotion to the Virgin Mary led to the establishment of Lady Day (March 25) as the beginning of the year in the French chancery after 1112 and in England in the latter part of the twelfth century. After the middle of the thirteenth century, possibly as a result of the study of Roman law and the increasing use of almanacs, there was a gradual return to the Roman system in which the year began on January 1. It was not until 1752 that the beginning of the year was moved from March 25 to January 1 in England.[26] The pagan form of reckoning was gradually restored by the modern state. As in Egypt and in Rome control over time by the church was emphasized by architecture notably in the enduring monuments of the Gothic cathedral.

Gregory XIII introduced a calendar reform in 1582 in which the cumulative inaccuracies of a year based on $365\frac{1}{4}$ days were corrected and October 5 reckoned as October 15. While the Roman Catholic church exercised a dominant control over time other religions Jewish and Protestant asserted their rights notably in the determination of holidays. This division weakened the state in the creation of friction and strengthened it by compelling an insistence on unity. Significantly Protestant states grudgingly conceded the advantage of the change but it was not until 1750 that Great Britain ordered September 2, 1752, to be followed by September 14. It was only after the overthrow of the Tsarist régime in Russia that the Julian calendar was superseded by the Gregorian.

[24]R. L. Poole, *Chronicles and Annals: A Brief Outline of Their Origin and Growth* (Oxford, 1926), p. 26.
[25]R. L. Poole, *Lectures on the History of the Papal Chancery Down to the Time of Innocent III* (Cambridge, 1915), p. 38.
[26]See R. L. Poole, "The Beginning of the Year in the Middle Ages," *Proceedings of the British Academy*, X.

The Christian system followed Roman religion in giving a fixed year, that of the birth of Christ, a unique position. Control over time was not only evident in chronology but also in its place in the life of the Middle Ages. Spread of monasticism and the use of bells to mark the periods of the day and the place of religious services introduced regularity in the life of the West. Sun-dials, whose usefulness was limited in the more cloudy skies of the north, gave way to water clocks and finally to devices for measuring time with greater precision.[27] The modern hour came into general use with the striking clock in the fourteenth century.[28]

Regularity of work brought administration, increase in production, trade, and the growth of cities. The spread of mathematics from India to Baghdad and the Moorish universities of Spain implied the gradual substitution of Arabic for Roman numerals and an enormous increase in the efficiency of calculation.[29] Measurement of time facilitated the use of credit, the rise of exchanges, and calculations of the predictable future essential to the development of insurance. Introduction of paper, and invention of the printing press hastened the decline of Latin and the rise of the vernaculars. Science met the demands of navigation, industry, trade, and finance by the development of astronomy and refined measurements of time which left little place for myth or religion. The printing press supported the Reformation and destroyed the monopoly of the church over time though the persistence of its interest is evident in feast days. The church recognized at an early date the threat of astronomers to the monopoly over time and treated them accordingly.

The struggle between church and state for control over time had centred about a series of measures in the states in the West and the iconoclastic controversy in the Byzantine Empire in the East. The fall of Constantinople in 1453 which followed the perfection of artillery came as a profound shock to Europe. A bulwark of opposition to the absolute supremacy of the papacy had been removed and new states became attracted to the problem of duration and to the possibility

[27]A. P. Usher, *A History of Mechanical Inventions* (New York, 1929); also Lewis Mumford, *Technics and Civilization* (New York, 1934).
    [28]M. P. Nilsson, *Primitive Time-reckoning* (London, 1920).
    [29]L. T. Hogben, *From Cave Painting to Comic Strip* (London, 1949), pp. 103 ff.; see also Etienne Hajnal, "Le rôle social de l'écriture et l'évolution européenne," *Revue de l'Institut de Sociologie*, 1934.

of devices which had contributed to the solution of problems of longevity in the Byzantine Empire. The experiment of the Tudors[30] had many parallels with that of the Byzantine Empire—notably the emphasis on a sort of Caesaropapism by Henry VIII in becoming head of the Anglican church, on the destruction of monasteries paralleling the iconoclastic controversy, and on the position of women on the throne in contrast with the prohibitions of Salic law. As the Tudors assumed the mantle of divine right from the papacy they laid the foundation for internal struggles for control over time evident in the contention over monopolies[31] under Elizabeth and James I, and in the absolute supremacy of parliament. The interest of parliament in time was evident in the statute of limitations, restrictions on the period for patents and copyright, the rule against perpetuity in wills, and abolition of entail. The interest of the state in the subject of mortmain has been followed by estate taxes to check control over time beyond life itself. It was not until 1774 that perpetual copyright in common law was destroyed by a decision of the courts following the refusal of Scottish courts to recognize the pretensions of English common law and London booksellers. The concern of the Crown in the problem of time and in the permanence of dynasties was evident in the choice of names for monarchs, to mention only the four Georges. A growing interest in problems of permanence of the British Empire was evident in Gibbon's *Decline and Fall of 'the Roman Empire*. The struggle over control of time on the Continent led the French to start a new era at the birth of the republic on September 22, 1792. Names descriptive of the seasons, such as Thermidor for the summer, were introduced. The arrangement was brought to an end in 1805 following the Concordat of 1802. Holidays determined by the church were suppressed and new holidays were created by the modern state. Economic inefficiencies incidental to the growth in numbers of religious holidays were paralleled by industrial controversies over shorter working weeks.

[30]Byzantine policy also had implications for the French. The Edict of Nantes was supported by an illustration of tolerance told by Jacques-Auguste de Thoʋ (1533-1617) in *Continuation of the History of His Time,* to the effect that th. Pope visited Constantinople in 526 to plead against the persecution of Arianism. See A. A. Vasiliev, *Justin the First: An Introduction to the Epoch of Justinian the Great* (Cambridge, Mass., 1950), pp. 220-1.

[31]C. H. McIlwain, *Constitutionalism, Ancient and Modern* (Ithaca, N.Y., 1940), p. 124.

Weakening of control over time by the church and limited control by the state left a vacuum which was occupied by industry. The church, particularly in the monastic orders, had introduced a rigorous division of time for services following the spread in the use of clocks and the bell. But industrial demands meant fresh emphasis on the ceaseless flow of mechanical time. Establishment of time zones facilitated the introduction of uniformity in regions. An advance in the state of industrialism reflected in the speed of the newspaper press and the radio meant a decline in the importance of biological time determined by agriculture. Demands for the reform of the calendar and daylight saving schemes follow the impact of industrialism. The persistence of Easter as a movable feast points to the conservative character of time arrangements.

The demands of industry on time have been paralleled by the demands of business. Family concerns extending over generations were followed by more flexible and permanent arrangements in partnerships and corporations. Certain types of industries such as communication, particularly newspapers, were apparently suited to family control, partly because of the need for advertising and use of the same name over a long period to give an appearance of permanence where permanence and dependability were important. The length of life of corporations has been dependent on concern of management with policies affecting duration and with the character of an industry. Centennial volumes are published to reflect the element of permanency and as a form of institutional advertising. The long history of the Hudson's Bay Company was perhaps in part a result of the necessity of conducting operations extending over a period of five or six years between the date of purchase of goods and the date of the sale of furs. Periods of expansion and consolidation imply an alternative interest in time and place.

Conflict between different groups over monopolies of time hastened the intervention of the state. Devices emphasizing rapid turnover of goods, whether technological (for example, in the substitution of buses for street railways), or commercial (for example, in the introduction of pennies to secure newspaper sales and in an emphasis on changing fashions as in the case of motor cars or the publication of books by popular authors), tend to conflict with long-term investment supported by savings voluntary or compulsory, whether insurance or old age pensions. Competition between consumers' goods with rapid turnover and durable goods implies conflict within an economy and conflict between nations emphasizing the durable character of goods, such as England, and those emphasizing a less durable character, such as North America. As a result the state intervenes with policies ranging from the breaking of trusts to the devices of socialism. In fields concerned with durable goods and involving long-term investment of capital, such as railways, electric power, forests, and steel, state intervention has been marked. The ultimate steps are taken in a concern with long-term budgets and long-term capital arrangements and with five-year plans. The need for a sane and balanced approach to the problem of time in the control of monopolies, and in the whole field of interest theory and in other directions, is evident in the growth of a bureaucracy in a totalitarian state. The static approach to economic theory has been of limited assistance in meeting the problems of time.

A balanced civilization in its concern with the problem of duration or time and of extent or space is faced with several difficulties. Systems of government concerned with problems of duration have been defeated in part by biology, when dynasties fail to provide a continued stream of governing capacity, and by technology,[32] when invaders are able to exploit improvements in the methods of warfare at the expense of peoples who have neglected them. Writing as a means of communication provides a system of administration of territory for the conquerors and in religion a system of continuity but in turn tends to develop monopolies of complexity which check an interest in industrial technology and encourage new invaders. "For where there is no fear of god, it [the state] must either fall to destruction, or be supported by the reverence shown to a good Prince; which indeed may sustain it for a while, and supply the want of religion in his subjects. But as human life is short, its government must of course sink into decay when its virtue, that upheld and informed it, is extinct." (Machiavelli.) A balanced concern with space or extent of territory and duration or time appears

[32]See Benjamin Farrington, *Head and Hand in Ancient Greece: Four Studies in the Social Relations of Thought* (London, 1947).

to depend on a dual arrangement in which the church is subordinate to the state and ensures that the mobilization of the intellectual resources of the civilization concerned, by religion or by the state, will be at the disposal of both and that they will be used in planning for a calculated future in relation to the government of territory of definite extent. If social stratification is too rigid and social advancement is denied to active individuals as it is in plutocracies a transpersonal power structure will be threatened with revolt.[33]

The tendency of a monopoly over time in religion to lead to an accumulation of wealth invites attacks from the state with demands for redistribution evident in the embarrassments of the church in the Middle Ages, and in the attacks on monasteries in England and in the Byzantine Empire, and in confiscation of the property of the Jews. The linking of church and state in an absolute monarchy and the accumulation of wealth may lead to revolution as it did in France and Russia. This implies a fundamental break with a concept of time increasingly out of line with the demands of a bureaucracy centring on space. The bias of communication in space or in time involves a sponge theory of the distribution of wealth which assumes violence.

It is beyond the bounds of this paper to enumerate the inventions for the measurement of time or to suggest their implications in the various developments of modern industrialism. It is concerned with the change in attitudes toward time preceding the modern obsession with present-mindedness, which suggests that the balance between time and space has been seriously disturbed with disastrous consequences to Western civilization. Lack of interest in problems of duration in Western civilization suggests that the bias of paper and printing has persisted in a concern with space. The state has been interested in the enlargement of territories and the imposition of cultural uniformity on its peoples, and, losing touch with the problems of time, has been willing to engage in wars to carry out immediate objectives. Printing has emphasized vernaculars and divisions between states based on language without implying a concern with time. The effects of division have been evident in development of the book, the pamphlet, and the newspaper and in the growth of regionalism as

[33]N. S. Timasheff, *An Introduction to the Sociology of Law* (Cambridge, Mass., 1939), p. 207.

new monopolies have been built up. The revolt of the American colonies, division between north and south, and extension westward of the United States have been to an important extent a result of the spread of the printing industry. In the British Empire the growth of autonomy and independence among members of the Commonwealth may be attributed in part to the same development. In Europe division between languages has been accentuated by varying rates of development of the printing industry. Technological change in printing under constitutional protection of freedom of the press in the United States has supported rapid growth of the newspaper industry. Its spread to Anglo-Saxon countries has sharpened the division between English and languages spoken in other areas and in turn contributed to the outbreak of the First World War. Not only has the press accentuated the importance of the English language in relation to other languages, it has also created divisions between classes within English-speaking countries. Emphasis on literacy and compulsory education has meant concentration on magazines and books with general appeal and widened the gap between the artist concerned with improvement of his craft and the writer concerned with the widest market. The writing of history is distorted by an interest in sensationalism and war. The library catalogue reflects an obsession of commercialism with special topics, events, periods, and individuals, to mention only the names of Lincoln, Napoleon, Churchill, Roosevelt, and others.

Large-scale production of newsprint made from wood in the second half of the nineteenth century supported large-scale development of newspaper plants and a demand for effective devices for widening markets for newspapers. The excitement and sensationalism of the South African War in Great Britain and of the Spanish-American War in the United States were not unrelated to the demands of large newspapers for markets. Emergence of the comics[34] coincided with the struggle for circulation between Hearst and Pulitzer in New York. Increased newspaper circulation supported a demand for advertising and for new methods of marketing, notably the department store. The type of news essential to an increase in circulation, to an increase in advertising, and to an increase in the

[34]Coulton Waugh, *The Comics* (New York, 1947).

sale of news was necessarily that which catered to excitement. A prevailing interest in orgies and excitement was harnessed in the interests of trade. The necessity for excitement and sensationalism had serious implications for the development of a consistent policy in foreign affairs which became increasingly the source of news. The reports of MacGahan, an American newspaper man, on Turkish activities were seized upon by Gladstone and led to the defeat of Disraeli.[35] The activity of W. T. Stead in the *Pall Mall Gazette* was an important factor in the fiasco of Gordon's expedition to Egypt. While it would be fatal to accept the views of journalists as to their power over events it is perhaps safe to say that Northcliffe played an important role in shifting the interest of Great Britain from Germany to France and in policy leading to the outbreak of the First World War.

Technological advance in the production of newspapers accompanied the development of metropolitan centres. In the period of western expansion "all these interests bring the newspaper; the newspaper starts up politics, and a railroad."[36] A large number of small centres were gradually dwarfed by the rise of large cities. In turn the opinion of large centres was reflected in their newspapers and in an emphasis on differences. "No," said Mr. Dooley, "They've got to print what's different."[37] Large centres became sources of news for distribution through press associations and in turn press associations became competitive with an emphasis on types of news which were mutually exclusive. The United Press became a competitor of the International News Service (Hearst) and of the Associated Press. The limitations of news as a basis of a steady circulation led to the development of features and in particular the comics and photography. Improvements in the reproduction of photographs coincided with the development of the cinema. News and the cinema complemented each other in the emphasis on instability. As a result of the struggle between various regions or metropolitan centres political stability was difficult to achieve. "It is one of the peculiar weaknesses

    [35]Archibald Forbes, *Souvenirs of Some Continents* (London, 1894).
    [36]Matthew Josephson, *The Robber Barons: The Great American Capitalists, 1861-1901* (New York, 1934), p. 27.
    [37]Cited by L. M. Salmon, *The Newspaper and the Historian* (New York, 1923), p. 29.

A PLEA FOR TIME 79

of our political system that our strongest men cannot be kept very long in Congress."[38] While Congress was weakened the power of the president was strengthened. Theodore Roosevelt appealed to the mass psychology of the middle class and significantly gave the press a permanent room in the White House.[39] Oswald Garrison Villard claimed that "Theodore Roosevelt did more to corrupt the press than anyone else."[40]

The steadying influence of the book as a product of sustained intellectual effort was destroyed by new developments in periodicals and newspapers. As early as 1831 Lamartine would write: "Le livre arrive trop tard; le seul livre possible dès aujourd'hui, c'est un journal." The effect of instability on international affairs has been described by Moltke: "It is no longer the ambition of princes; it is the moods of the people, the discomfort in the face of interior conditions, the doings of parties, particularly of their leaders, which endanger peace."[41] The Western community was atomized by the pulverizing effects of the application of machine industry to communication. J. G. Bennett is said to have replied to someone charging him with inconsistency in the New York Herald, "I bring the paper out every day." He was consistent in inconsistency. "Advertisement dwells [in] a one-day world."[42]

Philosophy and religions reflected the general change. In the words of Punch: "It was the gradually extended use of the printing press that dragged the obscure horrors of political economy into the full light of day: and in the western countries of Europe the new sect became rampant." Hedonism gained in importance through the work of Bentham. Keynes has described his early belief by stating that he belonged to the first generation to throw hedonism out the window and to escape from the Benthamite tradition. ". . . I do now regard that as the worm which has been gnawing at the insides of modern civilisation and is responsible for its present moral decay. We used to regard the Christians as the enemy, because they appeared

[38]Brand Whitlock, Forty Years of It (New York, 1925), p. 157.
[39]Matthew Josephson, The President Makers, 1896-1919 (New York, 1940), p. 145.
[40]Oswald Garrison Villard, Fighting Years: Memoirs of a Liberal Editor (New York, 1939), p. 151.
[41]Vagts, A History of Militarism, p. 173.
[42]Wyndham Lewis, Time and Western Man (London, 1927), p. 28.

as the representatives of tradition, convention and hocus-pocus. In truth it was the Benthamite calculus, based on an over-valuation of the economic criterion, which was destroying the quality of the popular Ideal. Moreover, it was this escape from Bentham, joined with the unsurpassable individualism of our philosophy, which has served to protect the whole lot of us from the final *reductio ad absurdum* of Benthamism known as Marxism."[43] But Keynes was to conclude "we carried the individualism of our individuals too far" and thus to bear further testimony to the atomization of society. In religion "the new interest in the future and the progress of the race" unconsciously undermined "the old interest in a life beyond the grave; and it has dissolved the blighting doctrine of the radical corruption of man."[44] We should remind ourselves of Dean Inge's remarks that popular religion follows the enslavement of philosophy to superstition. The philosophies of Hegel, Comte, and Darwin became enslaved to the superstition of progress. In the corruption of political science confident predictions, irritating and incapable of refutation, replaced discussion of right and wrong.[45] Economists (the Physiocrats) "believed in the future progress of society towards a state of happiness through the increase of opulence which would itself depend on the growth of justice and 'liberty'; and they insisted on the importance of the increase and diffusion of knowledge."[46] The monopoly of knowledge which emerged with technological advances in the printing industry and insistence on freedom of the press checked this development.

The Treaty of Versailles recognized the impact of printing by accepting the principle of the rights of self-determination and destroyed large political organizations such as the Austrian Empire. Communication based on the eye in terms of printing and photography had developed a monopoly which threatened to destroy Western civilization first in war and then in peace. This monopoly emphasized individualism and in turn instability and created illusions

[43] John Maynard Keynes, *Two Memoirs* (London, 1949), pp. 96-7.
[44] J. B. Bury, *A History of Freedom of Thought* (London, 1928), p. 227.
[45] W. R. Inge, *Diary of a Dean, St. Paul's 1911-1934* (London, 1950), pp. 193-198.
[46] J. B. Bury, *The Idea of Progress, an Inquiry into Its Origin and Growth* (London, 1920), p. 175.

in catchwords such as democracy, freedom of the press, and freedom of speech.

The disastrous effect of the monopoly of communication based on the eye hastened the development of a competitive type of communication based on the ear, in the radio and in the linking of sound to the cinema and to television. Printed material gave way in effectiveness to the broadcast and to the loud speaker.[47] Political leaders were able to appeal directly to constituents and to build up a pressure of public opinion on legislatures. In 1924 Al. Smith, Governor of the State of New York, appealed directly by radio to the people and secured the passage of legislation threatened by Republican opposition. President F. D. Roosevelt exploited the radio as Theodore Roosevelt had exploited the press. He was concerned to have the opposition of newspapers in order that he might exploit their antagonism. It is scarcely necessary to elaborate on his success with the new medium.

In Europe an appeal to the ear made it possible to destroy the results of the Treaty of Versailles as registered in the political map based on self-determination. The rise of Hitler to power was facilitated by the use of the loud speaker and the radio. By the spoken language he could appeal to minority groups and to minority nations. Germans in Czechoslovakia could be reached by radio as could Germans in Austria. Political boundaries related to the demands of the printing industry disappeared with the new instrument of communication. The spoken language provided a new base for the exploitation of nationalism and a far more effective device for appealing to larger numbers. Illiteracy was no longer a serious barrier.

The effects of new media of communication evident in the outbreak of the Second World War were intensified during the progress of the war. They were used by the armed forces in the immediate prosecution of the war and in propaganda both at home and against the enemy. In Germany moving pictures of battles were taken[48] and shown in theatres almost immediately afterwards. The German

[47]William Albig, *Public Opinion* (New York, 1939), p. 220.
[48]S. Kracauer, *From Caligari to Hitler* (Princeton, N.J., 1947), pp. 297-8. "The camera's possibility of choosing and presenting but one aspect of reality invites it to the worst kinds of deceit." *The Journals of André Gide,* trans. Justin O'Brien, IV (New York, 1951), 91.

people were given an impression of realism which compelled them to believe in the superiority of German arms; realism became not only most convincing but also with the collapse of the German front most disastrous. In some sense the problem of the German people is the problem of Western civilization. As modern developments in communication have made for greater realism they have made for greater possibilities of delusion. "It is curious to see scientific teaching used everywhere as a means to stifle all freedom of investigation in moral questions under a dead weight of facts. Materialism is the auxiliary doctrine of every tyranny, whether of the one or of the masses."[49] We are under the spell of Whitehead's fallacy of misplaced concreteness. The shell and pea game of the country fair has been magnified and elevated to a universal level.

The printing industry had been characterized by decentralization and regionalism such as had marked the division of the Western world in nationalism and the division and instability incidental to regions within nations. The radio appealed to vast areas, overcame the division between classes in its escape from literacy, and favoured centralization and bureaucracy. A single individual could appeal at one time to vast numbers of people speaking the same language and indirectly, though with less effect, through interpreters to numbers speaking other languages. Division was drawn along new lines based on language but within language units centralization and coherence became conspicuous. Stability within language units became more evident and instability between language units more dangerous.

The influence of mechanization on the printing industry had been evident in the increasing importance of the ephemeral. Superficiality became essential to meet the various demands of larger numbers of people and was developed as an art by those compelled to meet the demands. The radio accentuated the importance of the ephemeral and of the superficial. In the cinema and the broadcast it became necessary to search for entertainment and amusement. "Radio . . . has done more than its share to debase our intellectual standards."[50] The demands of the new media were imposed on the older media,

[49]Amiel, *Journal intime*, June 17, 1852.
[50]Ilka Chase, *Past Imperfect* (New York, 1942), p. 236. For a reference to the breath-taking feats of tight-rope walking to avoid any possible offence by the major networks see *ibid.*, p. 234.

the newspaper and the book. With these powerful developments time was destroyed and it became increasingly difficult to achieve continuity or to ask for a consideration of the future. An old maxim, "sixty diamond minutes set in a golden hour," illustrates the impact of commercialism on time. We would do well to remember the words of George Gissing: "Time is money—says the vulgarest saw known to any age or people. Turn it round about, and you get a precious truth—money is time."[51]

May I digress at this point on the effects of these trends on universities. William James held that the leadership of American thought was "passing away from the universities to the ten-cent magazines."[52] Today he might have argued that it had passed to the radio and television. But it is still necessary to say with Godkin in the last century: ". . . there is probably no way in which we could strike so deadly a blow at the happiness and progress of the United States as by sweeping away, by some process of proscription kept up during a few generations, the graduates of the principal colleges. In no other way could we make so great a drain on the reserved force of character, ambition, and mental culture which constitutes so large a portion of the national vitality."[53] By culture he meant "the art of doing easily what you don't like to do. It is the breaking-in of the powers to the service of the will."[54]

If we venture to use this definition we are aware immediately of the trends in universities to add courses because people like to do them or because they will be useful to people after they graduate and will enable them to earn more money. In turn courses are given because members of the staff of the universities like to give them, an additional course means a larger department and a larger budget and, moreover, enables one to keep up with the subject. These tendencies reflect a concern with information. They are supported by the text-book industry and other industries which might be described as information industries. Information is provided in vast

[51]George Gissing, *The Private Papers of Henry Ryecroft* (London, 1914), p. 287.
[52]Norman Hapgood, *The Changing Years: Reminiscences* (New York, 1930).
[53]E. L. Godkin, *Reflections and Comments, 1865-1895* (New York, 1895), p. 157.
[54]*Ibid.*, p. 202.

quantities in libraries, encylopaedias, and books. It is disseminated in universities by the new media of communication including moving pictures, loud speakers, with radio and television in the offing. Staff and students are tested in their ability to disseminate and receive information. Ingenious devices, questionnaires, intelligence tests are used to tell the student where he belongs and the student thus selected proceeds to apply similar devices to members of the staff. A vast army of research staff and students is concerned with simplifying language and making it easier for others to learn the English language and for more people to read and write what will be written in a simpler language. In the words of Santayana, "It doesn't matter *what* so long as they all read the *same* thing." Ezra Pound quotes the remark of an American professor: "The university is not here for the exceptional man."[55] Henry Adams in a discussion of teaching at Harvard summarized the problem in the remark, "It can not be done."[56] I have attempted to use the word information consistently though I am aware that the proper word is education. George Gissing has referred to "the host of the half-educated, characteristic and peril of our time." ". . . education is a thing of which only the few are capable; teach as you will, only a small percentage will profit by your most zealous energy."[57] "To trumpet the triumphs of human knowledge seems to me worse than childishness; now, as of old, we know but one thing—that we know nothing."[58]

The relative adaptability of various subjects to mechanical transmission has threatened to destroy the unity of the university. "The University, as distinct from the technological school, has no proper function other than to teach that the flower of vital energy is Thought, and that not Instinct but Intellect is the highest form of a supernatural Will."[59] It tends to become a congeries of hardened avid departments obsessed with an interest in funds in which the department which can best prove its superficiality or its usefulness is most successful. Governments have been insensitive to the crucial signi-

[55]*The Letters of Ezra Pound, 1907-1941,* ed. D. D. Paige (New York, 1950), p. xxiii.
[56]*Ibid.,* p. 338.
[57]George Gissing, *The Private Papers of Henry Ryecroft,* p. 70.
[58]*Ibid.,* p. 178.
[59]Henry Adams, *The Degradation of the Democratic Dogma* (New York, 1919), p. 206.

ficance of a balanced unity in universities and have responded to the
pleas of specific subjects with the result that an interest in unity has
been distorted to give that strange inartistic agglomeration of
struggling departments called the modern university. The University
of Oxford has recognized the threat and has set up a committee on
the effects of university grants on balance in university subjects. It
will probably be argued that social scientists have lost out in this race
for government grants or that they should suffer for views as to the
dangers of direct government intervention in the social sciences to
the political health of the community. But I am afraid that just as
with other subjects if the federal government should provide grants
the social sciences will be on hand with the most beautifully developed
projects for research that federal money can buy.

Under these circumstances we can begin to appreciate the
remarks of an Oxford don who said after solving a very difficult
problem in mathematics, "Thank God no one can use that." There
must be few university subjects which can claim immunity or few
universities which will refrain from pleading that their courses are
useful for some reason or other.[60] The blight of lying and subterfuge
in the interests of budgets has fallen over universities, and pleas are
made on the grounds that the universities are valuable because they
keep the country safe from socialism, they help the farmers and
industry, they help in measures of defence. Now of course they do
no such thing and when such topics are mentioned you and I are
able to detect the odour of dead fish. Culture is not concerned with
these questions. It is designed to train the individual to decide how
much information he needs and how little he needs, to give him a
sense of balance and proportion, and to protect him from the fanatic
who tells him that Canada will be lost to the Russians unless he
knows more geography or more history or more economics or more
science. Culture is concerned with the capacity of the individual to
appraise problems in terms of space and time and with enabling him
to take the proper steps at the right time. It is at this point that the

[60]For example, the teaching that "intellectual activity is worthy of esteem
to the extent that it is practical and to that extent alone. . . . the man who loves
science for its fruits commits the worst of blasphemies against that divinity."
Benda, *The Great Betrayal*, p. 121. The scholar's defeat "begins from the very
moment when he claims to be practical." *Ibid.*, p. 151.

tragedy of modern culture has arisen as inventions in commercialism have destroyed a sense of time. "Our spiritual life is disorganized, for the over-organization of our external environment leads to the organization of our absence of thought."[61] "There is room for much more than a vague doubt that this cult of science is not altogether a wholesome growth—that the unmitigated quest of knowledge, of this matter-of-fact kind, makes for race-deterioration and discomfort on the whole, both in its immediate effects upon the spiritual life of mankind, and in the material consequences that follow from a great advance in matter-of-fact knowledge."[62] "In the long run, utility, like everything else, is simply a figment of our imagination and may well be the fatal stupidity by which we shall one day perish" (Nietzsche).

The limitations of Western culture can perhaps be illustrated by reference to the subject with which I pretend some acquaintance, namely the social sciences. Enormous compilations of statistics confront the social scientist. He is compelled to interpret them or to discover patterns or trends which will enable him to predict the future. With the use of elaborate calculating machines and of refinements in mathematical technique he can develop formulae to be used by industry and business and by governments in the formulation of policy. But elaboration assumes prediction for short periods of time. Work in the social sciences has become increasingly concerned with topical problems and social science departments become schools of journalism. The difficulty of handling the concept of time in economic theory and of developing a reconciliation between the static and dynamic approaches is a reflection of the neglect of the time factor in Western civilization. It is significant that Keynes should have said that in the long run we are all dead and that we have little other interest than that of living for the immediate future. Planning is a word to be used for short periods—for long periods it is suspect and with it the planner. The dilemma has been aptly described by Polanyi, "laissez-faire was planned, planning is not." The results have been evident in the demand for wholesale govern-

[61]Albert Schweitzer, *The Decay and the Restoration of Civilization* (London, 1932), p. 32.
[62]Thorstein Veblen, *The Place of Science in Modern Civilization and Other Essays* (New York, 1919), p. 4.

ment activity during periods of intense difficulty. The luxury of the business cycle has been replaced by concerted measures directed toward the welfare state and full employment. Limited experience with the problem has involved expenditures on a large scale on armaments.

The trend towards centralization which has accompanied the development of a new medium of communication in the radio has compelled planning to a limited extent in other directions. Conservation of natural resources, government ownership of railways and hydro-electric power, for example in Canada and by T.V.A. in the United States, and flood control are illustrations of a growing concern with the problems of time but in the main are the result of acute emergencies of the present. Concern with the position of Western civilization in the year 2000 is unthinkable. An interest in 1984 is only found in the satirist or the utopian and is not applicable to North America. Attempts have been made to estimate population at late dates or the reserves of power or mineral resources but always with an emphasis on the resources of science and with reservations determined by income tax procedure, financial policy, or other expedients. Obsession with present-mindedness precludes speculation in terms of duration and time. Morley has written of the danger of a "growing tendency to substitute the narrowest political point of view for all the other ways of regarding the course of human affairs, and to raise the limitations which practical exigencies may happen to set to the application of general principles, into the very place of the principles themselves. Nor is the process of deteriorating conviction confined to the greater or noisier transactions of nations. . . . That process is due to causes which affect the mental temper as a whole, and pour round us an atmosphere that enervates our judgment from end to end, not more in politics than in morality, and not more in morality than in philosophy, in art, and in religion."[63]

Concern of the state with the weakening and destruction of monopolies over time has been supported by appeals to science whether in an emphasis on equilibrium suggested by the interest of the United States in a balanced constitution following Newtonian mathematics or in an emphasis on growth, competition, and survival of the fittest

[63]John, Viscount Morley, *On Compromise* (London, 1921), p. 6.

of Darwin. Attempts to escape from the eye of the state have been frustrated by succession duties, corporation laws, and anti-combine legislation. The demands of technology for continuity have been met by rapid expansion of the principle of limited liability and devices such as long-term leases guaranteeing duration but these have provided a base for active state intervention in income taxes. Little is known of the extent to which large corporations have blocked out the utilization of future resources other than in matters of general policy. A grasping price policy sacrifices indefinite possibilities of growth. A monopolist seeks expanding business at a reasonable profit rather than the utmost immediate profit.[64] Organization of markets and exchanges facilitates the determination of predictions and the working-out of calculations which in turn have their effect on immediate production as an attempt to provide continuity and stability, but limitations progressively increased as evident in business cycles and their destruction of time rigidities. The monopoly of equilibrium was ultimately destroyed in the great depression and gave way to the beginnings of the monopoly of a centralized state. The disappearance of time monopolies facilitated the rapid extension of control by the state and the development of new religions evident in fascism, communism, and our way of life.

The general restiveness inherent in an obsession with time has led to various attempts to restore concepts of community such as have appeared in earlier civilizations. The Middle Ages have appeared attractive to economic historians, guild socialists, and philosophers, particularly those interested in St. Thomas Aquinas. "The cultivation of form for its own sake is equally typical of Romanticism and Classicism when they are mutually exclusive, the Romantic cultivating form in detachment from actuality, the Classicist in subservience to tradition" (Fausset).[65] It is possible that we have become paralysed to the extent that an interest in duration is impossible or that only under the pressure of extreme urgency can we be induced to recognize the problem. Reluctance to appraise the Byzantine Empire may in part be a result of paralysis reinforced by a distaste for any discussion of possible precursors of Russian govern-

[64]J. M. Clark, *Alternative to Serfdom* (New York, 1948), p. 65.
[65]E. E. Kellett, *Fashion in Literature* (London, 1931), p. 282.

ment. But the concern of the Byzantine Empire in the Greek tradition was with form, with space and time. The sense of community built up by the Greeks assumed a concern with time in continuity and not in "a series of independent instantaneous flashes" (Keynes) such as appealed to the Romans and Western Christianity. "Immediacy of presentment was an inevitable enemy to construction. The elementary, passionate elements of the soul gave birth to utterances that would tend to be disconnected and uneven, as is the rhythm of emotion itself."[66] There was a "parallel emergence, in all the arts, of a movement away from a need which, whether in the ascendant or not, was always felt and honoured: the craving for some sort of continuity in form."[67] The effort to achieve continuity in form implies independence from the pressure of schools and fashions and modes of expression. In the words of Cazamian the indefinite duration of productive vitality in art and letters requires that the individual writer or reader be reinstated in the full enjoyment of his rights.[68]

Wyndham Lewis has argued that the fashionable mind is the time-denying mind. The results of developments in communication are reflected in the time philosophy of Bergson, Einstein, Whitehead, Alexander, and Russell. In Bergson we have glorification of the life of the moment, with no reference beyond itself and no absolute or universal value.[69] The modern "clerks" "consider everything only as it exists *in time,* that is as it constitutes a succession of particular states, a 'becoming,' a 'history,' and never as it presents a state of permanence beyond time under this succession of distinct cases." William James wrote: "That the philosophers since Socrates should have contended as to which should most scorn the knowledge of the particular and should most adore knowledge of the general, is something which passes understanding. For, after all, must not the most honourable knowledge be the knowledge of the most valuable realities!

[66]Louis Cazamian, *Criticism in the Making* (New York, 1929), p. 72.
[67]*Ibid.,* p. 64.
[68]*Ibid.,* p. 129. The novelists Smollett, Fielding, Sterne, Richardson, Defoe, and the cockney artist Hogarth all had "an intimate connection with early journalism, sharing its time-sense as a series of discrete moments, each without self-possession, as well as its notion of the 'concrete' as residing in the particular entity or event sensorily observed." Milton Klonsky, "Along the Midway of Mass Culture," *Partisan Review,* April, 1949, p. 351.
[69]Lewis, *Time and Western Man,* p. 27.

And is there a valuable reality which is not concrete and individual."[70] The form of mind from Plato to Kant which hallowed existence beyond change is proclaimed decadent. This contemporary attitude leads to the discouragement of all exercise of the will or the belief in individual power. The sense of power and the instinct for freedom have proved too costly and been replaced by the sham independence of democracy.[71] The political realization of democracy invariably encourages the hypnotist.[72] The behaviourist and the psychological tester have their way. In the words of one of them: "Great will be our good fortune if the lesson in human engineering which the war has taught us is carried over, directly and effectively, into our civil institutions and activities" (C. S. Yoakum).[73] Such tactlessness and offence to our good sense is becoming a professional hazard to psychologists. The essence of living in the moment and for the moment is to banish all individual continuity.[74] What Spengler has called the Faustian West is a result of living mentally and historically and is in contrast with other important civilizations which are "ahistoric." The enmity to Greek antiquity arises from the fact that its mind was ahistorical and without perspective.[75] In art classical man was in love with plastic whereas Faustian man is in love with music.[76] Sculpture has been sacrificed to music.[77]

The separation and separate treatment of the senses of sight and touch have produced both subjective disunity and external disunity.[78] We must somehow escape on the one hand from our obsession with the moment and on the other hand from our obsession with history. In freeing ourselves from time and attempting a balance between the demands of time and space we can develop conditions favourable to an interest in cultural activity.

It is sufficient for the purpose of this paper if attention can be drawn on the occasion of the 150th anniversary of a university on

[70]Benda, *The Great Betrayal*, pp. 78-80.
[71]Lewis, *Time and Western Man*, p. 316.
[72]*Ibid.*, p. 42.
[73]Cited *ibid.*, p. 342.
[74]*Ibid.*, p. 29.
[75]*Ibid.*, p. 285.
[76]*Ibid.*, p. 295.
[77]*Ibid.*, p. 299.
[78]*Ibid.*, p. 419. For a discussion of the effects of printing on music see Constant Lambert, *Music Ho! A Study of Music in Decline* (London, 1934).

this continent[79] to the role of the university in Western civilization. Anniversaries remind us of the significance of time. Though multiples of decades are misleading measures as the uniform retiring age of 65 is inhuman in its disrespect of biological differences they draw attention to a neglected factor. The university is probably older than Hellenistic civilization and has reflected the characteristics of the civilization in which it flourished, but in its association with religion and political organization it has been concerned with problems of time as well as of space. I can best close this paper by an appeal to Holy Writ. "Without vision the people perish."

[79]This paper was presented at the University of New Brunswick in 1950.

# THE PROBLEM OF SPACE

"SPACE AND TIME, and also their space-time product, fall into their places as mere mental frameworks of our own constitution."[1] Gauss held that whereas number was a product of the mind, space had a reality outside the mind whose laws cannot be described *a priori*. In the history of thought, especially of mathematics, Cassirer remarked, "at times, the concept of space, at other times, the concept of numbers, took the lead."[2]

A concern with problems of space and time appears to have marked the beginnings of civilization in Egypt and Mesopotamia. A change from a pre-dynastic to a dynastic society, or a precise recognition of time, in both regions appears to have coincided with writing, monumental architecture, and sculpture. In both regions surplus supplies of labour appear to have been the result of the pronounced seasonal character of agriculture incidental to floods.

The flow of the long Nile river to the north and dissipation of its regular floods in the numerous channels of the delta provided a background for the development of artificial canals and dykes by which the valley might be widened and the water held at the height of the flood for irrigation. The length of the river with the downward flow and the delta, and a shifting economic development incidental to dependence on a single line of transportation militated against a compact government and a stable political organization.[3]

[1]President of the British Association, 1934. Cited by F. M. Cornford, "The Invention of Space," in *Essays in Honour of Gilbert Murray* (London, 1936), p. 216.

[2]Ernst Cassirer, *The Problem of Knowledge: Philosophy, Science, and History since Hegel*, trans. by W. H. Woglom and C. W. Hendel (New Haven, Conn., 1950), p. 98.

[3]J. H. Breasted, *A History of Egypt, from the Earliest Times to the Persian Conquest* (New York, 1912), p. 7.

92

A kingship probably emerged to meet the demands for a uniform system of administration.[4] Its power was possibly strengthened with the beginnings of the measurement of time on July 19, 4241 B.C. when Sirius arose at sunrise and prediction of time became more certain with recognition of a year of 365 days. After 3400 B.C. the importance of the south became evident in its conquest of the north by a king, leader of the Falcon clan, and in the selection of a capital at Thinis under Menes to mark the consolidation of the two lands north and south. The growing importance of the delta and the north was reflected in the displacement at the end of the second dynasty, early in the thirtieth century B.C., of Thinis by Memphis as a capital with its location at a distance from Heliopolis, a centre of religious influence. As a means of increasing the prestige and power of the king in response to the demands of a vast increase in territory and of maintaining continuity of dynastic power, provision was made for the development of a state religion with elaborate temple endowments, rituals, priesthoods, and an increasing emphasis on the dead. With a new capital at Memphis[5] the pyramids were built by the fourth dynasty "to furnish a vast, impenetrable and indestructible resting place for the body of the king" and to reflect the "power of a far-reaching and comprehensive centralization effected by one controlling mind."[6] The permanency of death became a basis of continuity through the development of the idea of immortality, preservation of the body, and development of writing in the tombs by which the magical power of the spoken word was perpetuated in pictorial representation of the funeral ritual. The tombs of courtiers were placed

[4]For a description of the transition from the egalitarian and undivided totemic clan to territorially organized and individualized sovereign power, from matriarchal to patrilinear relationships, see A. Moret and G. Davy, *From Tribe to Empire* (London, 1926), pp. 1-106. V. Gordon Childe has argued that writing was necessitated by economic demands and that its development was generally connected with the change from kinship to a territorial basis of social organization; see *Man Makes Himself*, also *Progress and Archaeology* (London, 1945), p. ii. On the effects of political expansion on writing see W. F. Albright, *The Vocalization of the Egyptian Syllabic Orthography* (New Haven, Conn., 1934).
[5]Significantly Ptah, the god of Memphis, was the god of art and of all handicrafts. The high priest of Ptah was the chief of stone workers and artist to the king. Architecture as the chief force in the artist's life meant that sculpture became part of the decorations and subordinate. See M. A. Murray, *Egyptian Sculpture* (London, 1930), pp. xvii-xxiii.
[6]Breasted, *History of Egypt*, pp. 117, 119.

around the pyramid of the king; they shared his divine glory and had ultimate consubstantiality with him, partly derived from him and partly inherent in themselves. Control over large bodies of organized labour was tangibly indicated in a monument with a square base of 755 feet to each side, covering 13 acres, 481 feet in height, and involving the handling of 2,500,000 blocks of stone of 2½ tons each, without the advantage of pulleys.

The enormous economic drain of the pyramids enabled the priests of Ra or the sun cult at Heliopolis to exploit discontent. In this they were strengthened by the neglect of Horus, the god of the pre-dynastic kings. The fourth dynasty collapsed and in the fifth dynasty beginning about 2750 B.C. the king was regarded as the bodily son of Ra. The limitations of an hereditary family as a basis of continuity in spite of reliance on such devices as the pyramids pointed to the efficiency of a religious cult as a centre of control over time and in turn over space. Without the absolute power of kings of the fourth dynasty, the fifth and sixth dynasties were characterized by decentralization and a marked increase in the independence of local nobles. Civil servants, masters of the art of hieratic writing and supported by a papyrus industry, had brought agriculture to a high level over a period of five centuries but a highly centralized bureaucracy introduced a division of class between the learned and the unlearned. In a decentralized bureaucracy, the demands of administration increased, the art of writing was encouraged, a system of uniform orthography was established, and the civil service was opened to the middle class. In the twelfth dynasty of the middle kingdom the rights and privileges of the nobles were adjusted to the centralized authority of the king.

The official supremacy of Amon-Ra, the solar god, in the twelfth dynasty and decline in the power of the king accompanied a shift in power to the south and migration of the capital from Memphis to Thebes about the middle of the twenty-second century. Osiris, as a judge in the next world, god of the dead, and king of the realm of the blessed, achieved a victory among the people. Immortality was shared by the king with the people. Rights for the masses meant rites for the masses.[7] A belief in immortality became a source of strength in the

[7] V. Gordon Childe, *What Happened in History* (New York, 1946), p. 149. In the social revolution illusory gratifications were substituted for changes in social order. See Abram Kardiner, *The Psychological Frontiers of Society* (New York, 1945), p. 427.

army in Egypt, as it did later with the Druids and the Mohammedans. A stable organization emerged about 2000 B.C. The middle kingdom replaced the old kingdom.

A decline of centralized bureaucratic power and a shift from an emphasis on control over space reflected in the pyramid to a decentralized bureaucratic power with an emphasis on continuity and religion to be seen in the spread of writing and the use of papyrus, the extension of magical formulae from the hieroglyphic of the pyramids to that of papyrus, from the king to the people weakened control over space and invited the invasions of the Hyksos from the north. By mobilizing new resources, notably the horse[8] and the chariot, Ahmose I about 1580 B.C. expelled the Hyksos and restored control over space by making Egypt his personal estate and extinguishing the decentralized bureaucracy of the middle kingdom. In the eighteenth dynasty a concern with the problem of time was accompanied by the subordination of all priestly bodies to the high priest of Amon. A priest of Amon became Thutmose III in 1501 B.C. and destroyed the Hyksos army at Megiddo in 1479. Use of the horse meant success in attack and consolidation of control over space through improved communication. An attempt to build up an empire as an organization concerned with problems of duration or of time and of space was carried out through a powerful priesthood and marriage alliances with alien peoples, for example, the marriage of the daughter of Mitanni to Thutmose IV.

Extension of the empire to the north and organization of space, and inclusion of new peoples, imposed strains on a bureaucracy built up around Thebes, a southern capital, and brought an attempt at compromise in the decision of Amenhotep IV to gain support from the suppressed Ra cult, to establish a more northerly capital at Akhetaton, and to change his name to Ikhnaton. He attempted to destroy the magical properties of the hieroglyphics and to bring the

[8]The significance of the horse in the chariot and in the cavalry has been generally underestimated. It compelled an improvement in the standard of intelligence in the armed forces and probably led to the rise of humanitarianism. E. J. Dillon remarked concerning a mounted policeman that he was always surprised by the look of intelligence on the horse's face. The greater stability of the oriental empires of the second millennium as compared to those of the third has been attributed to the acceleration of official journeys by the use of chariots. The horse supported development of a separate military class. Childe, *Progress and Archaeology*, p. 68.

written and spoken languages into close accord but the power of the
Amon priesthood prevailed. His successor Tutenkhaton changed his
name to Tutenkhamon and returned to Thebes.

With the end of the eighteenth dynasty about 1350 B.C. and the
restoration of the Amon priesthood at Thebes the handicaps of a
southern capital became more obvious. Harmhab, a military leader,
as king attempted to eliminate inefficiency in the administration. His
successors through treaties and marriage alliances arranged a *condo-
minium* with the Hittites similar to the earlier arrangements with the
Mitanni from 1280 B.C. to 1260. The Amon priesthood became more
effective in its control over time. It was estimated that one of every
five persons and almost a third of the cultivable land were controlled
by the temples. Control over space was weakened, the empire contracted, and from 945 B.C. to 745 B.C. Egypt was ruled by Libyan
invaders. Ethopians gained control in 712 B.C. and the Assyrians
sacked Thebes in 668 B.C. Egyptian civilization failed to establish a
stable compromise between a bias dependent on stone in the pyramids
and a bias dependent on papyrus and hieroglyphics in the face of
difficulties imposed by dependence on the Nile.

In contrast with the centralizing tendencies of the Nile, the two
rivers of the Tigris and Euphrates dominated Mesopotamia and
flooding was irregular and incalculable. Clay was predominant and
fertile. Single enduring monuments of stone such as the pyramids in
Egypt were absent. The land was centrifugal in its influence and the
economy was separated. Each city developed as a community in
relation to its tall brick temple and though strongly democratic was
essentially a theocratic communism. The gods symbolized divine
powers and the communities. Several temple communities, each the
estate of a god, made up a city state under a god who owned one
of the largest temple communities of which his high priest was
governor charged with the integration of the component parts. The
communities were organized in relation to the problem of continuity
and time. With increased population, improved equipment, and
greater use of metal, fields became contiguous, conflict developed,
problems of space emerged, and a kingship was established,[9] first

[9]See Henri Frankfort, *Kingship and the Gods: A Study of Ancient Near
Eastern Religion as the Integration of Science and Nature* (Chicago, 1948),
pp. 217-19.

temporary and then permanent. With the high priest of the powerful temple the king provided the essential vigorous leadership.[10] He was a mortal endowed with a divine freedom, receiving his authority in divine election from the city god, acting in agreement with divine authority. Conflicts between the city states or between divine owners were settled by an assembly of the gods which assigned temporary rule of land to one city after another.[11]

The military limitations of a society concerned with problems of time and the importance of unification in developing an elaborate canal system were evident in the subjugation of Sumerians by the Akkadians, a Semitic people, and the temporary solution of problems of space in the development of an empire under Sargon. Under a monarchy and a vast empire the local customs of religious city states were replaced by personal legislation. Sumerian was displaced by Akkadian as a spoken language but the power of religion was evident in the persistence of Sumerian in the written word.[12] The two tongues became vehicles of profoundly different cultures and the friction between them provided the flexibility essential to political stability.

The economic advantage and vitality of a large political organization were indicated in a new artistic freedom: the abrupt appearance of modelling in relief as a vehicle of expression of physical reality and the escape by seal cutters from the limited outlook of a theocratic régime or the excessive demands of the market.[13] Problems of continuity of political organization appeared in the tenacity of religious city states and the difficulties of maintaining a dynastic line. It disappeared in the face of bands of invaders from Gutium and was eventually replaced by a Sumerian dynasty at Ur supported by a culture represented in temples, libraries, and schools. Theocratic Sumerian city states were brought under the control of native kings who had learned the advantages of political organization in a civil service from former conquerors. The effects of monopoly over time and continuity exercised by religion were offset by the development of a system of administration of justice. About 2450 Urukagina rescued classes of the population from the exactions of priests.

[10]*Ibid.*, pp. 218-23.
[11]*Ibid.*, pp. 237-44.
[12]*Ibid.*, p. 225.
[13]See Henri Frankfort, *Cylinder Seals: A Documentary Essay on the Art and Religion of the Ancient Near East* (London, 1939), p. 93.

The solution of problems of administration was influenced by the character of the medium of communication, namely clay. It compelled an early shift from pictographic writing to the symbol and the cuneiform. In turn these were adapted to the demands of mathematics and accounting and the development of writing essential to the economic organization of the temple community. A civilization dominated by monopolies of time had its own peculiarities, notably in abstractions implied in the development of mathematics. The interrelation between writing and arithmetic in the conduct of affairs stimulated mathematical speculation and the land of Sumer and Akkad became the cradle of algebra. Limitations were reflected in problems of political organization and of control over space and it was significant that in the second half of the third dynasty of Ur innumerable contracts, receipts, and agreements were in evidence, that written documents increased "one thousand fold,"[14] and that seal cutters lost interest in a variety of designs and emphasized the ritual scene as a predominant pictorial element.

Again the political organization proved unable to withstand the attacks of invaders; a new empire was built up under Hammurabi, with Babylon as a capital. Babylon was destroyed by the Hittites about 1600 B.C. and in turn relative stability was reached in the Kassite dynasty. Marduk became the god of Babylon, chosen by divine assembly through Anu, the god of the sky[15] and influencing the whole universe as an organized society, and Enlil, god of the storm representing force and defining society as the state.[16] The gods of the various city states were bound in a higher unity and the tendency toward political unification was sanctioned by the most violent measures. The successful conqueror as Enlil's representative on earth became the moderator and judge between the city states.[17] He stood at the head of the clergy[18] and appointed the high priest, was the chosen servant of the gods, absolute masters whom man was

[14]*Ibid.*, p. 12.
[15]H. and H. A. Frankfort, J. A. Wilson, T. Jacobsen, and W. A. Irwin, *The Intellectual Adventure of Ancient Man: An Essay on Speculative Thought in the Ancient Near East* (Chicago, 1946), p. 139.
[16]*Ibid.*, p. 43.
[17]*Ibid.*, pp. 192-5.
[18]Frankfort, *Kingship and the Gods*, p. 252.

created to serve,[19] and interpreted their will.[20] In New Year celebrations the main actors were the gods but participation of the king was essential.

A more stable political organization accompanied more effective control over space in the use of horses and the replacement of heavy solid wheels by light spoked wheels.[21] Control over time was strengthened by the practice ot reckoning in terms of the years of the reign of the king. The Sumerian language became sacred and a source of strength to religion and continuity in contrast with the language of the conquerors concerned with problems of space and administration of law. The king and the god became the joint sources of law and order but law freed itself from religion and the judge became a secular authority. The scribe drew up contracts and acted as a professional notary without a necessary connection with the temples.[22] The code of Hammurabi was inscribed on stone. A large, effective political organization provided a powerful stimulus to commerce.

The power of the Babylonian priesthood was evident in the establishment of the era of Nabonnasar in 747 B.C. with the discovery that every 18 years and 11 days the moon returned to almost its original position with reference to the sun.[23] The discovery of periodicity in the heavens enormously strengthened the position of religion in its control over time and continuity. In 729 B.C. Tiglath-Pileser III became King of Babylon; Ashur assumed the leading position in the pantheon succeeding Marduk[24] and Assyrian kings made annual visits to take part in the ceremonies of Babylon.[25] After Sargon seized the throne in 722 B.C. and built a palace at Dur-Sharukin an attempt was made to offset the influence of the Babylonian priesthood by construction of a library. Its resources were extended by his

[19]Ibid., p. 309.
[20]Ibid., p. 258.
[21]Childe, What Happened in History, p. 245.
[22]L. R. Farnell, Greece and Babylon: A Comparative Sketch of Mesopotamian, Anatolian and Hellenic Religions (Edinburgh, 1911), p. 132.
[23]See J. T. Shotwell, An Introduction to the History of History (New York, 1922), p. 45.
[24]Frankfort, et al., The Intellectual Adventure of Ancient Man, p. 169.
[25]Frankfort, Kingship and the Gods, p. 327.

son who also built a new palace. Difficulties with the Babylonian priesthood led Sennacherib to destroy Babylon in 689 B.C. but his son Esar-haddon was compelled to restore it. After the successful conquest of Egypt the royal library and archives were rapidly extended at Nineveh under Ashur-bani-pal (668-626 B.C.). In 625 B.C. Nabopolassar, of a native dynasty in Babylon, threw off the Assyrian yoke. He was followed by Nebuchadrezzar (605-562 B.C.). Finally opposition of the priesthood to Nabonidus who attempted to introduce new gods in Babylonia encouraged invasion by the Persians in 539 B.C. and was followed by the consecration of Cyrus as king in 536 B.C. The apparatus by which the Mesopotamian ruler was set aside as an intermediary between society and the divine process continued.[26]

In contrast with an absolute king in Egypt who cultivated an interest in the next world and immortality, Sumerian and Babylonian priests by virtue of the importance of religion had little interest in the hereafter but were concerned with the systematizing of knowledge[27] and an emphasis on a sense of order and law. The significance of religion in Mesopotamia enabled the priesthood to withstand the effects of sudden change and to compel conquerors concerned to recognize the importance of continuity. The importance of systematized knowledge in Babylonia forced the Assyrians to emphasize libraries in a new capital. On the other hand the adaptability of the priesthood to the demands of conquerors made religion malleable and laid the foundations essential to the development of an enduring empire. Compromises between the demands of a monopoly of space and of a monopoly of time, between a monopoly emphasizing capitals and a Semitic language and a monopoly emphasizing architecture and writing determined by clay and the Sumerian language, between barbarian invaders and an earlier culture, implied ultimate instability and adjustments. The maintenance of separate languages checked the encroachment of cultures on each other and facilitated political and technological adjustment.

The written tradition has left a powerful stamp on knowledge regarding the civilizations of Egypt and Babylonia. An oral tradition may be presumed from the emphasis in Egypt on the spoken word. The systematic revision of documents in the Near East by cuneiform

    [26]*Ibid.*, p. 338.
    [27]W. F. Albright, *From the Stone Age to Christianity: Monotheism and the Historical Process* (Baltimore, 1940), pp. 146-9.

scribes to eliminate archaic spelling and grammar points to an extended familiarity with writing.[28] Sacred and profane documents were copied with great care. Semitic peoples between the civilizations of Egypt and Babylonia adapted elements of Egyptian writing to the demands of an extensive oral tradition and the alphabet was developed and spread in Phoenicia and Palestine.[29] Devices had been used to facilitate continuous repetitions and to strengthen memories, including the knot.[30] Aids to memory began with constant diligent repetition and developed form in metre and rhyme, in knot symbols as mnemonics, and finally in writing.[31] As a most radical innovation the latter was undertaken with religious sanction. Moses introduced the art of writing at the command of God. According to the rabbis,[32] shortly before his death he reduced the Torah to writing on thirteen scrolls, one for each tribe and one for the tribe of Levi, the latter to serve for collation, to prevent the possibility of disappearance of the oral tradition through the death of elders. The Torah was not intended for practical use and was practically a sealed book until the discovery of the Book of the Law under Josiah about 622 B.C. Even five hundred years after its official publication in the time of Ezra about 444 B.C. men were able to recite the whole Bible from memory. By the time of Ezra Jews spoke Aramaic but portions of the Pentateuch were recited in Hebrew, which had become sacred and continuing the oral tradition contained divine revelation in oracles and prophecies. Each word was full of deep meaning with mysteries and magic powers. Language recited and preserved with the use of metre and rhyme to support the memory became poetry.[33] Writing became sacred after it was associated with the sacred book and the written word became the principle of authority.

Ancestors of some of the Israelites had probably lived several centuries in Egypt before migrating to Palestine.[34] After the conquest

[28]Ibid., pp. 45-6.

[29]It was known to the Canaanites between 1700 and 1500 B.C. Ibid., p. 43.

[30]Solomon Gandz, "The Knot in Hebrew Literature, or From the Knot to the Alphabet," Isis, XIV, 1930, 190-214.

[31]Solomon Gandz, "Oral Tradition in the Bible," in Jewish Studies in Memory of George A. Kohut, 1874-1933, ed. S. W. Baron and A. Marx (New York, 1936), pp. 254-5.

[32]Ibid., p. 286.

[33]Solomon Gandz, "The Dawn of Literature: Prolegomena to a History of Unwritten Literature," Osiris, VII, 1939, 290-1.

[34]Albright, From the Stone Age to Christianity, p. 184.

of Canaan an epic nucleus was probably extended to include the story of Moses and the combined narratives recited by Levites or rhapsodists. The Hebrew alphabet was written in ink and used in the fourteenth and thirteenth centuries. Writing was practised in the early eleventh century. Quantities of papyrus were exported from Egypt to Phoenicia about 1100 B.C. After the break-up of the amphictyonic organization of Israel by the Philistines in the eleventh century the epic was written down separately as J in the south and E in the north before 750 B.C.; was combined in the JE recension of the eighth or seventh century.[35] The oral as compared with the written transmission of tradition was inherently more consistent and logical in its results because of the constant sifting, refining, and modifying of what did not fit into the tradition.[36] In the cumulative effects of the oral tradition the pieces of an edifice were carried to another site and worked into the structure of a different novel. Fact shifted into legend, legend into myth. Facts worked loose and became detached from their roots in space and time. The story was moulded and remoulded by imagination, passion, prejudice, religious presumption, or aesthetic instinct.[37] The oral tradition probably transmitted the Song of Deborah, Amos, Hosea, Isaiah and much of Joshua, Judges, and Samuel, part of Kings, and the prophetic books. Some of the contents of Joshua and Judges were probably written in the tenth century though the form belongs to the seventh century.[38] Most of the prophetic books were anthologies attributed to certain prophets, circulating in written and oral form, and brought together by collectors. The apodictic laws of Israel with commands not to sin because Yahweh so wills were unique and original. The introduction of writing was an important factor in unifying the people and the power of the scriptures was reinforced by the selection of a fixed capital at Jerusalem at the expense of local sanctuaries.

The oral tradition and its relation to poetry implied a concern with time and religion. "The artist represents *coexistence in space,* the poet *succession in time*" (Lessing at the University of Berlin,

[35]*Ibid.,* p. 190.
[36]*Ibid.,* p. 209.
[37]F. M. Cornford, *Thucydides Mythistoricus* (London, 1907), p. 131.
[38]Albright, *From the Stone Age to Christianity,* p. 209.

1810).[39] The oral tradition reflected the positive influence of Egypt in the name of Moses, the doctrine that God is the sole creator and the formula from which his name Yahweh derived, the concept of a single god and the establishment of doctrine based on monotheism, and the recognition of the international, cosmic character of the reigning deity. The negative influence appeared in the revolt against "virtually every external aspect of Egyptian religion," the complex, grotesque iconography, the dominance of magic over daily life evident in the nineteenth dynasty, and the materialistic absorption in preparation for a selfish existence in the hereafter. Distinctive Hebrew elements included a close association between God and his worshippers illustrated by the giving of personal names and by sacrificial rites, a contractual relation or covenant between the deity and his people, and the association of terrestrial manifestations of deity with storms and mountains.[40] As a migratory people, the Hebrews were compelled to abandon a god attached to a site and to develop a bond between Yahweh and a chosen people.

In the face of attacks from the Philistines who had the advantage of a monopoly of iron, the amphictyonic principle of confederation of the Israelites was replaced by the selection of a king, Saul, from Benjamin, the weakest and most central tribe, and in turn of David (about 1000-960).[41] The burdens of Solomon's lavish régime led to revolt of the northern tribes after his death and division of the monarchy about 925 B.C. In the reaction against centralization of secular and religious government and to offset the appeal of Solomon's temple which contained the Ark of the Covenant, Jeroboam I built sanctuaries to Yahweh at Bethel and Dan.[42]

Empires which had achieved relative equilibrium between religious organization with its emphasis on time and political organization with its emphasis on space were subjected to disturbance with technological change incidental to a shift from dependence on bronze

[39]Sir John Edwin Sandys, *A Short History of Classical Scholarship from the Sixth Century B.C. to the Present Day* (Cambridge, 1915), p. 294.
[40]Albright, *From the Stone Age to Christianity*, p. 206.
[41]*Ibid.*, p. 221-2. For the emphasis on a written constitution by the priests to limit the authority of the king see Deuteronomy 17: 18-20.
[42]Albright, *From the Stone Age to Christianity*, p. 228.

to dependence on iron. The horse-drawn chariot which displaced the wheel cart about 1500 B.C. was followed by horse training in North Syria after the fourteenth century. The command of a mobile arm which could be dispatched quickly in war and used to maintain contact over wide areas with officials and overseers contributed to the expansion of the Egyptian empires.[43] Discovery of iron by the Hittites and its greater abundance and cheapness brought the Bronze Age to an end about 1200 B.C. With the use of iron and the crossing of light Libyan horses with heavy Asiatic horses, the Assyrians developed the cavalry arm with horse-riding rather than horse-driving units. Their attempts to build up new organizations of space in relation to an organization of time were defeated by the entrenched organizations of time in Babylon and Thebes. The Assyrian Empire collapsed with the fall of Nineveh in 612 B.C.

In the political realignments which followed the fall of the Assyrians the Babylonians held Jerusalem from 587 to 539 B.C. and the Persians re-established a political organization comparable to that of the Assyrians by conquering Babylonia and, in 525 B.C., Egypt. With improved communication, the building of roads, the organization of posts, the simplification of script, an increase in the use of papyrus after the conquest of Egypt, and with a system of decentralization implied in the use of satrapies, the Persians established a more efficient empire. Toleration of religious organization was evident in the return of the Jews to Palestine from 538 to 522 B.C. and the building of the Temple from 520 to 515. In 444 B.C., under Artaxerxes I, Nehemiah, the autonomous governor of Judaea, made the official practice of the Temple in Jerusalem, embodied in the priestly code, standard for Judaism. In 397 B.C. Ezra as priest and scribe had special royal authority to reorganize the ecclesiastical administration of Judaea; he "ushers in the period of the autonomous theocratic state of Judah."[44]

The early Persian religion was substantially identical with the faith of the Rig-Veda. The Avesta was transmitted orally for from five to eight centuries and probably reduced to writing in the first century A.D. and to canonical form in the third century A.D. In the

[43]Childe, *What Happened in History*, p. 167.
[44]Albright, *From the Stone Age to Christianity*, p. 248.

seventh or sixth century B.C. Zoroaster preached a new gospel in favour of one supreme being, Ahura-Mazda, which abolished blood sacrifices and purified worship and relegated the old Iranian gods to the ranks of demons. The religion involved a dualism of the god with an organized angelic hierarchy and a personal antagonist and a belief in the last judgment and rewards and punishment after death. Its influence on Judaism became apparent after the second century B.C. About 400 B.C. Mazdayasnian phraseology was abandoned by Artaxerxes II.[45] The problem of organization of time contributed to the difficulties of the Persian Empire and to its disappearance at the hands of Alexander in 331 B.C.

As in Palestine the oral tradition in Greece implied an emphasis on continuity. It created recognized standards and lasting moral and social institutions;[46] it built up the soul of social organizations and maintained their continuity;[47] and it developed ways of perpetuating itself. The oral tradition and religion served almost the same purpose. Language was the physiological basis of oral traditions, and religion was the sociological mechanism through which traditions were established, directing and enforcing the co-operation of individuals in the interest of the community, maintaining group life, and creating a lasting organization of society independent of a living leader.[48] Education involved training, cultivating, and strengthening the memory. The specialized reciter was the carrier of social traditions. The memory took the place of logical process in writing and supported an immense burden of vocabulary and grammatical complexity with the help of verse, metre, rhyme, and proverbs. "Poetry is the chain of the stories" (Arab saying).[49] What was once well said was not to be changed but repeated in the very words of its original author. In oral intercourse the eye, ear, and brain, the senses and the faculties acted together in busy co-operation and rivalry each eliciting, stimulating, and supplementing the other.[50]

[45]Ibid., pp. 277-8.
[46]Gandz, "The Dawn of Literature," p. 274.
[47]Ibid., p. 261.
[48]Ibid., p. 294.
[49]Ibid., p. 306.
[50]S. H. Butcher, "The Written and the Spoken Word," in Some Aspects of the Greek Genius (London, 1891), p. 167.

A concern with communication by the ear assumes reliance on time. Persistence of the oral tradition in Greece implied an emphasis on poetry intimately associated with music and a time art.[51] Verbal poetry goes back to the fundamental reality of time. The poetic form requires a regular flexible sequence as plastic as thought, reproducing a transference of force from the agent to the object which occupies time and requires the same temporal order in imagination. Migration and conquest weakened the influence of place on religion, accentuated the importance of the oral tradition, and enhanced the adaptability of religion to the demands of new areas. The emotional colour of localities faded and primitive concepts and concrete orientations were destroyed. The oral tradition in the Homeric epics reflected the character of early Greek society.[52] The *Iliad* reflected a monarchy and the *Odyssey* an oligarchy. The Olympian tradition and its influence on philosophy was evident in its emphasis on the *Moirai* and spatial relationships. Among peoples accustomed to migration, the position of the religious sanctuary was weak and priesthoods had limited influence compared with their standing in communities with relative permanence and the possession of writing.

The use of armed force in conquest and defence emphasized the spatial concept and organization of the society in terms of space rather than time and continuity. It meant demands for more effective control over space and for more efficiency than was implied in a religious organization. In Greece, a country with poor pasturage and unsuited for horse breeding, military strength depended on the hoplites; this revolution in tactics in the eighth century compelled the Eupatrids to rely on the non-Eupatrids.[53] As a result of military compromise Eleusis was joined to Athens about 700 B.C., and the Eupatridae in two sections of Attica, and the Eleusinian sanctuary, represented three regions with three annual archonships. In the struggle against the Eupatridae as a privileged caste Draco published

[51]Ernest Fenollosa, "An Essay on the Chinese Written Character," in *Instigations* of Ezra Pound (New York, 1920), pp. 360-1.

[52]F. M. Cornford, *From Religion to Philosophy: A Study in the Origins of Western Speculation* (London, 1912), p. 143. See also Frankfort *et al.*, *The Intellectual Adventure of Ancient Man*, on the significance of Babylonian epics for an understanding of Sumerian society.

[53]J. H. Oliver, *The Athenian Expounders of the Sacred and Ancestral Law* (Baltimore, 1950), p. 67.

a code of laws and set up a council with a majority of non-Eupatrid hoplites in addition to the Areopagus.[54] The time element represented by the Eupatridae and representatives of the Eleusinian sanctuary was compelled to compromise with the space element. Solon recognized the time or religious element by making the tribe a political unit to cut across regional sectors.[55] His abolition of the personal security of the debtor favoured urban migration and encouragement of industry was followed by immigration of alien elements.[56] The highlands and the rural classes represented by Pisistratus, the tyrant, were temporarily defeated by a coalition of the men of the coast and of the plain, but were finally successful through a personal alliance between Pisistratus and Megacles, the Alcmaeonid leader of the coastal region. Dionysus was favoured by a new religion. The tyrants in Athens as in other Greek cities, for example, in Corinth (657-586 B.C.), emerged between periods dominated by old methods of government and newer powers more closely adapted to economic and social difficulties incidental to problems of spatial organization. Later the Alcmaeonidae with the aid of the Spartans expelled the tyrants, and Cleisthenes, the Alcmaeonid, with ex-slaves and immigrants of the urban areas of the coast enrolled in the citizen body, defeated Isagoras. Solon had left the great families too strong and Cleisthenes attempted to neutralize politically the historical division into three regions by rearranging the tribes in artificial units. He avoided the odium of interfering with religious customs and obtained sanction from Delphi to offset the religious sanctions of the system discarded.[57] The artificial units broke up regionalism and destroyed control over time.

Draco's publication of the code broke the Eupatrid monopoly of the interpretation of the laws and Solon their monopoly of political office. Cleisthenes destroyed their hold over the electorate and prevented the state falling into the hands of the rural classes which had supported the tyrants. The democratic reforms of the fifth century implied the capture of the Areopagus from the Eupatridae. The decline of the oral tradition and its monopoly over time evident in

[54]*Ibid.*, p. 68.
[55]*Ibid.*, p. 69.
[56]*Ibid.*, p. 70.
[57]*Ibid.*, p. 71.

the weakening of the Eupatridae and the Areopagus under Draco, Solon, and Cleisthenes reflected an increasing importance of problems of space, the rise of the Demos, and the spread of writing. With the appointment of official exegetes by the end of the fifth century, the space element became dominant. Apollo proved adaptable to the demands of Rome.

The change in military tactics which accompanied the revolution at the close of the eighth century and in which the polis emerged, saw the epic tradition developed in the art of recitation sink to the level of the cycle. The danger of the insertion of lines which might prove advantageous to contemporary interests led to a demand for protection against infiltration.[58] The carriers of the oral tradition, the rhapsodes and minstrels, resisted the threats of the written tradition by the use of writing as a means of guaranteeing accuracy. Writing and accuracy were religious necessities. Their success has been evident in the continued dominant influence of the great religious books, the Bible, the Vedas, the Koran, the New Testament, and Homer. After about 675 B.C. the schools for training rhapsodes became concerned for the preservation of the epics and the oral tradition, and resisted pressure for change. The demand for an exact rendering paralleled an interest in the seventh and sixth centuries in Egypt and western Asia in the recovery of ancient religious literature in its true wording and in the restoration of ancient cult forms. Scribal groups in Judah turned back to the Mosaic tradition, collected and wrote down the material for JE. The search for Mosaic traditions led to the Book of Deuteronomy. A revival of interest in the past was evident in the seventh century in Phoenicia and a flood of allusions to Canaanite literature appeared in Hebrew works from the seventh to the third centuries. In Assyria and Babylonia, Sargon II (722-705) filled his inscriptions with archaisms. A library was collected by Sardanapalus (668-626) and his brother Saosduchinus, King of Babylonia, had official inscriptions in the Sumerian tongue. Nabonidus was concerned with religious revivals. The Libyan princes of Sais, the Saite kings (660-526 B.C.), the twenty-sixth dynasty, deliberately attempted to

[58]H. L. Lorimer, "Homer and the Art of Writing: A Sketch of Opinion between 1713 and 1939," *American Journal of Archaeology*, LII, 1948, 22.

revive the ancient gods and forms of cult and to restore the pyramid age.[59]

Possibly the examples of Egypt and Babylonia supported the interest in the appearance of written copies of Greek poems during the religious movement in Athens in the sixth century and in transference from the spoken to the written word. Hesiod had promoted religious legalism and the severe ritualism of the sixth century. Influenced also by examples of the Saite kings, Solon possibly proposed the preparation of a state copy of the ancient religious literature with exact wording. Pisistratus, as a tyrant without religious sanction, was probably concerned with an accurate writing down of texts. At the great Panathenaea festival in 566 B.C. a musical contest between the rhapsodes provided a means of collecting the text of Homer. The great bulk of the oracular literature from the archaic period was presented in the form of hexameter.[60] The corpus of ancient verses of Orpheus and Musaeus, or *chresmoi,* the inspired utterances of oracles and wandering prophets with ritual prescriptions and predictions of future events, collected and written out, was interpreted by individuals of Eupatrid descent or *chresmologoi* who could thus tie the ancestral law into the framework of the polis.[61] It was significant that their disappearance should have been linked to their inability to adapt themselves to military demands or to problems of space. The failure of the Sicilian expedition destroyed their unlimited pretensions to expert knowledge. They were under continued attack from the old comedy poets from 410 to 400 B.C. and following revision of the laws of Solon in 399 B.C. were probably replaced by official exegetes who were given limited but undisputed authority to expound the non-statutory sacred law. The Eupatridae were stripped of the last tool by which they could exert pressure on political life. Their right to authoritative exegesis was put on a clear basis but their special influence was restricted to the religious and moral fields.[62]

The changing position of spatial organization became apparent not only in relation to political structure but also to art. Geometrical

[59]See Albright, *From the Stone Age to Christianity,* p. 242.
[60]Oliver, *The Athenian Expounders of the Sacred and Ancestral Law,* pp. 1-4.
[61]*Ibid.,* p. 17.
[62]*Ibid.,* p. 30.

design on the vases of Athens and the province of Attica from 900 to 700 B.C. was finally replaced by pictorial representation which under the influence of literature reflected the fundamental principle of progressive narration[63] especially in the black figured vases. The ear and the concern with time began to have its influence on the arts concerned with the eye and space. The painter attempted to create an impression of a single scene in which time was not fixed but transitory and in which several actions took place at the same time. In the fifth century this device was rapidly displaced by a method emphasizing unity of time and space and in the fourth century a single action represented in a picture became dominant.[64] A mono-scenic method concentrated on a single action within the limits of one scene.[65] Similarly in the drama the unseen supernatural action paralleled by human action on the stage was represented in pictorial scenes at upper and lower tiers on vases.[66] Literature was adapted to the demands of space in an emphasis on unity with time.

The philosophical implications of the growing importance of spatial organization were evident in the field of mathematics. In Egypt geometry had developed as an empirical art of mensuration but in Greece it was seized upon as the very centre of the true philosophical sort of knowledge. Mathematics was recognized as something which could be reduced to general laws with a scientific content.[67] The Ionians were under the spell of an undissolved relation between man and nature but saw the possibility of establishing an intelligible coherence in the phenomenal world. For Thales "all things are full of gods" but he was concerned with coherence of the things. The passionate concern for consistency involved a disregard of the data of experience but a recognition of the autonomy of thought. For Anaximander the infinite was boundless. The ground of all determinate existence could not itself be determinate. Opposites were separated out from the boundless. The power of abstraction reached

    [63]See Kurt Weitzmann, *Illustrations in Roll and Codex: A Study of the Origin and Method of Text Illustration* (Princeton, N.J., 1947), pp. 12-13.
    [64]*Ibid.*, p. 14.
    [65]*Ibid.*, p. 16. See also F. H. Robinson, "The Tridimensional Problem in Greek Sculpture," *Memoirs of the American Academy in Rome*, VII, 1929, 119-68.
    [66]Cornford, *Thucydides Mythistoricus*, p. 196.
    [67]Cassirer, *The Problem of Knowledge*, p. 47.

new levels when Heraclitus concentrated attention on the knowing of things rather than the thing known. As thought constitutes the thinker it controls phenomena. Since thought controls all things the universe was intelligible. The whole was a perpetual flux of change. The cosmos was the dynamics of existence. Being was a perpetual becoming. In attempting to meet the problem of correlating being and becoming or space and time Parmenides declared the two to be mutually exclusive and that only being was real. His philosophical absolute was "the unshaken heart of well-rounded truth."[68]

Pythagoras was anxious to determine existence quantitatively. From his time there was an intimate association, "not to say an indissoluble correlation between the theory of numbers and the theory of extension: between arithmetic and geometry."[69] In the boundless sphere of Anaximander and Anaximenes he represented numbers by patterns of dots arranged in geometric figures. The void distinguished their nature in blank intervals between the units or in gaps separating the terms in a series of natural integers. Units of number were identified with geometrical points having a position in actual space and an indivisible magnitude.[70] The mathematical void was invoked to separate units of number. From about 450 B.C. geometers realized that they needed space which was continuous and of infinite extent and not a space made up of points that could be identified with units of number separated by intervals of emptiness as in the discontinuous arithmetical void of Pythagoras. Geometry detached itself from arithmetic. Leucippus and Democritus accepted the framework of geometers and maintained the existence of an unlimited void. They ascribed to the physical void the infinite extent of geometrical space. Atoms were unlimited in number and demanded an unlimited extent in space. Infinite space, postulated for the construction of geometrical figures, was paralleled by recognition of an unlimited void in nature by the atomists or physicists. The ancient boundaries of spherical space were broken down and space robbed of circumference and centre.[71] The static shapes discovered by Greek mathematics supported the Platonic concept of the theory of ideas. Geometry in-

[68]Frankfort et al., The Intellectual Adventure of Ancient Man, pp. 378 ff.
[69]Cassirer, The Problem of Knowledge, p. 37.
[70]Frankfort et al., The Intellectual Adventure of Ancient Man, p. 230.
[71]Cornford, "The Invention of Space," p. 224.

fluenced in turn by Plato was codified and brought to completion by Euclid at Alexandria about 300 B.C. For a brief period the Greeks escaped from the oral tradition and from the written tradition. The oral tradition was sufficiently strong to check complete submergence in the written. The oral tradition supported Greek scepticism and evaded monopolies of religious literature.

The increasing importance of problems of space was accompanied by improvements in the efficiency of military tactics leading to the conquests of Philip and Alexander. With an abundance of good horses and a numerous and hardy nobility in Macedonia, they developed effectively the support of light armed troops and cavalry to the hoplites. The phalanx became a more heavily armed and a more immobile body in the interests of solidarity and rigidity and the heavy cavalry force the striking arm. Military success depended on the co-ordination of various kinds of troops. The Persian Empire was followed by the Alexandrian Empire.

The Persian Empire had succeeded in part through the possession of an organization of continuity in religion and through a recognition of the existence of other organizations in Babylon, Judaea, and Egypt. Alexander had no comparable organization other than that of the divine king, a concept tempered by the Platonic doctrine of wisdom to govern, and, with his death, the Empire broke up into the Hellenistic kingdoms. The Seleucid dynasty attempted to exploit possible division between Babylonian religion and Persian religion but the latter became the basis of expansion of the Parthian Empire. Babylon fell in 125 B.C. and the Seleucid kingdom retreated and disappeared. Hellenizing priests, Jason and Menelaus (175-165 B.C.) proposed a reorganization of Judaism as a Syro-Hellenic religion in the interests of the Seleucids but pious Jews supported the Maccabees and under Simon (143-135 B.C.) secured the autonomy of Judaea and the purification of Jerusalem.[72] The Ptolemies established a new capital at Alexandria and attempted to offset the religious influences of Thebes and of Babylonia by a new religion and the organization of knowledge in a university, a library, and a museum. Recognition of problems of space was shown in the work of Euclid and of time in the study of astronomy and in the revisions of the texts of Homer and the Old Testament.

The trend of development in Rome paralleled roughly the trend

[72]Albright, *From the Stone Age to Christianity*, pp. 271-2.

described in Athens. A monarchy was followed by an aristocracy of
patricians and the laws were controlled by four colleges of priests.
The struggle against the Eupatridae in Athens for control of the oral
tradition in law was not dissimilar to the struggle against the patricians
in Rome. The appointment of exegetes in Athens in the latter part of
the fifth century or early in the fourth century and the influence of
Greece on Rome probably contributed to the early development of a
specialized class in Rome when ancestral law still had great importance. The Roman pontiffs acquired enormous influence in contrast
with the Athenian exegetes.[73] The oral tradition and religion provided an organization of continuity which persisted through the
republic. With Scipio the idea emerged that religion could be used
by the government but with this development religion lost significance
among the people. Polybius wrote: "A scrupulous fear of the gods is
the very thing which keeps the Roman commonwealth together." As
problems of organization of space incidental to the success of Roman
arms in Italy, North Africa, Spain and Gaul, and the eastern Mediterranean became more pronounced, the problems of religious organization and continuity increased. Following the defeat of Roman arms
in 9 A.D. by Arminius, an attempt was made to consolidate the
territory of the empire behind lines of defence such as the Rhine and
Danube rivers and to solve the problem of continuity by reliance on
constitutionalism and dynasties. Augustus attempted to revive a dying
religion to support morality and the state. "The alliance of throne
and altar dates from that time." The tendency of Caesarism toward
absolute monarchy necessitated increasing dependence on oriental
clergy.[74] An interest in problems of space was evident in Strabo's
geography, an attempt to present an unified view of the universe,
and in the work of Ptolemy in collecting all the known geographical
information and in constructing a cartographical map of the earth.
Force became increasingly important and the dynastic problem more
acute. Dependence on war and organized force weakened the possibility of extended dynasties, increased dependence on successful
leaders of the army, and involved lack of continuity. The deification

[73]Oliver, *The Athenian Expounders of the Sacred and Ancestral Law*, p. 121.
On the effects of the introduction of the phalanx from Greece on Roman political development see G. W. Botsford, *The Roman Assemblies from Their Origin
to the End of the Republic* (New York, 1909), pp. 58-71.

[74]Franz Cumont, *The Oriental Religions in Roman Paganism* (Chicago,
1911), p. 39.

of emperors, following the acquisition of Egypt, development of the legal concept of adoption, an emphasis on architecture especially in Rome, the capital, propaganda devices in literature, gladiatorial games, coins, and columns, and effective control over the calendar especially in the names July and August, were designed to strengthen the position of various dynasties. Roman religion as a basis of continuity became less effective and the significance of the bureaucracy increased. Its demands required a division of the empire between east and west, and the necessity of establishing a new capital in the East at Constantinople weakened the influence of the sacred place in Roman religion.

Expansion to the East and contact with Eastern religions compelled the Roman Empire to face the problems of earlier empires, namely the problems of control over religion and organized time. Elements of the Persian religion which had been transmitted orally were written down and became the basis of expansion of the Parthian Empire. The Sassanid dynasty of 228 A.D. selected a new capital at Ctesiphon, supported a ruling hierarchy in charge of revived Mazdaism and gave the Avesta a place as a sacred book. In the struggle between Rome and Persia, Rome extended the policy of exploiting religions and Mithraism spread rapidly throughout the armed forces of the Empire.

An attempt to meet the problem of Persia led to difficulties with Judaism. In the last two centuries B.C. the influence of Iran on Judaism was pronounced.[75] The dualistic conception of Iranian religion had an important triumph in solving the problem of evil. The idea of the seven chief angels was taken from Iranian sources. After the translation of the Bible from Hebrew into Greek in Alexandria, the influence of Hellenistic thought on Judaism became pronounced. In the strife between the Sadducees and the Pharisees from 130 B.C. to 70 A.D., the Sadducees held that a belief in a future life, a divine judgment, bodily resurrection, and an angelic hierarchy was unscriptural and insisted on freedom of the human will, in opposition to the Stoic doctrine of predestination; the Pharisees recognized a duality, predestination or the providence of God and the free action of man's will. Under the influence of Hellenism, the Pharisees developed ritual law by exegetic and dialectic methods, emphasized

[75]Albright, *From the Stone Age to Christianity*, pp. 278-80.

the study of law and the formation of schools of disciples.[76] The scope of canonical legislation was extended by hedging the rules of Torah with new regulations protecting the observance of the original rules. As rigorous legalists the Pharisees aimed to perpetuate the Torah in the purest form.[77] They favoured the oral tradition and appealed to popular support in contrast with the Sadducees who were chiefly aristocratic and insisted upon the written Bible and Greek speculation. The oral tradition checked the possibility of translation and left the Pharisees in exclusive possession. The Talmud and the Mishnah were kept from being written down, translation and transmission to others was prevented, and religion was protected.[78] The early Christians repudiated the Pharisaic content. "The strength of sin is in the law." They developed their own oral tradition, traced back through the disciples to the apostles. The Greek Gospels were possibly based on an Aramaic sub-stratum of an oral tradition. Mnemotechnic devices were essential to oral transmission; the first and third Gospels, which reveal these, were developed from related oral sources.[79] The oral tradition of early Israel had been associated with an anthropomorphic god; the hardening effects of a written tradition had necessitated a return to the oral tradition and an anthropomorphic god in Christianity.[80] The Gospels and Acts, narratives of the life of Christ and the work of the apostles, were compiled for purposes of dissemination. In the face of persecution, transcription and circulation were difficult and the variety of readings increased.[81] About the end of the fourth century, the Byzantine received text was given recognition in the church of Constantinople. Increasing recognition of other texts led to the Revised version of 1881.[82] As compared with the accurate, authoritative texts of the classics transmitted through Alexandria and Constantinople the New Testament emerged from a variety of texts, the work of comparatively illiterate scribes.[83]

Cheap copies of works suited to Christians as a persecuted sect were probably written on papyrus in the form of a codex in the

[76]*Ibid.,* pp. 272-3. See also E. R. Goodenough, *By Light, Light: The Mystic Gospel of Hellenistic Judaism* (New Haven, Conn., 1935).
[77]Albright, *From the Stone Age to Christianity,* p. 301.
[78]Gandz, "The Dawn of Literature," p. 447.
[79]Albright, *From the Stone Age to Christianity,* pp. 296-7. [80]*Ibid.,* pp. 303-4.
[81]F. G. Kenyon, *The Text of the Greek Bible* (London, 1949), pp. 245-7.
[82]*Ibid.,* pp. 165 ff.
[83]F. G. Kenyon, *Ancient Books and Modern Discoveries* (Chicago, 1927), pp. 42-3.

second century A.D.[84] The codex form carried more material and was more convenient. Use of the roll would restrict content to single Gospels or the Acts. Vellum had an advantage over papyrus in that it could be carried without fraying. It was fully developed as a writing material by the beginning of the second century B.C. and was used at Pergamum and later for notebooks and books of second grade at Rome, Athens, and Alexandria. With recognition of Christianity in the Empire, papyrus was displaced by vellum. The demand for authoritative Christian scriptures led to a determination of the canon of the New Testament and the production of complete Bibles. A marked increase in the demand for copies of the scriptures following the end of persecution probably hastened the revolution in the change from papyrus to vellum. The narrow two- to three-inch column of the papyrus roll was continued in the early vellum manuscripts, which contained three or four columns to a page.[85]

The transformation from the papyrus roll to the parchment codex in the fourth century A.D. presented the miniaturist with a durable material, papyrus being generally limited to a life of three generations, with a surface more suited to delicate techniques. Book illumination was raised to a high artistic level. The artist on papyrus was limited to line drawing and water colouring and parchment prevented the use of thick layers of paint. While the parchment roll persisted as it permitted an intimate connection between picture and text, the proportions of a single page of the codex led the painter to adjust the picture to the new format.[86] With the change from a square format to one in which height is greater than width, the number of columns was reduced to two and to one. Libraries were recopied on vellum, that of Pamphilus at Caesarea having vellum copies by 350 A.D. The Vaticanus and Sinaiticus vellum codices belong to the same period.

Mithraism proved unacceptable to the Hellenistic population of the eastern Mediterranean and it became necessary for an administrative bureaucracy to give more direct attention to the wealthier portions of the Empire and for the emperor to choose a more defensible site for the capital. Constantinople was chosen and Christianity

[84]*Ibid.*, p. 40.
[85]*Ibid.*, pp. 56-9.
[86]Weitzmann, *Illustrations in Roll and Codex*, pp. 77-84.

became the official religion. It had syncretistic elements and included with other religions the virgin birth of a god, his astral associations, birth among cattle, imprisonment, death, descent to the underworld, disappearance for three days, resurrection and exaltation to heaven.[87] The holidays of other religions, such as the 25th of December of Mithraism, were taken over by Christianity. The element of time had been organized in relation to religion to meet the demands of an organization of space in relation to the Empire. "We must regard as altogether divine that which alone and really exists and whose power endures through all time" (Constantine). A bureaucracy built up in relation to papyrus and the alphabet was supplemented by a hierarchy built up in relation to parchment. The consequent stability was evident in the continuity of the Byzantine Empire to 1453. The success of the Ptolemies in Egypt in adapting a religion to their needs had not been lost on the Roman emperors.

The development of the church in relation to the New Testament, the writings of the Fathers, and the oral tradition was accompanied by heresies centring about the spelling and interpretation of words and the problem of continuing powerful religious organizations in Egypt. Constantine became concerned to secure the support of a unified Christianity.[88] With the summoning of a universal council of the whole church to settle the Arian controversy, Constantine secured acceptance of an inclusive formula, proposed by Western bishops but derived from the concept of consubstantiality of Egyptian religion, that "homoiousios" or "of one essence" should describe the Father and Son whereas the East, possibly continuing Babylonian tradition, held that the Son cannot be in the same sense God.[89] The importance of unity on the other hand and the strength of Arianism in the East and among the Goths explained the return of Constantine to the Arian faith and the persistence of its influence until 381.

The imposition of the Trinity on the Christian world by a small number of bishops from the West was followed by the Pelagian,

[87]Albright, *From the Stone Age to Christianity*, p. 306. See also L. G. Rylands, *The Beginnings of Gnostic Christianity* (London, 1940), and W. B. Smith, *Ecce Deus: Studies of Primitive Christianity* (Chicago, 1913).

[88]See N. H. Baynes, "Constantine the Great and the Christian Church," *Proceedings of the British Academy*, IV, 1929, 367.

[89]A. H. M. Jones, *Constantine and the Conversion of Europe* (London, 1948), pp. 140-62.

# 118        THE BIAS OF COMMUNICATION

Nestorian, and other heresies. The precedent set for the Eastern church by Constantine that only an emperor could call a general council left the initiative in the settling of heresies with the emperor. The attempts of Gregory of Nazianzus and Basil of Caesarea to temper the doctrine to the East failed to meet the demands of monophysitism. Rejection of the latter in the Council of Chalcedon in 451 was followed by discontent in Syria and Egypt. The position of the church in the West was strengthened as the political position of the Empire was weakened. Establishment of Constantinople in itself probably weakened the Empire and hastened its collapse, as it controlled the wealthy provinces of Asia Minor and the best recruiting ground, the Illyrian provinces.[90] Since the Roman religion did not permit a priestly caste and the pontifices and augurs were lay experts on religion,[91] the way was open for the growth of the papacy.

The fundamental bases of the unwritten constitution of the Byzantine Empire were the senate, the army, the demes, and the church.[92] The emperor was the central figure in religion and in politics. The effectiveness of organized force in the Byzantine Empire arose in part from the ruthless recognition of military capacity in the army. "Every man in the Byzantine army had an imperial sceptre in his hands." Justin, for example, was born in Thrace, of peasant stock, and became Emperor to be succeeded by his nephew, Justinian. The capacity of Justinian was evident in his administration. They strengthened the position of the Chalcedonians and weakened the position of the monophysites. Acacius, Patriarch of Constantinople, had attempted to reconcile Chalcedonians and monophysites in the Edict of Union in 482 under the Emperor Zeno, but had been anathematized by the pope. The Egyptian tradition in religion, which had been strengthened by Alexandrian theologians, first in opposition to Babylonian religion, resisted pressure from Constantinople. The first breach between the Eastern and the Western churches was brought to an end with Justin's accession on July 9, 518. A Chalcedonian policy implied opposition to Theodoric, the Ostrogoth, an Arian, in Italy and the West. Arian religion provided no central organization

[90]*Ibid.*, p. 237.
[91]*Ibid.*, p. 250.
[92]A. A. Vasiliev, *Justin the First: An Introduction to the Epoch of Justinian the Great* (Cambridge, Mass., 1950), p. 75.

of time to maintain political power and he attempted to maintain independence of the Eastern Empire by matrimonial alliances with his German neighbours.[93] The weakness of political organization based on these alliances led Justinian to press toward the West, as did his difficulties with Persia and with Egypt. The papacy attempted to check persecution of Gothic Arians in the Eastern Empire, but John I, who succeeded Pope Hormisdas in 523, went to Constantinople in 526 and crowned Justin Emperor of the Orient. The papacy came under the domination of the Byzantine Empire until Pope Zacharias (741-52), the last Greek on the papal throne.[94]

Control over the papacy in Rome was acquired at the expense of increasing difficulty with the monophysites in Egypt. This weakness of the Empire was the opportunity of Mohammedanism. Among the Arabs poetry contributed to the rise of a standard, national language and later to political unity.[95] It was sacred and linked to the pagan religion, but at the time of Mohammed both were on the decline. In the four sacred months, when war was forbidden, rival poets declaimed their verses at the fairs which were centres of social and literary life.[96] Mohammed began by oral recitals (Koran=recital) inspired by God through the angel Gabriel. After the death of Mohammed and the loss of many reciters at the battle of al-Yemama in 633, steps were taken to write down the tradition and to provide an official written text. The memory was the seat of the book. A final recension was established in 651.[97]

Restriction of writing to the sacred book and the limitations of legal and ritual matter in the Koran were followed by the growth of an oral tradition in the Hadith, a new saga, which replaced the old prose saga of the Arabs. It gained the force of law and the authority of inspiration and became a system of law and religion. Writing slowly extended its influence to the Hadith. The late recognition of writing was due in part to the cost and effort of writing down a large volume like the Koran. Disapproval of writing compelled Moham-medans to concentrate on the Koran and kept them from other books.

[93]*Ibid.*, p. 321.
[94]*Ibid.*, p. 216.
[95]Gandz, "The Dawn of Literature," p. 485.
[96]*Ibid.*, p. 491.
[97]*Ibid.*, p. 498.

Professional memorizers whose repetitions depended on memory and not on what they committed to writing, opposed the writing down of the Hadith. As the Jews had forbidden the composition of fresh books in addition to the Old Testament so the Mohammedans opposed possible rivals to the Koran.

The earlier pagan religion began to return in the secular anti-religious reaction of the Umayyad dynasty (651-750) and Islam made a compromise with the old poetry. In turn the supporters of the poetry of tradition developed hostility to the Umayyads as descendants of the pagan aristocracy which had persecuted Mohammed and were joined by the Abbasid revolutionaries who came into power in 750.[98] The capital was moved from Damascus to Baghdad, and the Umayyads set up an independent capital at Cordova in Spain.

The Byzantine Empire with its close relation between church and state was an absolutism which was always in danger of being tempted to the persecution of heresy.[99] Heretics became a source of strength to enemies of the Empire. The Nestorians expelled by Zeno were welcomed in the Sassanid Empire.[100] "It was by the genius of Muhammad that Nestorius' doctrine was to be restored to the realm of religion" (F. W. Buckler).[101] Athenian scholars migrated to Persia after the closing of the schools in 529. Extension of Byzantine interests to the West was at the expense of conciliation with Persia. Disaffection of the monophysites facilitated the conquest of Palestine and Egypt by the Persians. Though territory was reconquered by Heraclius, the struggle between Persians and Byzantines and continued religious disaffection enabled the Mohammedans with the zeal of a new religion to extend their conquests from Palestine to Spain. The failure of Nestorius in the Christian church made restoration outside in Islam inevitable. Byzantine Christianity as monophysitism became one of the main foundations of Islam and the early caliphates followed the methods and system of Byzantium and Sassanid Persia.[102] They were eventually checked by Leo III at Constantinople in 718 and by

[98]*Ibid.*, p. 512.
[99]*Byzantium: An Introduction to East Roman Civilization*, ed. N. H. Baynes and H. St. L. B. Moss (Oxford, 1948), xxv.
[100]*Ibid.*, p. 117.
[101]Cited *ibid.*, p. 309.
[102]*Ibid.*, p. 310.

Charles Martel in the West in 732. This resistance increased the difficulties of Mohammedanism as a political organization and contributed to the revival of Persian influence evident in the rise of the Abbasids and the break between Baghdad and Cordova. The limitations of the organization of space in relation to the demands of religion and of the organization of time and continuity persisted in the weakness of Mohammedanism.

Retreat of the Byzantine Empire in Egypt weakened its position in the West particularly as the Franks had defeated the Mohammedans. The attempt of the church in the East to strengthen its power at the expense of the emperor through monasticism had led to the resistance of the latter and had created difficulties for it in the iconoclastic controversy from 730 to 787. In the Byzantine Empire as in the principate "the imperial power is an autocracy tempered by the legal right of revolution" (Mommsen). An organization adapted to problems of space and of time such as the Byzantine Empire was faced with difficulties of balance which were met by contraction in space. "Belief and unbelief never follow men's commands" (Hobbes). The precedents of the coronations of Anastasius I by the Patriarch Euphemius in 491, by which the appearance of encroachment on the omnipotence of imperial power was scrupulously avoided but in which the Patriarch participated on condition that the Emperor would "introduce no innovations into the holy Church of God,"[103] and of Justin by Pope John I in 526, ultimately had sinister results for the Eastern Empire. The patriarch participated in the coronation as a representative of the people who co-operated with the army and the senate in the election of the emperor. The papacy in the West made coronation one of the most important rights of the church.

As a result of Byzantine weakness Pope Zacharias approved the consecration of Pippin as King of the Franks by Boniface in 751 and enabled him to dispossess the Merovingian dynasty. In turn the Frankish church was reformed and Frankish rulers were brought into close relation with the papacy. The Carolingian renaissance was accompanied by the crowning of Charlemagne[104] by the pope. Friendship between Haroun-al-Raschid and Charles the Great eventually

[103]Vasiliev, *Justin the First*, pp. 78-80.
[104]F. M. Stenton, *Anglo-Saxon England* (Oxford, 1943), p. 170.

compelled the Byzantine Empire to recognize Charles as Emperor in 812.[105]

The independence of the papacy and its relation with the Franks had unfortunate implications because of the number of bad popes from the ninth to the eleventh centuries. The papacy fell into slavery whereas the Eastern patriarchs retained their independence conscious of their strength, dignity, and privileges.[106] The political organization of Europe after the invasion of the barbarians lacked a significant basis of continuity. Monasticism had been introduced in Gaul by Athanasius and had spread rapidly. As Roman organization was submerged by the invaders, the Roman aristocracy became the hierarchy of the Roman church.[107]

The Roman conquests and extension of political organization had involved destruction of the oral tradition of the conquered and the imposition of writing. The oral tradition of the Druids reported by Caesar as designed to train the memory and to keep learning from becoming generally accessible had been wiped out. In Ireland and in Germany, beyond the bounds of the Roman conquest, the oral tradition persisted. In Ireland the oral system was retained with the native secular education while the official religion was recognized in foreign schools with writing. With the introduction of Christianity the Druids were eliminated, but the fili, or official poets attached to a central monarchy, renounced paganism and made peace with the church, thus preserving the mythological heroic literature in the oral tradition in spite of Christianity with writing and books.[108] The file was replaced by the bard with the fall of the central monarchy. By 575 the rapacity of the bards became intolerable and measures were taken against them. After the eleventh century, official secular and ecclesiastical scribes collected stories, and genealogical tales which had persisted in the oral tradition. Assemblies of poets or of the learned were held as late as 1351 and were of political significance.[109]

[105]F. W. Buckler, *Harunu'l-Rashid and Charles the Great* (Cambridge, Mass., 1931), p. 27.

[106]*Byzantium*, ed. Baynes and Moss, p. 123.

[107]See Theodore Haarhoff, *Schools of Gaul: A Study of Pagan and Christian Education in the Last Century of the Western Empire* (Oxford, 1920); also C. E. Stevens, *Sidonius Appollinaris and His Age* (Oxford, 1933).

[108]Gandz, "The Dawn of Literature," pp. 353-60.

[109]*Ibid.*, p. 368.

The insistence of the Pharisees on the oral tradition of native religion in opposition to Greek writing was paralleled by the insistence of Irish poets on the oral tradition in contrast with Christian writing and led, on the one hand, to Jewish, and, on the other, to Irish nationalism.

In Germany heroic poems were of courtly origin. Minstrels recited metrical speeches accompanied by the harp.[110] Court poems became the basis of epic and narrative poems from the fourth to the sixth centuries. In the heroic age bonds of kinship were disintegrating, the primitive sanctity of the family was giving way.[111] Tribal obligations broke down.[112] The Teutonic poems, like the Homeric poems of the heroic age, were a characteristic of a period of long-standing relations between semi-civilized people and civilized people.[113] On the other hand the Greeks maintained their language intact whereas the Teutons were exposed to the influence of Latin. Indeed the Greek oral tradition in surviving the impact of oriental civilizations influenced Rome, and destroyed the oral tradition of the Franks. Charlemagne attempted to collect existing poems and in the twelfth and later centuries they came into favour with the upper classes. They continued as testimony of freedom from Roman conquest and became a support to German nationalism. It has been significant that the national propaganda of the small nations of Europe has been largely in anthologies of poetry as the media best designed to protect them from the influences of "products of pure intelligence."[114] Plato's concern with expulsion of the poets was perhaps not unrelated to his appreciation of their role.

The limitations imposed on Christianity in Ireland by the persistence of the oral tradition released its energies for missionary activity to Scotland and England and to the Continent. Christian missions to the Continent gave momentum to the Carolingian renaissance and strengthened the position of the empire of the West, in which the papacy at Rome occupied a position parallel to that of the patriarch of Constantinople in the Byzantine Empire. The Carolingian revival of ancient Latin literature in the ninth century paralleled the

[110]H. M. Chadwick, *The Heroic Age* (Cambridge, 1926), p. 93.
[111]*Ibid.*, p. 347.
[112]*Ibid.*, p. 443.
[113]*Ibid.*, p. 458.
[114]Julien Benda, *The Great Betrayal* (London, 1928), p. 64.

revival of Greek at Constantinople in the same period and followed the outburst of activity in learning at Baghdad. These revivals did much to enable the classics to survive.[115] But the Byzantine Empire had no dark ages such as had followed the invasions of the barbarians for the Western church. The Western church had become independent of the Eastern church and of the Byzantine Empire but had allied itself with a new emperor who had not been disciplined by a church.

The Western Empire had the elements of a Caesaropapism in its capacity for organizing space and its relations with the church for organizing time and securing continuity. But it lacked elements of political strength. After the death of Charlemagne the Teutonic principle of division among the heirs was preserved and the vast area controlled by Charlemagne was divided. Nuclei of force were organized to meet the invasions of the Norsemen and of the Magyars. At Paris resistance to the invaders led to the emergence of the Capet family which followed the hereditary principle and became the basis of a dynastic kingship. In Germany the principle of election meant that the emperor was not attached to any one region and that dukedoms broke into small municipalities.[116] The church escaped from political influence and, as a step toward independence, in 1059, organized a school of cardinals which selected popes and in turn the cardinals. Control over time and continuity was wrenched from the state. A monopoly over time was built up centring around the name of Rome, the use of Latin, celibacy of the clergy, freedom from the state, and a monastic system. The church sponsored the Crusades and extended the decentralizing forces which accompanied the barbarian invasion in the West to the East and in 1204 erased "the last vestige of Rome's unification."[117]

A monopoly over time stimulated competitive elements in the organization of space. The introduction of paper from China to Baghdad and to Cordova and to Italy and France contributed to the development of cursive writing and to the organization of space in relation to the vernaculars. Venice, Pisa, and Genoa exploited the growing weakness of the Byzantine Empire. Uniformity in writing

[115]Werner Jaeger, *Humanism and Theology* (Milwaukee, Wisc., 1943), p. 24.
[116]See H. M. Chadwick, *The Nationalities of Europe and the Growth of National Ideologies* (Cambridge, 1945), pp. 94-7.
[117]*Byzantium*, ed. Baynes and Moss, p. 32.

followed the work of Charlemagne in the development and spread of the Carolingian minuscule to Italy. Arabic numerals displaced the cumbersome Roman numerals and facilitated calculation. In Italy writing[118] continued as an instrument of secular life after antiquity. Florence led in the practical aspects of writing in domestic industry and as a means of organizing trade in the twelfth century. Wool became an industrial and commercial product introducing profound transformations in Europe. Life could be organized legally and politically over vast territories. Toward the end of the twelfth century Florence had about six hundred notaries employed in industrial and commercial work and early in the thirteenth century a guild was formed with masters to whom children were apprenticed. Notaries specializing in commercial law were sent to distant countries where they acted as collaborators with banks and brought Florence in touch with the business and politics of Europe and of foreign countries. The notariat was transformed in a practical sense. Manuals of commercial calculation were produced. With a knowledge of reading, writing, and calculation artisans could become masters. About 1330, 8,000 to 10,000 children in Florence knew how to read, of whom 1,000 to 1,200 had a knowledge of the abacus and 500 to 600 a knowledge of grammar and logic. Schools were conducted as private enterprise and studies had a practical purpose. The corporations of Florence were based on a system of writing in Italian, accounts, central control of "boutiques," matricules, registers, scribes, and postal services. Writing compelled the individual to reflect more intensively. Discipline brought greater aptitude for expression. Calculability had intellectual consequences. Commercial property developed with contracts and economic relations lost their personal colour. Great artists and individuals rose from the ranks of the notaries. Writing played a decisive role in the intellectual and artistic revolution.

In Flanders and the low countries a civilization similar to that of Tuscany emerged. The Dutch language had an existence separate from Germany because it was fixed early in writing. Outside Italy only Flanders had an original renaissance.[119]

[118]Etienne Hajnal, "Le rôle social de l'écriture et l'évolution européenne," *Revue de l'Institut de Sociologie*, 1934, pp. 255-9.
[119]*Ibid.*, p. 266.

The impact of paper and writing on the monopoly over time exercised by the church was evident in the growing importance of the vernacular, and the development of industry and trade. In defence against the stubborn and varied assaults on the most precious beliefs of Catholic Christianity, the apostolic rule of faith and the apostolic order of bishops had been developed as a guarantee of truth in addition to reliance on the Old and New Testaments.[120] Limits were set to the compass of Holy Scripture; baptism and the Lord's Supper were given the form of mysteries; it was forbidden to put the baptismal symbol in writing and part of the public worship was forbidden to profane eyes. Bible reading was emphasized and the church became a great elementary school. Every Christian must know what he believed.[121] The Greek church pressed on to the translation of the Bible into other tongues and laid the foundations of national literature among other peoples. Cyrillic and Glagolitic alphabets, developed to make the scriptures and the liturgy available to the Slavs, more adequately represented the sounds of the Slavonic language and provided a more effective bridge between the oral and the written traditions.[122] Christianity as the daughter of Judaism had defended the sacred writings from the encroachment of a priesthood in a world of mystery religions.[123]

In the church of Rome, monasticism and monastic theology had become established before the elements of a mystery religion became important. In the struggle against barbarism, the church emphasized exclusion by concentrating on Latin and supported its position by monastic orders (notably the friars), architecture (notably the Gothic cathedrals), and manuscripts (notably in the work of illumination) and music. Stone in architecture and scripture emphasized permanence and durability. In the thirteenth century "Tout ce que' les théologiens, les encyclopédistes, les interprètes de la Bible ont dit d'essentiel a été exprimé par la peinture sur verre ou par la sculpture."[124] Psalm singing created, in the words of Ambrose, "a great

---

[120]Adolf von Harnack, *Bible Reading in the Early Church*, trans. J. R. Wilkinson (New York, 1912), pp. 48-9.

[121]*Ibid.*, pp. 85-6.

[122]D. Diringer, *The Alphabet, a Key to the History of Mankind* (London, n.d.), p. 476.

[123]Von Harnack, *Bible Reading in the Early Church*, pp. 145-8.

[124]Emile Mâle, *L'Art religieux du XIII^e siècle en France* (Paris, 1910), p. 3.

bond of unity when the whole people raise their voices in one choir."[125] Music was handicapped by limitations of writing "for if music is not retained by man's memory, it is lost, since it cannot be written down."[126] Early in the eleventh century Guido wrote regarding his system of notation: "For since I have undertaken to teach this method to my boys, certain of them have succeeded, easily, within three days, in singing melodies previously unknown to them; a result which formerly, by the other methods, could not have been brought about in many weeks."[127] Counterpoint in which the aim is "to perform several melodies simultaneously and bind them together by good and well-regulated consonances" developed about 1300.[128]

The manufacture of paper near urban centres because of demand and of cheap supplies of linen rags as raw material hastened the shift of writing from the monasteries to urban communities. The writing master emerged in the fourteenth and fifteenth centuries and in turn printing in the trend toward urbanization.[129] Machine industry, of which printing was an early and conspicuous illustration, made effective inroads on a society dominated by the manuscript. The interrelation and unity of the arts in which the production of manuscripts meant writing and painting, which in turn were influenced by sculpture and architecture, was destroyed. The perfection of the sculpture of Michelangelo supported by the wealth of Italian cities and the papacy and combining Christian and pagan traditions was the last gesture of a society destined to fall with the Italian city state, following the French invasions and the influence of the book. The horrors of the Bible illustrated by the statues of the cathedrals were offset by classical influence. The painting of the Last Judgment reflected the doom of a culture based on stone, parchment, and painting. Stone was a medium of expression of immortality for the artist and the culture. The attack of Savonarola was based on the book and it was symbolic of an end of a period that Michelangelo should have designed the Vatican library.

That the sacred character of the scriptures in the Middle Ages

[125]P. H. Lang, *Music in Western Civilization* (New York, 1941), p. 43.
[126]*Ibid.*, p. 85.
[127]H. E. Woolridge, *The Oxford History of Music* (Oxford, 1929), I, 281.
[128]Lang, *Music in Western Civilization*, p. 162.
[129]Hellmuth Lehmann-Haupt, *Peter Schoeffer of Gernsheim and Mainz* (Rochester, N.Y., 1950), p. 9; also S. H. Steinberg, "Medieval Writing Masters," *The Library*, 4th series, XXII, 1942.

was expressed in sculpture and architecture had disastrous implications following the expansion of printing with its emphasis on the scriptures. Greek scriptures following the translations of Erasmus and a concern with the possibility of translation into the vernaculars destroyed the monopoly of the church as expressed in Latin. In the Reformation print was used to overwhelm sculpture and architecture as interpreters of the scriptures. Translations into the vernaculars gave them a sacred character and gave a powerful drive to nationalism. Milton was concerned with the production of an epic in English which would combine nationalism and Christianity.

The printing industry made rapid advance in regions in which the effects of the Roman conquest were limited such as Germany and England or in regions marginal to areas dominated by a bureaucracy based on papyrus. Regions in which Latin was strong or regions of the Romance languages developed opposition to mechanized print partly through other arts including literature. In England the strength of the oral tradition was evident in Shakespeare, and in Germany in the absence of a uniform dialect until after Luther's Bible was printed. In these regions Protestantism made rapid headway and supported the growth of the state. New monopolies of space began to emerge as the monopoly over time was weakened.

A new interest in space was evident in the development of the mariner's compass and the lens.[130] Columbus discovered the New World, Magellan proved the earth a sphere, and in astronomy the Ptolemaic system was undermined especially after the invention and improvement of the telescope. The architect Brunelleschi has been credited with first constructing a scene according to a focused system of perspective. Dürer advanced from the empirical to mathematical construction.[131] In Florence the new conception of space was translated into artistic terms as a counterpart of the modern notion of individualism.[132] Its immediate effect on architecture was evident in the baroque. In philosophy Leibniz was the first to explain space as

[130]M. S. Bunim, *Space in Medieval Painting and the Forerunners of Perspective* (New York, 1940), p. 105.
    [131]*Ibid.*, pp. 187-91.
    [132]Sigfried Giedion, *Space, Time and Architecture: The Growth of a New Tradition* (Cambridge, Mass., 1941), p. 31.

pure form, an order of existence, and time as an order of succession. The paper and printing industries supported the development of monopolies of space in nationalism and the state. Printing emphasized vernaculars, reduced the speed of movement of ideas, and divided the European mind. Formerly philosophy directed scientific knowledge but an increase in printed material has compelled science to go now in one direction and now in another. Germany became more isolated from England in part because of the difficulty of its language as compared with that of France. It would be interesting to conjecture as to the history of Europe in the nineteenth century if Newman and Comte had known German. The vested interests of the printing industry tend to check the movement of ideas and to contribute to the building-up of monopolies, and, ultimately, to the breaking-over into other languages and to the ebb and flow of movements. The delay in the industrial development of Germany followed by its rapid development after 1870 described by Veblen is in part an illustration. Even science with its emphasis on a common vernacular and on translations has come under the influence of monopolies of knowledge in patents, secret processes, and military "security" measures. Science had gained in the escape from the monopoly of knowledge in terms of time but eventually lost in the development of knowledge in terms of space. An obsession with monopolies of space has been evident in the effects of militarism on geography. As a military instrument it was especially effective in propaganda in its adaptations to regionalism and nationalism. "We must know about our own country." Geopolitics was developed in Germany by seizing on Mackinder's thesis and attempting to create an impression of fatalism and inevitability. But, as Cornford remarked, when war is described as inevitable, its causes are not known.

The destruction of time and the increasing importance of monopolies of space were evident in the writings of Hegel for whom progress was perpetual movement and strife or of Marx who regarded time as "formless inevitability."[133] For Schopenhauer music was the highest because the most irrational form of art, the most naked un-

[133]Hans Kohn, *The Twentieth Century: A Mid-Way Account of the Western World* (New York, 1949), p. 55.

reflected expression of the essence of life, of the will.[134] Wagner expressed in music the resistance to Rome and Christianity. "What I
have never forgiven Wagner is his condescending to Germany"
(Nietzsche).[135] The destruction of Germany's contribution to
Western civilization based on the book and on music was followed
by attempts at recovery from the standpoint of militarism and the
state and the aberrations of German culture incidental to the effects
of war.

The increasing influence of print has been reflected in republican-
ism with the bias toward constitutions and documents and guarantees
of freedom of the press and of the right of the individuals. Demands
for control over time were reflected in the separation of church and
state. George Washington wrote in a statement to Tripoli: "The
government of the United States is not in any sense founded upon the
Christian religion." More significant perhaps have been the varying
attitudes of peoples toward the state, as between East and West,
between common law countries and Roman law countries, and
between countries at different stages of industrial development. The
concept of the state as an economic factor has become an indication
of economic activity. Without religion as an anchorage the state has
become more dependent on cultural development. With cultural
maturity as in France the state becomes a cloak to put on and off
at will during periods of emergency in the form of constitutional
changes. In nations without cultural maturity such drastic changes
become unthinkable and the statute books become cluttered with
constitutional amendments and legislation. The totalitarian state or
the welfare state with rigid constitutions is compelled to resort to
endless administrative activity.

The oral tradition implies the spirit but writing and printing are
inherently materialistic. The influence of the oral tradition through
resort to writing and printing and a stress on its sacredness—thus
paralysing its possible rivals, turning the weapons of its enemies
against them—persisted in the Bible and Homer. The accumulation
of poetry under the oral tradition dominated the history of the West.
Greece and Rome kept their respect for the oral tradition.[136] A decline
of the oral tradition meant an emphasis on writing (and hence on

[134]*Ibid.*, p. 47.
[135]Cited by Benda, *The Great Betrayal*, p. 47.
[136]Albright, *From the Stone Age to Christianity*, p. 46.

the eye rather than the ear) and on visual arts, architecture, sculpture, and painting (and hence on space rather than time). The significance of time persisted in the character of materials notably in the use of stone in architecture and sculpture because of their permanence and durability. The emphasis on capitals in Egypt, Babylonia, Assyria, Persia, Greece, Rome, Constantinople, Paris, Berlin, London, Washington, and Moscow reflected a concern with the problems of control over time and over space. The burden of capitals on the peoples concerned has not been unrelated to their decline and to revolutions, for example in France and Russia. Religious monopolies concerned with time relied on the oral tradition. It had resort to the support of architecture in its sacred places as in Rome, Jerusalem, and Mecca. Again revolutions were in part protests against the burden of capitals, as in the case of Protestantism. The destruction of the Temple in Jerusalem by the Romans accentuated the importance of the oral tradition among the Jews and made Judaism inadaptable to political demands. The rise of Palestine has been a tribute to the persistence of the oral tradition as a basis for the organization of time on the one hand and to the increasing pressure of the written and printed tradition toward the organization of space on the other.

In the clash between types of monopoly, an unpredictable freedom has been achieved. The Roman Catholic church, with its control over time, absorbed elements of administration of the Roman Empire essential to control over space and attempted to maintain a balance comparable to that of the Byzantine Empire. In a sense they supported each other and destroyed each other. The spread of paper and printing from China and the Mohammedan world upset the balance and compelled new adjustments. Germany's escape from the discipline of Rome permitted the clash of ideas between France and the Holy Roman Empire and between England and Germany. In the West the demands of faith—it is certain because it is impossible (Tertullian)— when disseminated by translation into different languages were too heavy. The fanaticism of faith and the fanaticism of reason tore Europe apart and intensified the problem of adjustment between obsession for the state and obsession for the church and led to the growth in the name of science of new monopolies to exploit faith and incredibility.

# INDUSTRIALISM
# AND CULTURAL VALUES[1]

WE MUST ALL be aware of the extraordinary, perhaps insuperable, difficulty of assessing the quality of a culture of which we are a part or of assessing the quality of a culture of which we are not a part. In using other cultures as mirrors in which we may see our own culture we are affected by the astigma of our own eyesight and the defects of the mirror, with the result that we are apt to see nothing in other cultures but the virtues of our own. During the twentieth century machine industry has made it possible to amass enormous quantities of information evident in encyclopaedias, histories of civilization, and quiz programmes. The concern with the study of civilization in this century is probably a result of the character of our civilization. Certainly such studies reflect our civilization. Spengler in *The Decline of the West* could not have been unaffected by the position of Germany, nor could Toynbee free himself from the traditions of English-speaking countries, nor could Kroeber escape the influence of the United States and the obsession with the objective qualities of science. I shall assume that cultural values, or the way in which or the reasons why people of a culture think about themselves, are part of the culture.

It is perhaps a unique characteristic of civilization that each civilization believes in its uniqueness and its superiority to other civilizations. Indeed this may be the meaning of culture—i.e., something which we have that others have not. It is probably for this reason that writings on culture can be divided into those attempting to weaken other cultures and those attempting to strengthen their own. The emphasis of St. Augustine on original sin implied an attack on those representing the secular state, as the emphasis of John Locke on the *tabula rasa* was the basis of an attack on ecclesiastical hier-

[1]A paper read on December 30, 1950, at the meetings of the American Economic Association at Chicago.

archy, and the work of Spencer on progress was the basis for the claim to supremacy of Anglo-Saxons. "Reason is and ought only to be the slave of the passions and can never pretend to any other office than to serve and obey them"—a statement as true of this quotation and of Hume's writings as of others. Perhaps the obsession of each culture with its uniqueness is the ultimate basis of its decline. Dean Inge has remarked that civilization is a disease almost invariably fatal unless the cause is checked in time. The Hindus and the Chinese have survived by marking time.[2]

A brief survey of cultural development in the West may indicate the peculiarity or uniqueness of culture and elements which make for duration and extension. Cultures will reflect their influence in terms of space and in terms of duration. How large an area did they cover and how long did they last? The limitations of culture, in point of duration, are in part a result of the inability to muster the intellectual resources of a people to the point where stagnation can be avoided and where boredom can be evaded. The history of boredom or stagnation has yet to be written but it might well include the story of the ostracism of Aristides the Just on the ground that the Greeks became weary of hearing him called the Just. Hume wrote that "when the arts and sciences come to perfection in any state, from that moment, they naturally or rather necessarily decline and seldom or never revive in that nation where they formerly flourished." Intense cultural activity is followed by fatigue.

The capacity to concentrate on intense cultural activity during a short period of time and to mobilize intellectual resources over a vast territory assumes to an important extent the development of armed force to a high state of efficiency. Cultural activity, evident in architecture and sculpture, capable of impressing peoples over a wide area, is designed to emphasize prestige. It becomes an index of power. A concern for continuity, the biological limitations of the patriarchal system as a basis for dynasties, and the difficulties of maintaining a high cultural level over a long period of time will involve an emphasis on types of architecture calculated to reflect a control over time as well as over space. The pyramids were an index of power over time but dynasties represented by them were displaced and in turn new

[2]W. R. Inge, *Diary of a Dean, St. Paul's 1911-1934* (London, 1950), p. 195.

dynasties concentrated on new monuments to enhance their prestige. Old capital sites scattered along the Nile valley are a memorial of the demands of successive dynasties for prestige. The Egyptian Empire was a tribute to their success. But such monuments as capitals with tombs, palaces, temples, and sculpture were expensive and did much to bring the Empire to an end. Political power reflected in capitals was supported by such cultural activities as writing evident in successive bureaucracies.

Civilization in the Tigris and Euphrates valleys developed along lines similar to that in the Nile but solutions to the problem of time appear to have been reached before the problem of space and organized force became acute. Religious communities with hierarchical organizations characterized Sumerian civilization. Though architecture dependent on bricks made from the clay of the delta regions became important, writing on clay was a basis for communication, administration, and trade. Organized force represented by Sargon of the Akkadians brought religious communities under control and with access to writing made possible a vast empire. With religion based on writing Sumerian culture proved sufficiently strong to throw off control of a foreign ruler and to support a capital at Ur for a limited number of dynasties. In turn this culture came under the control of fresh conquerors and a new capital of palaces and temples emerged at Babylon. The effectiveness with which control over time reflected in religion was fused with control over space was evident in the long period in which Babylon persisted as a capital under the Kassite dynasty.

The success of organized force was dependent in part on technological advance, notably, in early civilizations, in the use of the horse, the crossing of the light African horse with the heavier Asiatic horse, the introduction of horse riding and cavalry to replace horse driving and chariots, and the use of iron as a substitute for bronze. The Hittites with the use of iron succeeded in building an empire with a capital which emphasized sculpture and architecture but it was checked on the south by Babylon and on the north and west by the Greeks with their control over the sea at Troy. They were followed by the Assyrians who exploited technological advance in warfare and made fresh contributions to its development. With a new capital at

Nineveh they succeeded in offsetting the prestige of the Nile and of Babylon and establishing an empire to include the civilizations of both. Prestige was secured not only by architecture and sculpture but also by writing. The library became a great instrument of imperial power and set an example which has influenced the history of the West until the present time. The concern of the Assyrian Empire with the collection of Sumerian documents for the library at Nineveh has been paralleled at Alexandria, Rome, Paris, Berlin, London, Moscow, and Washington. In Canada we are attempting to follow in our own way at Ottawa. The Assyrians attempted to maintain their prestige not only by libraries but also by development of a reputation for war-like ferocity, paralleled in this century. Failure of the Assyrian Empire was in part a result of the tenacity and diversity of civilization in Babylon and Egypt.

Persia succeeded where Assyria had failed by emphasizing the importance of a single capital by architecture and sculpture and of small capitals of districts or satrapies governed from a centre. The beginnings of the principle "divide and rule" were evident in recognition of the religions of Babylon and Egypt and encouragement of the religion of the Hebrews at Jerusalem. But as in the case of Assyria the political organization of Persia was unable to meet the demands of continuity.

Political organizations determined to an important extent by the limitations of armed force and characterized by centralized power emphasized the capital city and left their impress on cultural activity in architecture and sculpture. They emerged in land areas, from the Nile valley to Asia Minor. They provided a shelter for the development of communication facilities and for the growth of trade such as that of the Aramaeans on land and of the Phoenicians on the Mediterranean. Communication was subordinated to the demands of centralized power in religion and in political organization; it was characterized by the use of the eye rather than the ear. The scribe occupied a strategic position in centralized bureaucracies.

In attempting to use other civilizations as mirrors by which we may understand our own we are exposed to much greater dangers in studying Greek culture and its successors since our own culture has been profoundly influenced by it. Civilizations of the Nile and Asia

Minor had a limited influence on peoples along the north shore of the Mediterranean. Minoan civilization was an attempt to encroach on the sea which failed in the face of opposition from the north. Mycenean civilization on the mainland proved more adaptable but in turn succumbed. The Greeks escaped the centralizing tendencies of river civilizations with their effects on capitals, architecture, and sculpture and on writing with its implications for bureaucracy. In their settlements on the islands and along the coast, the Greeks emphasized cultural aspects suited to their needs. The oral tradition rather than writing provided a basis for the epic and for literature designed to unite scattered groups in a consciousness of Greek culture. The alphabet borrowed from the Phoenicians was given vowels and adapted to the demands of speech. The ear replaced the eye. With the spread of writing the oral tradition developed fresh powers of resistance evident in the flowering of Greek culture in the sixth and fifth centuries. A concern with the Eastern concept of the capital was apparent in the age of tyrants in the sixth century notably in Athens and in the fifth century notably in the Athenian Empire. But as the epic and tragedy reflected the character of Greek civilization so too did architecture and sculpture. "The statues of the classic artists are the relics of ancient dancing" (S. H. Butcher). "After art had been toiling in India, in Persia, and in Egypt to produce monsters, beauty and grace were discovered in Greece" (Sir James Mackintosh). "Nothing over-much" was a maxim which implied distrust of specialization in all phases of cultural life. Greek culture was destroyed in the growth of writing and of individualism in the latter part of the fifth century.

The vitality of Greek culture was evident finally in the flowering of military skill in the conquests of Philip and Alexander. Greek culture with its political organization reflected in the city state came in contact with concepts peculiar to early civilizations and compromised with them in the Hellenistic kingdoms. The capital to a limited extent was restored. In Egypt the Ptolemies established a new capital at Alexandria and created a new deity to destroy the influence of the old capital at Thebes, and built up a library to exploit the limitations of Athens and to offset the influence of Babylon. At Pergamum, the Attalids developed a capital with a library designed to offset the prestige of Alexandria. The Seleucids were eventually defeated by a revival of Persian civilization.

In the east, along the north coast of the Mediterranean, Rome came under the cultural influence of Greece, and after destroying Carthage, which had inherited the commercial traditions of Phoenicia, extended her influence to the Hellenistic kingdoms to the east, and to Spain and Gaul in the north and west. The influence of Egypt was evident in the deification of the ruler, in the decline of the Roman Republic and the emergence of the Roman Empire, and in the increasing centralization of a bureaucracy. The attempt to offset the influence of Persian civilization was evident in the orientalization of the emperors and eventually in the establishment of Constantinople as a capital to take advantage of the support of Hellenistic culture including Christianity. The inroads of the barbarians were followed by the decline of Rome and the rise of Constantinople as a political centre. The difficulty of subordinating cultural capitals with their roots in earlier civilizations reflected in the religious controversies of the period led to the emergence of Rome as the religious capital of the West, and to the spread of Mohammedanism in the East. With Mohammedanism new capitals arose at Baghdad and at Cordova in Spain. Access to a medium other than papyrus and parchment, namely paper, enabled these centres to build up libraries and compelled Constantinople to take a fresh interest in learning. In the West the Holy Roman Empire became an institution designed to strengthen the prestige of Rome. In turn the political influence of Rome led to the increasing prestige of Paris as a theological centre. The attempt of the papacy to recapture Jerusalem and the Eastern church in the Crusades was followed by the growth of small Italian city republics notably at Venice, Florence, and Genoa. The final collapse of Constantinople and of the Byzantine Empire in 1453 following the use of artillery brought new efforts to regain prestige in the East at Kiev and in the West at Paris.

The capitals of the northern Mediterranean and Europe while reflecting the influence of the capitals of the Nile and the Tigris and Euphrates valleys were dominated by the oral tradition of Greece. The absolute monarchy of Egypt and the East became the Roman emperor, the English Tudors, Louis XIV, and the czars of Russia, and its influence was evident in the courts of Rome and Constantinople, London, Paris, and St. Petersburg. The city state of Greece was revived in the city republics of Italy and Germany and in the Renaissance, and its influence softened the tyranny of the courts. In some sense the culture represented by the courts had solved the problem of time and space. The Byzantine Empire persisted as a unique achievement in duration, and while the size of its territory fluctuated, its achievement in the solution of problems of space was scarcely less remarkable. Paris became the cultural centre of the West notably under Louis XIV and the influence of the French court was evident in the England of Charles II, in the courts of Russia, and indeed wherever culture in the Western sense raised its head. Antwerp, Amsterdam, London, Berlin, St. Petersburg, Moscow, and Washington were influenced directly and indirectly by the dominance of Paris. French culture persisted after the Revolution and after the occupation of the recent war, and survived the state. Like Paris, London became more dependent on cultural influence than on political organization as is evident in the British Commonwealth of Nations.

After this brief survey of earlier civilizations we can attempt an appraisal of the possibilities in terms of duration and extent of our own civilization. We have emphasized the significance of communication in determining the characteristics of earlier civilizations and of changes in methods of communication. The discovery of printing in the middle of the fifteenth century implied the beginning of a return to a type of civilization dominated by the eye rather than the ear. With printing and an increase in the use and manufacture of paper German cities strengthened their position and facilitated a break from the church in Holland, Germany, and England. Their advance was registered in the concern for the word of the Bible, the Reformation, and the rise of Protestantism. The full impact of printing did not become possible until the adoption of the Bill of Rights in the United States with its guarantee of freedom of the press. A guarantee of freedom of the press in print was intended to further sanctify the printed word and to provide a rigid bulwark for the shelter of vested interests. Printing assumed mass production or reproduction of words and once it escaped from the pattern of the parchment manuscript it compelled the production of vast quantities of new material including material to meet the demands of science and technology. Improvement of communication hastened the development of markets and of industry. The Industrial Revolution followed the printing industry and in turn in the nineteenth century, with the use of steam power in the manufacture of paper and of printed material, supported rapid expansion of the printing industry.

We are perhaps too much a part of the civilization which followed the spread of the printing industry to be able to detect its characteristics. Education in the words of Laski became the art of teaching men to be deceived by the printed word. "The most important service rendered by the press and the magazines is that of educating people to approach printed matter with distrust."[3] But there are unmistakable signs that ours is a civilization which partakes of the character of all civilizations in its belief in its uniqueness and superiority over other civilizations. We are all familiar with the claims of the printing industry to the effect that it has ushered in a new and superior civilization. No other civilization, we are told, has enjoyed our advantages. Democracy, education, progress, individualism, and other blessed words describe our new heaven. At this point the water becomes swift and we are in grave danger of being swept off our feet by the phenomenon we are describing. We are in danger on the one hand of losing our objectivity and on the other hand of being placed under arrest. Freedom of the press has been regarded as a great bulwark of our civilization and it would be dangerous to say that it has become the great bulwark of monopolies of the press. Civilizations have their sacred cows. The Middle Ages burned its heretics and the modern age threatens them with atom bombs.

In contrast with the civilization dominated by Greek culture with its maxim "nothing in excess," modern civilization dominated by machine industry is concerned always with specialization which might be described as always in excess. Economics, beginning with Adam Smith, and indeed other social sciences have an obsession with specialization. Specialization and industrialism support an emphasis on equality. An interest in material goods which characterized the Scottish people, represented notably in Adam Smith, has been followed

[3]*Further Extracts from the Note-Books of Samuel Butler,* ed. A. T. Bartholomew (London, 1934), p. 261.

by an attitude described by Samuel Butler: "All progress is based upon a universal innate desire on the part of every organism to live beyond its income." The concern with specialization and excess, making more and better mousetraps, precludes the possibility of understanding a preceding civilization concerned with balance and proportion. Industrialism implies technology and the cutting of time into precise fragments suited to the needs of the engineer and the accountant. The inability to escape the demands of industrialism on time weakens the possibility of an appraisal of limitations of space. Constant changes in technology particularly as they affect communication, a crucial factor in determining cultural values (for example, the development of radio and television), increase the difficulties of recognizing balance let alone achieving it.

The cultural values of an industrial society are not the cultural values of other societies. The equation of ethical values between cultures is possibly more difficult than the equation of other values, though Professor V. Gordon Childe has described the implications of cultural change in such fields of abstraction as mathematics. The outburst of rich artistic activity in Greece coincided with a decline in the status of women. Dean Inge has reminded us that the extreme sensitivity of modern civilization, for example in the attitude toward cruelty to animals, and the extreme insensitivity toward unbelievable cruelty to human beings have synchronized with the complete collapse of spontaneous and unconscious artistic production.[4] The ugliness of English and American towns and the disappearance of beauty accompanied the invention of machinery and great industries. Von Eicken's thesis that the master key to history lies in the conclusion that human movements provoke violent reactions has much to support it. Roman imperialism created by intense nationalism ended by destroying the nationality of rulers and subjects. The nationalism of the Jews left them without a country. The Catholic church renounced the world and became the heir of the defunct Roman empire. Universal suffrage heralded the end of parliamentary government. The more successful a democracy in levelling population the less the resistance to despotism. The interest of the French Revolution in humanity kindled the

[4]See his essay in *The Legacy of Greece*, ed. R. W. Livingstone (Oxford, 1923), p. 40.

fire of patriotism and nationalism in Spain, Germany, and Russia.[5]

Anthropologists, notably Pitt-Rivers, have explored the dangers of the intrusion of one culture on other cultures. Historians have commented on the unsatisfactory results which followed the importation of the parliamentary system to the European continent. The disasters which overtook North American civilization following the coming of Europeans have been described at length. The disturbances which have characterized a shift from a culture dominated by one form of communication to another culture dominated by another form of communication whether in the campaigns of Alexander, the Thirty Years' War, or the wars of the present century point to the costs of cultural change. The impact of Point Four on other cultures, the clash of so-called "backward" and so-called "forward" countries involve such unpaid costs as the enormous loss of life directly through war and indirectly through cultural change. The spread of communism from France to Russia and China is a further illustration of the instability of Western civilization. Stability which characterized certain periods in earlier civilizations is not the obvious objective of this civilization. Each civilization has its own methods of suicide.

[5]Inge, *Diary of a Dean*, pp. 208, 210.

# THE ENGLISH PUBLISHING TRADE
# IN THE EIGHTEENTH CENTURY

THE MONOPOLY POSITION of the publishing trade had significant implications for the age of enlightenment in England. After the revolution of 1689 and the growing importance of parliament, public opinion became more effective as the basis of power. The demands for greater responsiveness to public opinion continued throughout the eighteenth century and in the latter half parliament made numerous concessions.

The role of public opinion was determined in part by the availability of paper and the cost of printing. In the early part of the eighteenth century England had about 150 mills producing 60,000 reams annually including all "the lower sorts" used for domestic consumption and white paper, to the value of £30,000 to £40,000. In a total of 400,000 reams consumed, about two-thirds was produced in England. Partly as a result of a protective tariff imposed in 1712, England and Wales had 278 paper mills with 338 vats in 1739. Les Frères Gautier, a firm handling imports from Holland, wrote from London in 1742, "We are pretty much out of Business and intirely discouraged out of the Paper Trade, which is brought here to a very low ebb, and will decrease more and more, by reason of the great Quantity made in England, which Manufactory increases every day."[1] By the end of the century there were about 500 mills in the United Kingdom producing 10,000 tons of hand-made paper annually. Rags were imported to the extent of 9,000 to 10,000 tons annually. Expansion of mills was restricted by a limited number of sites with abundance of water and room. The age of machinery in the making of paper and in the press had not yet appeared. Intellectual interest was not yet dominated by the machine.

[1]Cited by Charles Wilson, *Anglo-Dutch Commerce and Finance in the Eighteenth Century* (Cambridge, 1941), p. 61.

The extremely slow growth of the paper industry, as compared with that of the nineteenth century,[2] strengthened the position of monopoly in the publishing industry. John Locke complained near the beginning of the century that the monopoly of classical authors held by the Company of Stationers meant that they were "scandalously ill printed, both for letter, paper, and correctness, and scarce one tolerable edition is made." ". . . our printing is so very bad, and yet so very dear in England."[3] The abandonment of the Licensing Act in 1694, partly a result of Locke's efforts, brought marked expansion in the publishing trade and excesses brought demands for restriction. As a result of a petition from printers, papermakers, and booksellers, a Copyright Act, effective April 10, 1710, gave protection to the extent of 21 years if the book had been published before that date and 14 years if published after that date, renewable for an additional 14 years if the author was still alive. Piracy was checked in England but not in Scotland and Ireland and smuggling from the Continent continued. Legislation in 1739 imposed a heavy tax on paper imported from France and Holland and imposed severe penalties on illegal importers of printed books.

Political strife and the European wars meant that writers were enlisted to support parties and the demand for news provided a market in the coffee-houses. News became a vendible commodity after the lapse of the Licensing Act. With the end of the war the position of newswriters, post men, and post boys in the words of Addison was "more hard than that of soldiers; considering that they have taken more towns and fought more battles. They have been upon parties and skirmishes when our armies have lain still, and given the general assault to many a place, when the besiegers were quiet in their trenches. They have made us masters of several strong towns many weeks before our generals could do it, and completed victories when our greatest captains have been glad to come off with a drawn battle. When Prince Eugene has slain his thousands, Boyer has slain his ten thousands."

Prior to 1710 literature was supported by patrons partly as a political weapon. "Nothing sells like good topical satire" and the

[2]H. A. Innis, *Political Economy and the Modern State* (Toronto, 1946), pp. 35-55.
[3]Lord King, *The Life and Letters of John Locke* (London, 1864), pp. 204-7.

support of Swift, Defoe, Addison, and Steele was enlisted in the interests of political parties. Harley was one of the first to appreciate how vital the press was to the prestige of the government. The mild support of the Tories by Defoe's *Review* was reinforced by Swift's weekly articles in the *Examiner* from November 2 to June 4, 1711. "Political writers had hitherto been hirelings and often little better than spies. No preceding, and, we may add, no succeeding writer ever achieved such a position by such means. The press has become more powerful as a whole: but no particular representative of the press has made such a leap into power. Swift came at the time when the influence of political writing was already great."[4] With the shift of the centre of gravity for the Tories from parliament to the press, Swift, in *The Conduct of the Allies*, contributed powerfully to the downfall of Marlborough and ultimately to the Treaty of Utrecht. With a sound education, a quick and accurate perception of public taste, and a shrewd knowledge of the times, he wrote with broad generalization supported by a mastery of detail. By the skilful use of subventions Swift left an efficient political and news organization when he returned to Dublin in 1713. The death of Anne in 1714 meant that government was free from the personal intervention of the sovereign. As Leslie Stephen remarked, "Everyone knew that George I had nothing to do with God Almighty."

Defoe became a journalist in that he knew that popularity depended on readers caring little or nothing about politics. He wrote for the day and for the greatest interest of the greatest number. As the oracle of the masses he introduced fresher and lighter material in broadsides and gave readers a *feuilleton* with sensational and supernatural incidents. Because of his knowledge of men his attachment to political parties was weak. Depending on subventions he shifted from Whig to Tory interests. He had an unrivalled genius for "lying like truth."[5] He combined pungent, persuasive, political criticism with domestic news and bright social excursions. He made the newspaper an organ of initiative and reform and attempted complete independence.

As Defoe's mildness had contributed to the enlistment of Swift by the Tories on the one side, it led to the enlistment of Addison by

[4]Leslie Stephen, *Swift* (London, 1931), p. 86.
[5]William Minto, *Daniel Defoe* (London, 1902), p. 143.

the Whigs on the other. Halifax had become convinced that the pamphlet as a political weapon must be displaced by the newspaper emphasizing news and well-conceived and concise observations. Addison introduced the leading article to replace the tract and the paragraph. The pamphlet and the brochure were adapted in the leading article and made a part of the newspapers as chronicles of news by Defoe and were developed by Addison. Whereas Swift had embittered relations between the land-owning aristocracy and the new plutocracy by his attacks on the latter, Addison and Steele tempered animosities and made the newspaper a purifying and constructive force of value to the divine and the philanthropist as well as the politician. The press performed duties which the church owed to the community. The *Spectator* and the *Tatler*, through the development of the periodical essay by Addison, and the emphasis on the position of women as readers in the reign of Queen Anne by Steele, bridged the gap between the irreligious licentiousness of the Restoration and Puritan rigidity. They created an organized public opinion in the clubs and coffee-houses. Addison wrote in 1716: "Of all the ways and means by which this political humour hath been propagated among the people of Great Britain, I cannot single out any so prevalent or universal as the late constant application of the press to the publishing of state matters."[6] Addison "reconciled wit and virtue, after a long and disastrous separation, during which wit had been led astray by profligacy and virtue by fanaticism" (Macaulay). He brought "philosophy out of closets and libraries, schools and colleges, to dwell at clubs and assemblies, at tea-tables and in coffee-houses."[7] Under Addison and Steele, journalism[8] moved away from dependence on the patron. The periodical essay offset the effects of "short lived gossipy newspapers, virulent pamphlets, indecent verses and salacious tales." Periodicals were collected in volumes and provided fresh ideas, instructive easy reading of a higher moral level, a more humane feeling, and milder manners. The *Spectator* was the first and best representative of a special style of literature which consists in talking to the public about itself, "the only really popular literature of our time" (Thomas Hill Greene).

[6]Cited by H. R. Fox Bourne, *English Newspapers* (London, 1887), I, 98.
[7]W. J. Courthope, *Addison* (London, 1919), p. 192.
[8]See James R. Sutherland, "The Circulation of Newspapers and Literary Periodicals, 1700-1730," *The Library*, 4th series, XV, 1934-5.

The stamp taxes imposed under 10 Anne c. 19 (1712) on pamphlets and newspapers and on advertisements compelled a rise in price, which meant a decline in circulation and more substantial subsidies from political parties. As Morison[9] has pointed out, the tax was evaded by a rapid development of weeklies of six pages, or one and a half sheets, which were not specified in the legislation. The weekly essay and the weekly newspaper were brought together and the moral dissertation and the critical essay became a staple. News was collected more cheaply by taking copy from daily or other papers. By 1720 the newspapers had ceased to be primarily purveyors of news.

With the rise of Walpole and weakening of the opposition, newspapers were brought under control.[10] Writers were no longer supported on a generous scale and turned to other interests. Swift effectively attacked the government through the *Drapier's Letters* in Ireland. His suggestion of "looking into history for some character bearing a resemblance to the person we would describe, and with the absolute power of altering, adding or suppressing what circumstances we please" was followed by the attacks of Thomas Gordon writing as Cato in the *London Journal* and by his own satire in *Gulliver's Travels*. Pope wrote his *Dunciad* and Gay produced *The Beggar's Opera*. Defoe followed his major interest in *Robinson Crusoe*. "The taut phraseology of Defoe gave way to a verbosity which aimed primarily at wrapping up the meaning sufficiently to avoid the possibility of arrest."[11] It was probably to be expected that journalistic powers developed in the heat of political battles of the period would produce literature which has survived in children's tales and in the productions of Gay. Pope's translation of Homer dominated English literature until the revolt of Coleridge and Wordsworth.

[9]Stanley Morison, *The English Newspapers: Some Account of the Physical Development of Journals Printed in London between 1622 and the Present Day* (Cambridge, 1932).
[10]See C. B. Realey, *The Early Opposition to Sir Robert Walpole, 1720-1727*, Humanistic Studies of the University of Kansas, IV, nos. 2, 3 (Lawrence, Kan., 1931), also *The London Journal and Its Authors, 1720-1723*, Humanistic Studies of the University of Kansas, V, no. 3 (Lawrence, Kan., 1935).
[11]Laurence Hanson, *Government and the Press, 1695-1763* (London, 1936), p. 25.

The régime of Walpole bridged the gap between regicide and parliamentary adaptability following changes in public opinion influenced by the press. Changes without involving the person of the Crown could be made as a result of the regularity of the newspapers and the emergence of a cabinet and a prime minister under a German king and a difficult Prince of Wales.[12] But the change was accompanied by numerous direct and indirect devices for the control of public opinion. The Riot Act was adopted in 1715. Regius professorships were established in Oxford and Cambridge "to create a general dependence and raise a general expectation among the clergy."[13] An act was passed requiring the licensing of theatres in 1737. According to the *Grub-Street Journal* of 18 February, 1731, among printers "the pillory 'is so universally esteemed, that he, who has had the honour to mount that rostrum, is always looked upon amongst them as a graduate in his profession.' "[14] Public opinion had moved from the position of Lord Chief Justice Holt, stated in the trial of John Tutchin in 1704, "if people should not be called to account for possessing the people with an ill opinion of government, no government can exist. For it is very necessary for all governments that the people should have a good opinion of it."[15] But suppression exercised a significant influence on the writings of the period.

The influence of the press had extended to the country, particularly after the reduction of the postal rates in 1710, and the development of postal routes. After 1723 Edward Cave as a clerk in the post office secured news from the provinces for the London papers and sent London news to provincial papers. After the tax of 1725 the price of newspapers was increased from $1\frac{1}{2}d$. to $2d$. but magazines published as pamphlets evaded the tax and sold for $6d$. In February, 1731, Cave started the *Gentleman's Magazine* and in the following year made parliamentary news a regular feature. He defeated Walpole's attempt to tax magazines and by presenting a monthly view of the contents of all newspapers, including over 200 half-sheets a month,

[12]See W. T. Laprade, *Public Opinion and Politics in Eighteenth Century England to the Fall of Walpole* (New York, 1936).
[13]Cited *ibid.*, p. 278.
[14]Cited by Hanson, *Government and the Press, 1695-1763*, p. 58.
[15]Cited *ibid.*, p. 2.

introduced stability in the publishing industry. He gave an impartial survey of news, and condensed the accounts of weekly journals in the tradition of the historical miscellanies.[16] An index enhanced the value of his magazine as a work of reference. Walpole exploited the weekly journals as regularly printed, controlled propaganda, and more effective than the irregularly published pamphlets of Queen Anne. The pamphlet age had come to an end and the opposition resorted to newspapers, particularly the *Craftsman* started with Bolingbroke's support on December 5, 1726. Parliamentary news crowded out the periodical essay. With prohibition of printing parliamentary debates in 1738 the *Gentleman's Magazine* and the *London Magazine* presented them under fictitious names and rivalry made for more lucid writing. The editors were tried and fined by the House of Lords in April, 1747, and publication of debates was dropped. More literary and scientific news and greater attention to foreign news helped release the magazine from bondage to the weekly. Poetry contests were designed to increase circulation and Samuel Johnson's connection with the magazine was given publicity in the competitive race of the *Gentleman's Magazine* with the *London Magazine*. Book reviews became a feature after 1750. Politics were reduced to a small space and the interest in literature and science supported a rival venture, the *Monthly Review*, published by Griffiths. The historian of the *Gentleman's Magazine* has noted its contribution to the growing consciousness of national importance and to the development of foreign business interests by its impartial, detached accounts. It built up a standard of evaluation of news and a critical public attitude toward reporting. The public became accustomed to demand consistent news, parliamentary debates, and liberation of the press. The democratic tradition that government was accountable to the people was stabilized.

The large number of small papers printed in London was a reflection of limitations of the hand press. Relays of experienced press men could print 2,000 sheets on one side in eight hours. A newspaper with a circulation of 3,000 required twelve hours' printing at top speed and a popular paper had four presses, two for each side of the

[16]C. L. Carson, *The First Magazine: A History of the Gentleman's Magazine* (Providence, R.I., 1938).

sheet, the whole paper being set at least twice. These difficulties not only facilitated the development of the magazine, but also led to an attempt to solve the problem of advertising. Representatives of the coffee-houses complained in 1728 that they were used as tools of large numbers of newspapers and did the advertising without securing the returns. They proposed setting up two daily papers giving news of the town and advertisements. The *Daily Advertiser* was intended to overcome the objections that a few persons advertised in each of a great number of newspapers, that only the most eminent coffee-houses took in all the daily printed papers, and that only a few people read all the papers.[17] At least three-fourths of the paper was advertisements and the position of the reader and the advertiser was improved. It circulated in business houses, clubs, and taverns and the stimulus to advertising strengthened the position of other papers. By 1760 the *Public Ledger* carried four pages of full folio size with four columns, or roughly five times as much as the double column, single half-sheet papers of Queen Anne. But the limits of the hand press had been reached and the standard was fixed.

Restrictions on newspapers had implications for the publication of books. The high cost of paper and the low cost of typesetting meant small editions and a change in format, beginning in Queen Anne's reign, from folio to quarto. The publisher quickly emerged to provide an efficient channel for the distribution of books and the printer declined rapidly in importance. Patronage declined with the contempt of the court for letters and the lack of interest in writers after 1721 and during Walpole's régime. Writers turned from the government to the publisher. Johnson's patron was "commonly a wretch who supports with insolence, and is paid with flattery" or "one who looks with unconcern on a man struggling for life in the water, and when he has reached ground, encumbers him with help," and by 1761 he had become negligible.[18]

The writer was left at the mercy of the publisher and the latter with a limited market for literature concentrated on compendia of

[17]See *Johnson's England: An Account of the Life and Manners of His Age*, ed. A. S. Turberville (Oxford, 1933), II, *passim*.

[18]See A. S. Collins, *Authorship in the Days of Johnson, being a Study of the Relation between Author, Patron, Publisher and Public, 1726-1780* (London, 1928).

information. Timidity of the printers favoured the publisher and in turn led him to concentrate on compilations which could be sold by subscription to take the place of patronage. In turn this type of production required a substantial outlay of capital and the formation of partnerships and share arrangements by which risk was reduced and capital mobilized. A printing conger of seven booksellers was started in 1719 and a new conger in 1736, both being replaced by a chapter. Proprietors of old copy banded together and reduced the risk of competition by placing the property in the hands of a large number of booksellers. After 1720 an army of scribblers became drudges of the pen, abridging, compiling, writing notes, and with scissors and paste preparing voyages and travels, histories and natural histories. Pope attempted to enlist the support of patrons for a few authors but assistance was limited. The dependence of authors on booksellers meant an emphasis on the market and the production of quantity rather than quality to please the many and not the few. The first edition of Ephraim Chambers's *Universal Dictionary of Arts and Sciences* was published by subscription in 1728 and translation into French was followed by the *Encyclopaedia* of Diderot. In 1746 eight partners agreed to pay Johnson £1,575 for his *Dictionary*.

Pope's *Dunciad* was an attack on unfortunate writers and unscrupulous publishers. The *Grub-Street Journal*,[19] started on January 8, 1730, made bitter attacks on booksellers who took advantage of low and ignorant writers and published "false histories, lewd or immoral treatises, novels, plays, or poems." It attacked newspapers and advertisements but in itself it represented a group of publishers who had broken with the trade and was accordingly "opposed and depreciated by the generality of booksellers and their hackney authors." Since the author tried to write as much as possible and the bookseller to allow as little as possible for writing, tedious compilations and miscellanies resulted. Writing was converted to a mechanic's trade in which booksellers were patrons and paymasters. Compilations occupied an important place in the history of publishing, bridging the gap between the expansion of printing and the growth in the reading and writing of literature.[20]

[19]See J. T. Hillhouse, *The Grub-Street Journal* (Durham, N.C., 1928).
[20]See E. E. Kent, *Goldsmith and His Booksellers* (Ithaca, N.Y., 1933), pp. 95 ff., also W. M. Sale, Jr., *Samuel Richardson: Master Printer* (Ithaca, N.Y., 1950).

In the second half of the century evidence of a reading public was at hand in the establishment of critical reviews. Ralph Griffiths' *Monthly Review* (1749) was followed by the *Critical Review* (1756), started by Archibald Hamilton and Tobias Smollett. After 1760, a writer of merit was able to command substantial sums from publishers, though drudgery was his lot even in the nineteenth century. Isaac D'Israeli wrote on the *Calamities of Authors* at the end of the eighteenth century and its theme was elaborated in *Exposition of the False Medium and Barriers Excluding Men of Genius from the Public*, written by R. H. Horne but published anonymously by the radical publisher Effingham Wilson. Thomas Campbell proposed a toast to Napoleon on the ground that he had shot a publisher and publishers were said to drink toasts to prosperity out of the skulls of authors.

The market for newspapers and books had been widened in 1741 by an extension of the post office and a more frequent service from London. Restrictions on the theatre and on the press with improved facilities for distribution hastened the development of the novel and children's books. Bunyan in *The Pilgrim's Progress* had introduced conversation which had been largely the medium of drama and Defoe introduced the story interest into the English novel. Richardson, a printer by trade, was commissioned by the firm of Rivington and Osborne to prepare a series of "familiar letters on the useful concerns of common life" as a model letter writer for "country readers . . . unable to indite for themselves." The first two volumes of *Pamela* were published in November, 1740, and the model letter writer in January, 1741. Fielding as a former playwright wrote a parody on *Pamela* in his first novel, *Joseph Andrews*, published in February, 1742. Richardson co-ordinated plot, character, description, and dialogue into the complete novel and enormously intensified its interest. Fielding relieved it from the tyranny and constraint of the letter form. Smollett and Sterne greatly widened its range.[21] The circulating library, "the evergreen tree of diabolical knowledge," expanded rapidly after its introduction in London in 1740.

Children's books emerged as "a clear but subordinate branch of English literature" about the middle of the century. In 1744 John

21See George Saintsbury, *The English Novel* (London, 1913), pp. 77 ff.

Newbery published *A Little Pretty Pocket Book* deliberately to provide amusement.[22] He was the "first publisher to conceive of the illustrated book for children as a specially produced article."[23] The market had been built up by the sale of chap books from pedlars' packs and the improvement of communication with the country districts. Books had been combined with drugs, Newbery being particularly interested in Dr. James's Fever Powder. A study of the trade in nostrums and literature is badly needed but it is clear that the rise of the bookseller and publisher owed much to the high profits from the sale of cures.

In spite of the extension of markets the monopoly power of the booksellers was strengthened. Dodsley's *Public Register* (1741) was killed by the threat to tax it as a newspaper and by pressure on newspapers to refuse his advertisements as was Arthur Young's *Universal Museum* (1762). Smollett was persuaded to write a history as a means of reducing the sale of Hume's *History*. Authors attempted to evade publishers by printing their own volumes but sales of such volumes were hampered. Legal protection of the monopoly position was destroyed in a decision of February 22, 1774, in *Donaldson* v. *Beckett,* denying the right to a perpetual copyright under common law. Destruction of the claims of old books enabled small booksellers to sell cheap and convenient reprints. The group formerly protected by the monopoly arranged mutual compacts and increased prices as a means of appealing to a smaller, more exclusive market and securing larger profits. Perhaps the development of competition stimulated bigger publishers to undertake the publication of the large works which distinguished the eighteenth century, including those of Robertson, Adam Smith, and Gibbon. In 1769 Hume wrote, "People now heed the theatre almost as little as the pulpit. History is now the favourite reading, and our friend [Robertson] the favourite historian."[24] Scottish writers had not been hampered by the long period of drudgery and Scottish booksellers seized on the opportunity of a monopoly market, by developing business either in London, or in

22F. J. Harvey Darton, *Children's Books in England: Five Centuries of Social Life* (Cambridge, 1932), chap. i.

23*Ibid.*, p. 138.

24*Letters of David Hume to William Strahan,* ed. G. Birkbeck Hill (Oxford, 1888), p. 15.

Scotland for sale in London. The first edition of the *Encyclopaedia Britannica* was published in Edinburgh in 1771. The vacuum created in England during the period of the monopoly was filled by the great pouring-in of Scottish influence culminating in Scott.

Restrictions on newspapers contributed to the expansion of book-selling following the breaking of the power of the monopoly. Circulation increased from 7,411,757 in 1753 to 14,035,739 in 1790 in spite of a doubling of price. The rise in prices and wages after 1750 gave newspapers with advertisements an advantage. Restriction on signs in London under 2 Geo. III c. 21, following the spread of literacy and the use of numbers on the buildings, drove advertising into the newspapers.[25] As a result of the efforts of Junius and Wilkes the right of publishing debates was exercised after 1774. Reporting of debates increased the power of the press and made parliament more sensitive to public opinion. But the threat of libel suits and stamp and advertisement taxes compelled dependence of the political press on advertisements. John Walter in *The Daily Universal Register*, which became *The Times* (March 25, 1788), planned to facilitate commerce through the "channel of advertisements; to record the principal occurrences of the times; and to abridge the account of debates during the sitting of Parliament." By 1777 the dailies had practically displaced the weeklies. Postage rates were raised in 1764 and at later dates, but in 1784 the first mail coach was started between London and Bristol and by 1792 sixteen mail coaches left the General Post Office in London.

Restrictions on the press were offset by the wide distribution of pamphlet literature inspired by the American and the French revolutions. Swift's *Conduct of the Allies* had sold 11,000, but Price's pamphlet on the American Revolution sold 60,000, and Paine's *Rights of Man* 150,000! The increasing demand for popular literature was reflected in the phenomenal success of William Lane's Minerva Press.[26] He built up enormous sales of romances and novels and established a circulating library. John Lackington during the same period built up an extensive second-hand book trade, selling over

[25]Jacob Larwood and John Camden Hotten, *The History of Signboards from Earliest Times to the Present Day* (London, 1900).
[26]See Dorothy Blakey, *The Minerva Press, 1790-1820* (London, 1939).

100,000 copies annually by the end of the century. Harrison's *Novelists' Magazine* was started in 1779 and began the publishing of numbers. It ran to twenty-three volumes selling up to 12,000 copies weekly. Women writers found a large market. After 1794 superficial reading displaced heavy reading and the age of romantics began. Saintsbury has noted a change beginning with the ninth decade of the century in which satirists, revolutionary propagandists, and the school of terror novelists were in evidence. The essay of Addison scarcely survived the century.

Decline in the influence of the Crown after the death of Anne, the difficulties of the Anglican church in the Hanoverian régime, and the increasing activities of dissenters contributed to the interest in deism. With deism on the one hand and the repression of political activity on the other, the evangelist movement under the direction of Whitefield and Wesley made rapid headway. Whereas in France attacks on the political and social order meant attacks on the church, in England the religious movement was independent of political control. Publishers seized on the possibilities of markets for their products. Robert Raikes, owner of the *Gloucester Journal*, started the Sunday School movement in 1780. Hannah More sold two million copies of her Cheap Repository Tracts (three tracts monthly from 1792 to 1795) in the first year.

The limitations of the hand press had been reflected in the diversion of English writing into numerous channels other than the newspaper. The results were shown in part in the development of a native type industry. Caslon established a type foundry in 1720, the year in which imports of type from other countries were prohibited. His type united the solidarity of Dutch characters with the distinction of the French and was used widely in newspapers and for export to the American colonies. Baskerville developed a type* which alternated the thick and thin lines and sharpened the angles. He also made distinctive contributions in improved quality of paper and of ink. In 1763 he printed at Cambridge under the patronage of the University a folio edition of the Bible as well as a prayer book of a size "calculated for people who begin to want spectacles but are ashamed to use them in church." He printed the first fine books in England but his work

*Used in the present book.

probably had more influence on the Continent than in England. John Bell started a type foundry in 1788 to repair a neglect of the art of printing, "expedition being attended to rather than excellence —and temporary gain is preferred to lasting advantage and reputation."[27] He produced newspapers which illustrated the effectiveness with which type could be handled and influenced other papers which bought his type. He had "no acquirements, . . . but his taste in putting forth a publication, and getting the best artists to adorn it, was new in those times, and may be admired in any."[28]

Throughout the eighteenth century restrictions on imports of paper and books and the relatively slow growth of paper production in England were accompanied during a large part of the century by the restrictions of a publishing monopoly under the protection of copyright and the suppression of political writing. The limited possibilities of newspaper expansion with the wooden hand press and the improvement of communication between London and other centres favoured the growth of a variety of literary forms. After the stamp taxes of 1712 and the beginning of the Walpole administration and the end of continental wars, writers were compelled to turn to satire, miscellanies and compendia, the weekly newspaper, the monthly magazine, the novel and children's books. Suppression of writing in the political field meant continuous broadening-out in other directions. Destruction of the legal monopoly of the publishing industry and increased restriction on newspapers, in spite of Junius, Wilkes, and Fox's Libel Act of 1792, brought further expansion at the expense of depth and the beginnings of romantic literature. They also contributed powerfully to the revolt of the American colonies.

[27]Stanley Morison, *John Bell, 1745-1831* (Cambridge, 1930), following p. 16.
[28]*The Autobiography of Leigh Hunt,* ed. Roger Ingpen (Westminster, 1903), I, 169.

# TECHNOLOGY AND PUBLIC OPINION IN THE UNITED STATES[1]

FEW SUBJECTS are exposed to more pitfalls than those concerned with public opinion since the student is so completely influenced by the phenomena he attempts to describe. Objectivity may be improved by considering its development over a long period of time but even a description of this character must register the results of an astigma adjusted to present environment.

Freedom of the press in the United States emerged as a result of a clash with restrictive policies in Great Britain in the eighteenth century. Attempts of the mother country to extend such policies to the colonies involved an attack on the moulders of public opinion at a most sensitive point. Newspapers had developed in connection with printing establishments set up for the purpose of printing laws for the various assemblies and with the post office through which news and advertisements were collected and from which they were distributed. The stamp tax of 1765 imposed a heavy burden on a commodity which sold at a low price and was not to be tolerated by those chiefly concerned. They provoked an agitation which secured its withdrawal. It was followed by controversies leading to the Revolution which attracted the contributions of able writers.[2] The active role of the press in the Revolution was crowned by a guarantee of freedom under the Bill of Rights.

The power of the press evident in the Bill of Rights was also reflected in the Postal Act of 1793; section 21 states "that every printer of newspapers may send one paper to each and every other printer of newspapers in the United States free of postage under such regulations as the Postmaster General may provide." Newspapers sent to subscribers required one cent postage for all distances within one hundred miles and a cent and a half for all greater distances without reference to their weight. "The theory was that the cost of the mail service was to be paid out of letter postage, and that the newspapers

[1] A revision of a paper presented at the University of Michigan on April 19, 1949.
[2] See Philip Davidson, *Propaganda and the American Revolution, 1763-1783* (Chapel Hill, N.C., 1941).

were to have the advantage of the revenue thus created for their contemporaneous transmission through the mails."[3]

The defeat of Adams, the election of Jefferson, and the repeal of the Alien and Sedition Acts of 1798 were tributes to the power of the press and to the recognition by politicians[4] of its possibilities as an instrument of strategy. Jefferson[5] encouraged the publication of the *National Gazette* under Philip Freneau, started on October 21, 1791, in opposition to the *Gazette of the United States* edited by John Fenno in the interests of the Federalists. He complained of the great trading towns that "though not 1/25th of the nation, they command 3/4 of its public papers."[6] Through his influence the *National Intelligencer* edited by S. H. Smith was moved from Philadelphia to Washington and given a monopoly of congressional news and a "generous share of the public printing."[7] To supplement the administration paper he encouraged establishment in 1804 of the Richmond *Enquirer* edited by Thomas Ritchie. These measures invited attacks from other newspapers and in 1807 he wrote, "nothing can now be believed which is seen in a newspaper." "No details can be relied on. I will add, that the man who never looks into a newspaper is better informed than he who reads them."[8] Freedom had become licence.

[3]S. N. D. North, *History and Present Condition of the Newspaper and Periodical Press of the United States, with a Catalogue of the Publications of the Census Year* (Washington, 1884), p. 138. "The circulation of political intelligence through these vehicles [newspapers] is justly reckoned among the surest means of preventing the degeneracy of a free government, as well as of recommending every salutary public measure to the confidence and co-operation of all virtuous citizens" (House of Representatives reply to message of 1792). W. E. Rich, *The History of the United States Post Office to the Year 1829* (Cambridge, Mass., 1924), p. 91.

[4]E. S. Corwin, *The Twilight of the Supreme Court* (New Haven, Conn., 1935), p. 5.

[5]See F. L. Mott, *Jefferson and the Press* (Baton Rouge, La., 1943).

[6]J. E. Pollard, *The Presidents and the Press* (New York, 1947), p. 75.

[7]*Ibid.*, p. 70.

[8]L. M. Salmon, *The Newspaper and the Historian* (New York, 1923), p. 426. The low level of journalism has been attributed to the vituperation introduced by journalists from England, such as Cobbett, and by Irishmen. Binns owned one of the bitterest organs against the English and William Duane, editor of the *Aurora*, was violent in denunciations. "The fiercest and basest libeller of the age, the apostate politician, the fraudulent debtor, the ungrateful friend, whom England has twice spewed out to America, whom America, *though far from squeamish*, has twice vomited back to England"—*Edinburgh Review*, June, 1827, on Cobbett. N. N. Luxon, *Niles' Weekly Register, News Magazine of the Nineteenth Century* (Baton Rouge, La., 1947), p. 45. See A. L. Burt, *The United States, Great Britain and British North America, from the Revolution to the Establishment of Peace after the War of 1812* (New Haven, Conn., 1940), p. 301.

By 1812 the dominance of Federalist newspapers in seaport centres was offset by the establishment of Republican newspapers accompanying the westward movement of population.[9] Newspapers in the "trading towns" had developed as a result of the needs of business for announcements and communications. After the Revolution advertising increased in importance as a source of revenue and hastened the appearance of daily papers. To meet its needs John Dunlap in Philadelphia increased the size of the *Pennsylvania Packet and General Advertiser* from 9" × 15" with four pages and three columns per page to 12" × 19½" with four columns of which two-thirds was advertising.[10] In 1783 the paper became a tri-weekly and in 1784 the first daily in the United States. In New York the *Daily Advertiser* was started by Francis Childs on September 1, 1785.

The increase in the demands of advertising necessitated devices designed to increase the supply of paper. Paper production was encouraged by an import duty of 7½ per cent in 1789 and 10 per cent in 1790. The duty on rags was removed in 1804. It was estimated that by 1810 the United States had 185 paper mills of which 40 were in Massachusetts and 60 in Pennsylvania. To conserve paper, the *Daily Advertiser* reduced the size of its largest type to 18 point and in turn its text type. A large number of small advertisements characterized the newspapers of the first quarter of the nineteenth century, "the legal notice period of display." Running advertisements were contracted for at $30 a year or $40 including subscriptions. Mechanical limitations restricted the size to four pages and advertising reduced the space available for copy. A relatively stable income in addition to returns from commercial printing enabled the printer to support a paper with a circulation of three or four hundred in spite of collections of about 75 per cent of the bills.[11] Consequently many new papers came into existence, the number more than doubling between 1800 (150) and 1810.[12]

After the War of 1812 newspapers suffered from depressed business conditions. In 1816 postage on newspapers conveyed more than one

[9]Mott, *Jefferson and the Press*, p. 53.
[10]Frank Presbrey, *The History and Development of Advertising* (New York, 1929), p. 159.
[11]*Ibid.*, p. 177.
[12]North, *History of the Newspaper and Periodical Press*, p. 38.

hundred miles in the same state in which they were printed was reduced to one cent, half the postage being paid to the postmaster who delivered the newspapers. To provide greater accommodation for small advertisements, and to enhance prestige, the size of the newspaper was increased to 24" × 35" by 1828 and the number of columns from four to six.[13] As a result of the importance of advertising as a source of revenue and the high costs of paper, $5.00 a ream or a cent a sheet, the prices of newspapers were increased to six cents.With larger supplies of paper and a decline in price it became possible by 1832 to produce a sheet from a quarter to a third larger at 25 per cent less cost. The monopoly position of high-priced blanket sheets, with their emphasis on small advertisements and types of reading material suited to the mercantile class, invited competition from the small penny paper in metropolitan centres.

Technological advances in the production of newspapers and of paper supported the competition of a new type of newspaper. The use of the screw in the hand press restricted output to 150 copies per hour but in 1828 the Napier press, a double cylinder press brought in from England, was installed by R. Hoe and Company in the New York *Commercial Advertiser* and the Philadelphia *Daily Chronicle*. For smaller papers the Washington press in which Samuel Rust had developed a series of levers in place of the screw increased capacity after 1829 to 250 pages per hour. A Fourdrinier machine was introduced and completed in 1829 at Beach Mill, Saugerties, New York. Since it was estimated to have cost $30,000, paper making became a more highly concentrated industry. Extension of railways and facilities for handling the raw material and the finished product, larger mills, and the demand for cheaper power led to the migration of mills from the seaboard particularly to Berkshire County in western Massachusetts. After 1830 a bleaching process was introduced making it possible to use coloured rags in the manufacture of white paper. In 1840 there were 426 mills in 20 states of which 292 were in Massachusetts, New York, Connecticut, New Jersey, and Pennsylvania.[14] Supplies of rags were imported from Europe. The restrictive

[13]Presbrey, *The History and Development of Advertising,* p. 186.
[14]See L. T. Stevenson, *The Background and Economics of American Paper Making* (New York, 1940), p. 14.

policies of European governments checked the consumption of paper and released rags as raw materials for export. "Taxes on knowledge" in Great Britain prior to 1861 restricted the development of newspapers, favoured a monopoly of *The Times*, reduced the demand for rags, and accelerated development of newspapers in the United States. Imports of rags into the United States were valued at $588,000 in the year ending September 30, 1839, and at $749,000 (20,697,000 lb. including 10,277,000 lb. from Italy) in the year ending June 30, 1850. By 1850 the total value of production of paper was estimated at $10,000,000.

I

The new type of newspaper, designed to destroy the monopoly of blanket sheets, emphasized more sensational news. Penny magazines which flourished as a result of exemption from the heavy burden of taxes on newspapers in England were imported in large quantities from London and provided types of material attractive to new groups of people. Demand for cheap literature[15] and a search for new business for a job printing plant during the cholera epidemic led B. H. Day to experiment with the publication of the New York *Sun*,[16] a penny paper. Since the paper was designed to advertise the job printing plant, news was selected to increase circulation. The first issue of September 5, 1833, measured $11\frac{1}{4}'' \times 8''$, had three columns on each of four pages, and included local news, small talk, items from exchanges, and advertisements. It was sold on the London plan, at 67 cents per 100, to carriers who collected 6 cents every Saturday from each subscriber, and to the unemployed who were given attractive discounts for street sales. By December 17, circulation reached 4,500 or a little less than the *Courier and Enquirer* which had the largest circulation in New York City. A machine press with a capacity of 1,000 impressions per hour replaced the press with a capacity of 200 and in November, 1834, circulation reached 10,000. A steam press installed by R. Hoe and Company in 1835 increased printing capacity to 22,000 copies, both sides, in less than eight hours.

[15]H. M. Hughes, *News and the Human Interest Story* (Chicago, 1940).
[16]G. W. Johnson *et al., The Sunpapers of Baltimore* (New York, 1937), p. 30.

The New York fire of August 12, 1835, was accompanied by a morning edition of 23,000 and an extra edition of 30,000. Sensational writing such as the moon hoax story of Richard Adams Locke and the disclosures of Maria Monk contributed to an increase to 27,000 daily circulation. The size of the paper was increased from 10″ × 14″ to 12″ × 19″ in 1836 and in the latter year it carried thirteen columns a day of advertising.

The collection and presentation of news and a low price appeared as dominant elements in the success of the *Sun* at the expense of an interest in political connections, but an appeal to low income groups exposed the paper to the effects of depressions. Decline in advertising, bank failures, and fires in 1837 brought a decline in circulation and the sale of the paper in 1838 for $40,000 to M. Y. Beach, an inventor of a rag-cutting machine and after 1829 part owner of the paper mill at Saugerties, New York. Increased paper production following the introduction of new inventions was directly linked to the new journalism. Beach became actively interested in markets for paper, in mechanical improvements in the production of newspapers, and in the organization of expresses for the collection of news. In 1839 a 24-column paper carried 17 columns of advertising. Interests allied to the *Sun* and the Philadelphia *Public Ledger*, gaining favour immediately by a more obvious interest in politics, joined in attacks on the Bank of the United States. Joint organization of an express to handle Harrison's message of March 4, 1841, strengthened their position among exchange papers in the South and enabled them to extend an express system to Halifax, Nova Scotia, in 1845. The *Public Ledger* installed Hoe's lightning press, in which the problem of holding the type to a rapidly revolving cylinder press was solved in 1847.

Following the example of the *Sun*, J. G. Bennett,[17] who had been an active supporter of the Jackson administration, established the *Morning Herald* as a penny paper in 1835, imitating the London penny magazines and disclaiming "all steel traps, all principle, as it is called, all party, all politics. Our only guide shall be good, sound, practical, common sense." Within six weeks circulation reached 7,000; by August 17, 1836, when the price was increased to two cents, it was

[17]See D. C. Seitz, *The James Gordon Bennetts, Father and Son, Proprietors of the New York Herald* (Indianapolis, Ind., 1928).

40,000, and in 1840, 51,000. Sensational news with a money article and a stock table attracted large numbers of readers during the depression of 1837. Wall Street was exploited for its news value as were the proceedings of annual religious meetings reported after 1839. Bennett's active interest in the organization of news services was evident in his voyage to Europe on the return trip of the *Sirius*, the first steamship to arrive in New York (April 23, 1838), to arrange for correspondence from European news centres, and in the establishment of the first Washington bureau and of the overland express during the Mexican war. Attacks by the churches and by commercial interests advertised his aggressiveness. He destroyed the monopoly of classified advertisements held by the *Sun* and by 1847 his paper had become the foremost advertising medium. The cheap press had emphasized technological improvements and recognized the importance of news as a device for advertising the paper as an advertising medium. With a change in the price of paper based on the pound rather than the ream and an increase to fourteen cents a pound in 1853, and the imposition of advertising rates of a cent a line per day, the blanket sheets came to an end.

## II

Advances in technology in metropolitan newspapers were a striking contrast with those of smaller centres in the interior and notably of political capitals.[18] The small populations of Albany, Richmond, and Washington could not support the technological advances of large newspapers. The party machine bridged the gap between the government and public opinion. "The two chief weapons which parties use in order to obtain success are the newspapers and public associations."[19] The post office became an object of intense political interest and after 1825 a federal postal department was separated from the revenue system and made independent.[20] The administration organ

[18]"The preponderance of capital cities is a . . . serious injury to the representative system; and it exposes modern republics to the same defect as the republics of antiquity which all perished from not having known this system." Alexis de Tocqueville, *American Institutions,* trans. Henry Reeve, rev. and ed. Francis Bowen (Cambridge, Mass., 1870), p. 371.

[19]*Ibid.,* p. 239.

[20]Rich, *The History of the United States Post Office to the Year 1829,* p. 165.

in Washington was linked, through the exchange system, with newspapers in the smaller centres of the interior. Washington became a
centre of news. Monroe was the first president after Washington to
show himself to the public. Great interest was shown in the choice of
a president in the election of 1824 and the exciting debates of that
year even led newspapers to send correspondents to the federal capital.

In a campaign for Andrew Jackson as president attacks on the
monopoly position of the administration organ began with the purchase of the *United States Telegraph* in Washington in 1825 by Duff
Green. A similar campaign was started in 1826 by Amos Kendall,
editor of the *Frankford Argus of Western America*. The bitterness of
the struggle was evident in Jackson's remarks. "The whole object
of the coalition is to calumniate me, cart loads of coffin handbills,
forgeries, and pamphlets of the most base calumnies are circulated by
the franking privileges [*sic*] of Members of Congress"[21] (August
16, 1828). With Jackson's election as president the support of
journalists was rewarded. John Quincy Adams wrote in 1829 that
the chief beneficiaries of his defeat were newspaper men, "the vilest
purveyors of slander during the late electioneering campaign, and an
excessive disproportion of places is given to editors of the foulest
presses."[22] Jackson wrote, "I refuse to consider the editorial calling as
unfit to offer a candidate for office." Without patronage "men of
uncompromising and sterling integrity will no longer be found in the
ranks of those who edit our public journals."[23] Three of five members
of Jackson's cabinet were experienced journalists. The postmaster-
general became a member in 1829. Amos Kendall, at first fourth
auditor of the treasury, later became postmaster-general. Ritchie
complained of a "systematic Effort to reward Editorial Partisans,
which will have the effect of bringing the vaunted Liberty of the
Press into a sort of Contempt."[24] Other rewards of patronage to
editorial partisans included government printing, advertising of letters
on hand in post offices, and appointments to the post office involving
the right to half the revenue from newspaper postage, the privilege

[21]Pollard, *The Presidents and the Press*, p. 152.
[22]*Ibid.*, p. 141.
[23]*Ibid.*, p. 163.
[24]*Ibid.*, p. 163. A large number of newspaper editors were appointed to local
postmasterships (*ibid.*, p. 161).

of franking, estimated to be worth four or five hundred dollars a year, the possibility of restricting newspapers with opposing views,[25] exemption from military and jury service, and the advantage of early intelligence.

The *United States Telegraph*, with Duff Green as editor and public printer to Congress, displaced the *National Intelligencer* as the administra·ve organ. As it began to favour Calhoun as a successor to Jackson, ·an Buren sponsored establishment of the *Globe*. The importance of such papers arose from the use of exchanges by which contents were taken from other papers. Adams wrote that "in our Presidential canvassing an editor has become as essential an appendage to a candidate as in the days of chivalry a 'squire' was to a knight."[26] The *Globe* was started on December 7, 1830, by F. P. Blair, who had been brought from Kentucky. It began as a semiweekly at $5.00 a year and a weekly at $2.50 and within a year had 4,000 subscribers. With funds from official advertising and departmental job printing and from friends, a Napier press was purchased and the paper issued daily. Blair published copious excerpts from country newspapers including those which had been planted by himself.

The success of Jackson was supported by journalistic developments not only in Washington but also in the important state capitals of Albany and Richmond. Van Buren wrote regarding the Albany *Argus* in 1823 of the need of an editor "sound, practicable, and, above all, discreet republican. Without a paper thus edited at Albany we may hang our harps on the willows. With it, the party can survive a thousand such convulsions as those which agitate and probably alarm most of those around you."[27] On October 8, 1824, the *Argus* became a daily as well as a semi-weekly and a weekly. As the voice of the Albany regency which "regulated the politics of the state" and reduced politics to a science, with the *Globe* and the Richmond *Enquirer*, it "made cabinet officers and custom house weighers, presi-

[25]Dorothy Ganfield Fowler, *The Cabinet Politician: The Postmasters General, 1829-1909* (New York, 1943), pp. 16-20.
[26]Pollard, *The Presidents and the Press*, p. 142.
[27]Frederic Hudson, *Journalism in the United States from 1690 to 1872* (New York, 1873), pp. 276-7.

dents and tide waiters, editors and envoys. They regulated state legislatures and dictated state policies."[28]

The influence of the press was evident in the campaign for discontinuance of election of presidents by caucus in 1832. *Niles' Weekly Register* and the Richmond *Enquirer* were particularly effective and it was claimed that only 3 of 35 papers in Virginia, 10 of 125 in New York, 3 of 100 in Pennsylvania and 1 of 48 in Ohio were in favour of caucus elections.[29] In the intense campaign of 1832 Jackson claimed that the Bank of the United States had used its funds to manipulate the press, and the *Extra Globe* was published by his party as a campaign sheet at $1.00 per subscription. In spite of an estimated opposition of two-thirds of the newspapers, the support of Blair in the *Globe*, of Isaac Hill, a member of the cabinet and formerly of the New Hampshire *Post*, and of Van Buren in the Albany *Argus* secured Jackson's re-election. The *Globe* has been described as the first presidential organ to become an institution of government and Jackson as the first president to rule through the newspaper press.[30] The Democratic party through the Kitchen Cabinet and the *Globe*, the Richmond junta and the *Enquirer*, and the Albany regency and the *Argus* effectively capitalized control over the post office and the press.

Postmaster-General Barry wrote in 1832: "The freedom of the press guaranteed by the Constitution, and the small share of postage with which these publications are charged, compared with the whole expense of their transportation, demonstrate the estimation in which they are held by the government."[31] Nevertheless advances in the metropolitan press began to threaten political power. In his annual message of 1835 President Jackson drew "attention to the painful excitement produced in the south by attempts to circulate through the mails inflammatory appeals addressed to the passions of slaves."[32] Low rates of postage on newspapers favoured the larger centres and

[28]*Ibid.*, p. 277.
[29]Luxon, *Niles' Weekly Register*, p. 132.
[30]Pollard, *The Presidents and the Press*, p. 195.
[31]North, *History of the Newspaper and Periodical Press*, p. 140.
[32]*Ibid.*, p. 142. William Lloyd Garrison started the *Liberator* in January, 1831, and "stirred the South into a fury." W. A. Butler, *A Retrospect of Forty Years, 1825-1865*, ed. H. A. Butler (New York, 1911), p. 80.

newspapers in the smaller centres became servile imitators in "tone, temper and opinion."[33] In 1836 Postmaster-General Kendall attacked "the great injustice done the local press for the benefit of the metropolitan journals" and proposed that postage should be graduated according to the size and weight of the material conveyed.[34] Complaints were made in 1838 that some publishers exchanged with five or six hundred others of which "not one hundred are of any practical use to them."[35] Postmaster-General Niles in 1840 wrote: "All newspapers now pay the same rates of postage, although some are ten times the dimension and weight of others. This is not only unjust to those who pay the taxes but equally so to publishers. It gives an undue advantage to the larger establishments in the commercial cities over the penny papers in the same place, and over the country newspapers, which are more removed from sinister influences and in general are the most independent channels of sound public opinion."[36]

In the presidential campaign of 1840 Van Buren appealed to the new metropolitan press and gave the first presidential interview to the *Herald* in 1839. The convention of the Democratic party in 1840 presented a national platform and the campaign was the first in which large numbers took an intense interest.[37] Kendall resigned as postmaster-general to edit the *Extra Globe* in 1840 and sent out confidential circulars to postmasters to secure subscriptions and to send them to Washington without postage, but the party was defeated.

The Whigs gained in 1840 through closer relations to new developments in the cheap metropolitan press. An enormous increase in railroad construction after 1827, the spread of the public school system, and increased literacy widened the market of the metropolitan press. New types of readers demanded facts rather than ideas. Thurlow Weed,[38] a supporter of Adams, was elected to the New York assembly

[33]North, *History of the Newspaper and Periodical Press*, p. 112.

[34]*Ibid.*, p. 143.

[35]*Ibid.*, p. 144.

[36]*Ibid.*, p. 148.

[37]A. K. McClure, *Our Presidents and How We Make Them* (New York, 1900), p. 70. Ostrogorski has suggested the influence of improved communication on parties by stating that the Erie Canal was followed by New York conventions, the railways by a national convention, and the telegraph by a national campaign directed from a single centre. See M. I. Ostrogorski, *Democracy and the Organization of Political Parties* (London, 1902), II, 53.

[38]See *Autobiography of Thurlow Weed*, ed. H. A. Weed (Boston, 1883-4).

in 1829 and became editor of the *Albany Evening Journal*. He fostered anti-masonic sentiment which developed following the alleged abduction of William Morgan in 1826. He represented the merchant class of the north and west and reflected its power in legislation enacted at Albany. His strategic position as a journalist became evident in the growing power of New York. Cancellation of the charter of the Bank of the United States and the panic of 1837 were effectively exploited. In the election campaign of 1838 Weed was supported by a weekly, the *Jeffersonian*, edited by Horace Greeley, a Whig majority was elected to the Assembly, and Seward became governor of New York State. In the campaign of 1840, the *Log Cabin*, again edited by Greeley, and the use of slogans suggesting the democratic character of W. H. Harrison, the first presidential candidate to take the stump, were important in securing his election. As a means of giving greater stability to the Whig party and offsetting the sensational journalism of the *Herald*, Greeley started the *Tribune* as a penny paper on April 10, 1841. By November, 1842, it had a circulation of 9,500. Its influence was powerfully supplemented by a weekly which was widely advertised and sold at a low subscription price.

## III

The cheap metropolitan press took full advantage of the invention and extension of the telegraph. A rapid, prompt supply of news was available and accurate information was provided to meet the demands of the stock and produce exchanges. Greeley stated[39] that "the tele-

[39]His views may be contrasted with those of Thoreau: "I sat up during the evening, reading by the light of the fire the scraps of newspapers in which some party had wrapped their luncheon; the prices current in New York and Boston, the advertisements, and the singular editorials which some had seen fit to publish, not foreseeing under what critical circumstances they would be read. I read these things at a vast advantage there, and it seemed to me that the advertisements, or what is called the business part of a paper, were greatly the best, the most useful, natural, and respectable. Almost all the opinions and sentiments expressed were so little considered, so shallow and flimsy, that I thought the very texture of the paper must be weaker in that part and tear the more easily. The advertisements and the prices current were most closely allied to nature, and were respectable in some measure as tide and meteorological tables are; but the reading-matter, which I remembered was most prized down below, unless it was some humble record of science, or an extract from some old classic, struck me as strangely whimsical, and crude, and one-idea'd like a school-boy's theme, such as youths write and after burn. The opinions were of that kind that are doomed to wear a different aspect to-morrow, like last year's fashions; as if mankind were very green indeed,

graphic despatch is the great point" and that editorials had less influence than in England. The telegraph compelled newspapers to pool their efforts in collecting and transmitting news. A co-operative news service was worked out in 1848 between the *Courier and Enquirer, Tribune, Sun, Herald, Express,* and *Journal of Commerce,* which became the basis of the Associated Press.[40] News was sold to the Philadelphia *Public Ledger* and to the Baltimore *Sun* and additional subscribers lowered costs of operation to New York readers.

Extension of the telegraph and an increase in news accentuated the demand for faster presses,[41] the prerequisite of large sales at low prices. In 1852 the New York *Tribune* installed a six cylinder press with a capacity of 15,000 sheets per hour. Other plants installed presses of up to ten cylinders with capacities of 25,000 sheets but the number of presses meant costs of duplication in setting up type and loss of time. Papers with the largest circulation were compelled to start earlier, to omit the latest news, to lose the earliest sales, and to suffer in out-of-town circulation. The restriction was removed with the use of the stereotype installed by the *Tribune* in 1861. In the same year automatic feeding replaced hand feeding following the invention by W. H. Bullock in Philadelphia of a web-perfecting press which printed the paper on both sides from two main cylinders. With these developments costs including wear and tear on type were reduced and papers with large circulations could be placed in the

and would be ashamed of themselves in a few years, when they had outgrown this verdant period. There was, moreover, a singular disposition to wit and humor, but rarely the slightest real success; and the apparent success was a terrible satire on the attempt; the Evil Genius of man laughed the loudest at his best jokes. The advertisements, as I have said, such as were serious, and not of the modern quack kind, suggested pleasing and poetic thoughts; for commerce is really as interesting as nature. The very names of the commodities were poetic, and as suggestive as if they had been inserted in a pleasing poem,—Lumber, Cotton, Sugar, Hides, Guano, Logwood. Some sober, private, and original thought would have been grateful to read there, and as much in harmony with the circumstances as if it had been written on a mountain-top; for it is of a fashion which never changes, and as respectable as hides and logwood, or any natural product. What an inestimable companion such a scrap of paper would have been, containing some fruit of a mature life. What a relic! What a recipe! It seemed a divine invention, by which not mere shining coin, but shining and current thoughts, could be brought up and left there." Henry D. Thoreau, *A Week on the Concord and Merrimack Rivers* (Boston, 1867), pp. 197-8.

[40]See Oliver Gramling, *AP: The Story of News* (New York, 1940).

[41]See Robert Hoe, *A Short History of the Printing Press and of the Improvements in Printing Machinery* (New York, 1902).

hands of the public more quickly. Following construction of railways and canals large presses were shipped to new centres, particularly Chicago, and hastened the growth of regionalism.

The telegraph weakened the system of political control through the post office and the newspaper exchange. The monopoly over news was destroyed and the regional daily press escaped from the dominance of the political and the metropolitan press. *Niles' Weekly Register* had flourished with the exchange system and disappeared with the telegraph.[42] The post office continued to reflect the power of the press in favouring cheap transmission of newspapers. In 1845 the injustice of high rates of letter postage was recognized and a substantial reduction in them was made, but newspapers were carried free for distances of 30 miles, for 1 cent over 30 and under 100 miles or for any distance within the state where they were published, and for 1½ cents over 100 miles or outside the state. "A limitation of the number of papers editors may interchange free through the mails" was proposed but without results.[43] The postmaster-general wrote in his report of December 2, 1848, that newspapers have "always been esteemed of so much importance to the public, as the best means of disseminating intelligence among the people, that the lowest rate has always been afforded for the purpose of encouraging their circulation."[44]

Under the circumstances the *Tribune* exercised a wide influence through its weekly,[45] as well as through its metropolitan, circulation. In 1848 Greeley, James Webb of the New York *Courier and Enquirer*, and Weed exploited the interest of the electorate in military heroes and secured the election of General Taylor. Distrust of Greeley's increasing influence, and disapproval of his interest in fads, led the Whigs to encourage H. J. Raymond to start the New York *Times* in 1851. Greeley seized on radical movements and attracted writers such

[42]Luxon, *Niles' Weekly Register*, p. 9; see also Victor Rosewater, *History of Coöperative News-Gathering in the United States* (New York, 1930), p. 95, and E. S. Watson, *A History of Newspaper Syndicates in the United States, 1865-1935* (Chicago, 1936).
[43]North, *History of the Newspaper and Periodical Press*, p. 150.
[44]*Ibid.*, p. 151.
[45]"The greatest single journalistic influence was the *New York Weekly Tribune* which had in 1854 a circulation of 112,000 and many times that number of readers." J. F. Rhodes, "Newspapers as Historical Sources," in *Historical Essays* (New York, 1909), p. 90.

as Brisbane on Fourierism, C. A. Dana, Margaret Fuller and others who had been associated with Brook Farm, and Karl Marx. Lord Acton described the *Tribune* as ultra-democratic in every question without being democratic. The *Times* was designed to attract a middle class of conservative readers, who disliked the *Herald* and the *Tribune*, by its respectability of manner and tone. It quickly reached a circulation of 26,000, although doubling the price to two cents in 1852 brought a decline to 18,000. Publication of bank statements was switched from the *Tribune* to the *Times* and Raymond was supported by Weed for the position of lieutenant-governor. Greeley dissolved "the firm of Seward, Weed and Greeley" in 1854. Following the collapse of the Whig party Greeley took an active part in linking up with the Free Soil party and with the co-operation of the Chicago *Tribune* laid the basis for the Republican party. At the convention of the Republican party in 1860 Greeley played an active role in the defeat of Seward[46] and the nomination of Lincoln as president.

The telegraph and the fast press in the metropolitan areas destroyed the power of party based on the post office, the exchange system, and state capitals. Instability weakened the position of a central authority after 1840. Power shifted from Washington and issues were no longer settled in Congress. The metropolitan press destroyed a centrally directed government. Buchanan was the last president to have an administration organ in Washington.

With the outbreak of the Civil War, Lincoln was compelled to work directly with newspaper editors and to elaborate devices for keeping them in control, including appointments to diplomatic posts. The power of the press was evident in General Sherman's remark that "the press has now killed McClellan, Buell, Fitz-John Porter, Sumner, Franklin and Burnside. Add my name and I am not ashamed of the association."[47] Andrew Johnson was unable to meet the demands of editors, and the interest of the press in his impeachment threatened the position of the executive.

The military prestige of Grant led to his election as president in 1868 but the corruption which marked his administration compelled

[46]Seward and Weed had exploited anti-masonic feeling but came under the influence of Roman Catholics. This involved the antagonism of the know-nothing party and the opposition of Pennsylvania, and facilitated the success of Greeley.

[47]Salmon, *The Newspaper and the Historian*, p. 203. See R. S. Harper, *Lincoln and the Press* (New York, 1951).

the press to mobilize opposition. Greeley was nominated by the Democratic party for president in 1872 but the power of the press to revive it was not sufficient particularly as the support of rival newspapers of the *Tribune* was withdrawn.

The limitations of the metropolitan press became evident in the essentially local character of its circulation, the decline in influence of weekly newspapers, and the increasing importance of newspapers in small centres.[48] The telegraph emphasized the importance of news with the result that the newspaper[49] was unable to meet the demands for a national medium. Paralleling the obsession with news was the exposure of the United States to the influence of imports of other types of reading material from England not restricted by "taxes on knowledge" as applied to newspapers. Absence of copyright and large-scale pirating of English writers began at an early date. Harriet Martineau wrote on November 8, 1836, of "the shameless aggressions of the Harpers of New York." Emerson reported the remark of an Englishman: "As long as you do not grant us copyright we shall have the teaching of you." American writers were driven into journalism, as in the case of W. C. Bryant, and found it advantageous to have their work published in England. With the introduction of Atlantic steamships, New York became the centre of a printing and publishing industry concerned largely with reprinting in the shortest possible time new books which arrived from England. Neglect of fiction by the newspapers enabled individuals such as Robert Bonner to achieve astounding success in the New York *Ledger* by attracting well-

[48]"All these interests bring the newspaper, and the newspaper starts up politics and a railroad." Matthew Josephson, *The Robber Barons: The Great American Capitalists, 1861-1901* (New York, 1934), p. 27. An agent of a mercantile firm with a catalogue and price list of about a thousand articles was ordered to stop "at every town in these States on the line of railway where there is a church spire, a bank and a newspaper office." J. M. Richards, *With John Bull and Jonathan* (New York, 1906), p. 19. He was sent to California in 1866. "Your first business is to advertise in all good family papers possible. Avoid all mining, scientific, and agricultural journals. Rely principally upon religious, secular, and literary weeklies. It will hardly pay to advertise in many dailies. . . . In all advertisements say 'Sold by all dealers.' Grant no favours, advertise no man. . . . In making newspaper contracts *please remember* you are *not limited* in *advertising* to *any amount of dollars.* 'Create a sensation.' " *Ibid.,* pp. 21-2.

[49]"Newspapers—conducted by rogues and dunces for dunces and rogues, they are faithful to nothing but the follies and vices of our system, strenuously opposing every intelligent attempt at their elimination. They fetter the feet of wisdom and stiffen the prejudices of the ignorant. They are sycophants to the mob, tyrants to the individual." Ambrose Bierce (March 26, 1881), cited in Carey McWilliams, *Ambrose Bierce: A Biography* (New York, 1929), p. 168.

advertised names such as Dickens with enormous sums. Longfellow was paid $3,000 for "The Hanging of the Crane." Neglect of advertising technique by the newspapers, particularly by the *Herald*, enabled P. T. Barnum as well as Bonner to develop its enormous possibilities. Inability of the newspapers to meet demands for a national medium made it possible for a weekly able to concentrate on illustrations to become extremely effective. Cartoons appealed to lower levels of intelligence and had a national circulation. The brutal, devastating, unforgettable, and irretrievable caricatures by Thomas Nast in *Harper's Weekly* offset the influence of newspapers in their support of Greeley. Grant stated: "Two things elected me, the sword of Sheridan and the pencil of Thomas Nast."[50] Finally the power of the metropolitan press was weakened by legislation in 1874 in which newspaper postage was prescribed by weight without reference to the distance carried and uniformly in advance of publication. Newspapers issued weekly or oftener paid 2 cents per pound and less frequently 3 cents per pound.[51] President Hayes could write regarding administration papers that *"no organ* is wisdom."[52]

## IV

Increased demands for paper during the Civil War hastened the development of substitutes for rags.[53] Straw was used extensively after 1850. In 1866 two Voelter pulp grinders were brought from Germany and set up at Curtisville, Massachusetts. The first chipped groundwood was sent to the Smith Paper Company on March 11, 1867. By 1870, eighteen paper mills were installed, chiefly in northern New York and New England. The speed of paper machines increased

[50]A. B. Paine, *Th. Nast, His Period and His Pictures* (New York, 1904), p. 129.

[51]North, *History of the Newspaper and Periodical Press*, p. 156. Through efforts of syndicate papers it was provided "that newspapers, one copy to each actual subscriber residing within the county where the same are printed, in whole or in part, and published, shall go free through the mails." Watson, *A History of Newspaper Syndicates in the United States, 1865-1935*, p. 21.

[52]Pollard, *The Presidents and the Press*, p. 467.

[53]Imports of rags into the United States were valued at $1,540,000 in the year ending June 30, 1860, at $1,245,000 (37,304,000 lb. including 16,678,000 lb. from Italy) in the year ending June 30, 1863, at $3,749,000 (103,520,000 lb. including 30,665,000 lb. from Italy and 43,404,000 lb. from England) in the year ending June 30, 1871.

from 100 feet per minute in 1867 to 175 feet in 1872 and 200 feet in 1880. The sulphite industry was introduced in Providence in 1884 and the basic raw materials, groundwood pulp and sulphite pulp, were made available for the manufacture of modern newsprint. Domestic production of newsprint increased to 196,000 tons in 1890 and 569,000 tons in 1899 and per capita consumption to 8 lb. in 1890 and 15 lb. in 1899. Prices of paper declined from $344 a ton in 1866 to $246 in 1870, $138 in 1880, $68 in 1890, and $36 in 1900. It was significant that the American Paper Association was organized in 1878 to develop an export trade and to stabilize the market. Increase in the production of paper and decline in price stimulated a search for inventions[54] designed to increase circulation particularly in metropolitan areas. The fast press was developed to the point that 96,000 copies of eight pages could be produced in an hour in 1893. The linotype with at least five times the typesetting speed of the compositor was introduced about 1886 and was followed by a marked increase in the use of typewriters. It made possible the modern newspaper. The régime of the tramp printer came gradually to an end. The telephone supplemented the telegraph for local news and the reporter saw his work divided between the leg man who visited the sources of news and the rewrite man to whom he telephoned his information and who prepared it for the paper. The existence of a large population with a single language gave the telephone a position of greater importance in the United States than that of the telegraph in Europe with its numerous languages.

Changes in postal rates, improvements in printing and in the press, and the increasing use of wood pulp accentuated development in the metropolitan areas and concentration by individual newspapers on special fields of interest. The New York *Times* in the seventies made a vigorous attack on the Tweed ring and destroyed the generous advertising subsidies paid by the political machine to its competitors, with the effect that 27 of 89 newspapers on the payroll of the ring suspended operations and others changed in ownership, management, personnel, and politics.[55] Aggressive publishers exploited technological

[54]See H. A. Innis, *The Press: A Neglected Factor in the Economic History of the Twentieth Century* (London, 1949).
[55]Paine, *Th. Nast, His Period and His Pictures*, p. 141.

advances at the expense of the conservative tradition of competitors. Joseph Pulitzer, with experience in St. Louis, purchased the *World* in New York, at a reasonable price since it had lost prestige under the control of Jay Gould, and was given a loan to purchase a new press by G. W. Childs of the Philadelphia *Public Ledger* in order that he might have revenge for attacks by C. A. Dana of the *Sun*.[56] Pulitzer introduced cheap large-scale advertising methods and destroyed the prominence of the *Herald* which, obsessed with news, had been extremely conservative in advertising methods. Aggressive competition from the *World* was followed by a decline of the *Herald*, the *Times*, and the *Sun*. The effectiveness of the *World* became evident in its support of the Democratic party and its attacks on the monopoly of political control exercised by Republicans. Control over civil service appointments over a long period brought charges of corruption which were given great force when Garfield was assassinated by a disappointed office-seeker. The *World* and independent papers played an important part in the defeat of Blaine and the election of Cleveland in 1884 and gave a sharp rebuke to "the bloody shirt and the bloodless mugwump."[57]

A press less subservient to the political control of the Republican party followed the introduction of new inventions, wider circulation, larger capital equipment, and corporate organization. Personal journalism began to decline and more important sources of revenue developed with advertising and department stores. With the linotype, advertisements could be changed daily and became a part of news. The advertising manager began to absorb responsibility, operations were controlled by the business department, and the publisher became more important.

The election of Cleveland opened a breach in the monopoly of the Republican party supported by the press and the army but it was of limited duration. "It is generally conceded that the Post Office and paper in our town should go together, the two making a business, profitable in a small degree,"[58] and it was inevitable that protests would be made against Cleveland that he left "offensive republicans

[56]J. H. Harper, *I Remember* (New York, 1934), p. 260.
[57]J. L. Heaton, *The Story of a Page* (New York, 1913), p. 141.
[58]Fowler, *The Cabinet Politician: The Postmasters General, 1829-1909*, p. 191.

in nearly all our country post offices—the very officials they [the public] meet almost daily."[59] Industrial interests became more strongly entrenched behind a protectionist policy and Cleveland's concentration on the tariff as an issue in 1888 contributed to his defeat[60] in spite of his plea that "though the people support the government, the government should not support the people." The interest of newspapers in the Republican party was evident in the nomination of Whitelaw Reid as vice-president in 1892. Again distrust of rival papers and the hostility of labour incidental to Reid's active interest in the introduction of the linotype contributed to defeat. The depression and an election in which in the words of Henry Adams "one of them [the candidates] had no friends; the other only enemies"[61] brought a return of the Democratic party for another brief period.

## V

In the period prior to 1896 political disturbances were in part a reflection of adjustments of newspapers in relation to the telegraph. Demand for news during the Civil War with rapid extension of newspapers in the large regional centres contributed to the development of a loosely affiliated Western Associated Press, which Joseph Medill of the Chicago *Tribune* urged in 1862 should be reorganized as a more closely knit unit. Medill regarded the Associated Press as "a most pernicious and crushing monopoly." Western newspapers were at a disadvantage in time since news tended to spread from east to west, and complaints arose regarding the dominance of New York papers over business information. New York interests had an advantage in market reports and Western papers held that this advantage was particularly serious since they were compelled to pay high charges for them.[62] The Atlantic cable, "that great rope, with a philistine at each end of it, talking inutilities" (Arnold), finally completed in

[59]*Ibid.*, p. 228.
[60]McClure, *Our Presidents and How We Make Them,* p. 334. The tariff more than any other element "rouses up the sectional feelings and interests and disturbs the passions of the country." *Life, Letters and Journals of George Ticknor* (Boston, 1880), p. 214.
[61]*The Education of Henry Adams* (Boston, 1918), p. 320.
[62]Rosewater, *History of Coöperative News-Gathering in the United States,* pp. 117-18.

1866, the consolidation of telegraph lines, and an increasing demand for news after the Civil War strengthened the movement toward independence in the West. When Daniel Craig was dismissed by the Associated Press on November 5, 1866, and organized a rival United States and Europe Telegraph News Association with the support of the Western Union Telegraph Company which absorbed the American Telegraph Company in the same year, he was made general agent of the Western Associated Press. The Associated Press retaliated by building up connections with European news agencies such as Havas, Wolff, Reuter's, and Stefani and by strengthening its hold on Washington and New York financial news. Control of the Western Associated Press over internal domestic news compelled the two groups to reach an agreement signed on January 11, 1867, which readmitted Western papers to the Associated Press and arranged for an exchange of news. The telegraph company found it impossible to provide a duplicated service and the agreement required Western Union lines to be used exclusively. The Western Union absorbed the Atlantic and Pacific Telegraph Company in 1877 and later the National Union Telegraph Company. New contracts signed in January, 1883, and in 1887 continued the complete control over news in the East and West.

Newspapers which were left outside the agreement began to build up the United Press and to secure foreign news through the United News Agency, a rival of Reuter's in England, and the Cable News Company. The support of J. R. Walsh of the Chicago *Herald* and of William Laffan of the *Sun* enabled the United Press to compete with the Associated Press to the point that the Chicago *Tribune* and other members of the Associated Press began to purchase news from it. The Chicago *Daily News*, started in 1876 by William Dougherty and Melville E. Stone, added the *Morning News* on March 20, 1881 and secured its news from the United Press. Violation of the rules of the Associated Press forbidding the use of a telegraph company other than the Western Union and the patronizing of competing news-gathering agencies, and threats of competing papers created difficulties. In 1882 the *News* was allowed to receive despatches from the Associated Press and in 1883 Stone was made a director. In 1888, V. F. Lawson purchased Stone's interest and immediately complained of the control of the money interests of New York over mechanized news. As a member of a reconstituted Western Press Association executive he pressed for reform. Western papers demanded a wider range of news, and employees capable of presenting well-written exclusive news displaced those who had been chosen for their technical knowledge of the telegraph. Changes were made in the handling of news and in the organization of territory west to the Pacific coast, and there was an increase in the number of representatives in the Western association. The Associated Press was forced to move from the reporting of routine news into journalism but it was held in check by the interest of metropolitan dailies such as the *Herald* and the Chicago *Times* anxious to display their enterprise by special reports of exciting events. A final clash came with the disclosure in 1892 that members of the Associated Press had a controlling interest in the United Press.[63] The ten-year arrangement came to an end, the New York Associated Press was absorbed by the United Press, and the Western Associated Press was incorporated as the Associated Press of Illinois with Melville E. Stone as manager.

The latter organization was developed as a national co-operative news-gathering association, the agent and servant of newspapers, but selling no news, making no profits, and paying no dividends. The World's Fair in Chicago gave an immediate advantage. A contract was arranged in 1893 with a group of foreign agencies in London. Various eastern papers, particularly those with editors who had formerly been with the Western Associated Press such as Pulitzer of the *World*, Horace White of the *Evening Post*, and John Cockerill of the *Commercial Advertiser*, joined the association. Pulitzer joined in order to prevent Hearst securing an Associated Press franchise. Eastern papers, burdened with the increasing costs of a declining membership in the United Press, turned to the Associated Press. The New York *Times*, brought to the verge of bankruptcy by membership in the United Press,[64] was purchased by A. S. Ochs of the Chattanooga *Times* and, after expiry of its contract with the United Press, was brought into the Associated Press where it took full advantage of the greater accessibility of news.[65] In 1897 the *Herald* and the *Tribune* joined the Associated Press. With only the *Sun* and the New York

[63] See Melville E. Stone, *Fifty Years a Journalist* (New York, 1921).
[64] Rosewater, *History of Coöperative News-Gathering in the United States*, p. 242; also G. W. Johnson, *An Honorable Titan: A Biographical Study of Adolph S. Ochs* (New York, 1946).
[65] M. Koenigsberg, *King News, an Autobiography* (New York, 1941), p. 172.

*Journal* left with the United Press, the latter was declared bankrupt on March 29, 1897. A small number of United Press members remaining outside the Associated Press formed the Publishers Press. The *Sun* developed the Laffan News Bureau; a former employee, G. W. Henman, becoming editor of the Chicago *Inter-Ocean* which had been purchased by C. T. Yerkes in 1897, used despatches from it and was suspended from membership in the Associated Press on May 16, 1898. Suit was brought against the Associated Press and the courts compelled its dissolution on September 12, 1900.

A new association was immediately incorporated in New York in which members became part owners, each member contributing a share and defraying a portion of the total cost. Arrangements were made for rapid extension in France, Italy, Germany, and Russia. Washington became more important as a news centre after Theodore Roosevelt became president. Collapse of the German-subsidized Prensa Asociada in 1918 led to an active interest of the Associated Press in South America. A feature syndicate organized by G. M. Adams in 1912 expanded rapidly but because of its attempts to raise prices the Associated Press entered the field. After 1925 the Associated Press permitted the broadcasting of important news. It made the first feature service release in 1928. In 1935-6 a wire photo service was introduced. The history of the Associated Press was to an important extent a history of the destruction of a parochial monopoly of New York newspapers by newspapers which had emerged in relation to the demand for news in the West and of the growth of a monopoly in response to the demands of the telegraph.

The power of the Associated Press in facilitating mobilization of the resources of Republican newspapers in a united front was evident in the election of McKinley in 1896. Melville Stone and Kohlsaat in Chicago insisted on a Republican platform excluding bimetallism and R. W. Patterson was only more moderate.[66] New developments in business organization were exploited in that trust methods were used to bring together Republican organizations in forty-five states. In the words of William Allen White, Mark Hanna personified a union of "greedy forces of business and greedy forces of politics." With the

[66]Stone, *Fifty Years a Journalist*; also H. H. Kohlsaat, *From McKinley to Harding* (New York, 1923).

exception of the Wilson period the monopoly of the Republican press persisted until the election of F. D. Roosevelt in 1932.

Opposition to the monopoly position of the Associated Press and the Republican party emerged at several points. Excluded from the Associated Press chiefly through the efforts of Pulitzer, William Randolph Hearst[67] built up the International News Service. He had studied the methods used by Pulitzer in building up the *World*, and acquired valuable experience in the tactics of increasing newspaper circulation on the San Francisco *Examiner*. On September 25, 1895, he bought the *Morning Journal* in New York for $180,000, changing the name to the *American* on October 17, 1902. Pulitzer's desertion of the Democratic party on the free silver issue enabled Hearst to become the leading Democratic publisher in the East. With encouragement from the Democratic party he started and acquired papers in various centres. By an attack on the personal columns of the *Herald* which were being used for immoral purposes he greatly weakened its position as a competitor in the Sunday field. His interest in local crusades and in the political activities of the Democratic party, evident in his attempts to become mayor of New York City, governor of New York State, and vice-president of the United States, were in part a result of the necessity of combatting the monopoly of the Associated Press. In the competitive struggle with Pulitzer following the defeat of the Democratic party, Hearst resorted to new devices to increase circulation, ranging from larger headlines to sensationalism in the Spanish-American War, large salaries to attract staff from Pulitzer, features, and comic strips.[68] Hearst has been regarded as responsible for the emergence of the best seller in David Harum in 1898 by creating a demand for fiction in the minds of vast numbers.[69] The emphasis on features probably explains the remark regarding Brisbane: "I never knew a brilliant mind make less sense of the political scene."[70] During the First World War relations between the Associated Press and established agencies in Europe led him to emphasize anti-English and anti-Allied news with the result that during the war the governments

[67]See J. K. Winkler, *W. R. Hearst, an American Phenomenon* (New York, 1928).

[68]See Coulton Waugh, *The Comics* (New York, 1947).

[69]J. L. Ford, *Forty-Odd Years in the Literary Shop* (New York, 1921), p. 286.

[70]Valentine Williams, *World of Action* (Boston, 1938), p. 142.

of Great Britain, France, Portugal, Japan, and Canada imposed restrictions on the Hearst press. Forced to rely on the Associated Press and other agencies, he was faced with charges of piracy. An appeal to the Supreme Court was followed by a decision stating that a commercial agency had no right to appropriate Associated Press despatches once they had been published. Property right in news was established and the monopoly of the Associated Press strengthened. It is perhaps a tribute to the power of the Associated Press that a Senate investigation in 1928 stated that Hearst's was "a black record, the blackest in American journalism, the most gross abuse of the right of a free press in this or any other country's history."[71] Though Josephus Daniels could write that "political ambition and journalistic usefulness are rarely combined"[72] and Grasty of the Baltimore *Sun* could say, "I do not think there is any office that you, or I, or any other earnest and intelligent editor can afford to accept"[73] (November 9, 1912), Hearst's influence was evident in the nomination and election of Garner as vice-president in 1932. "Journalism and politics make a great combination" (La Guardia).[74]

The monopoly position of the Associated Press was conspicuous in the morning-paper field with the result that competition developed particularly in the evening-paper field. Improvements in the telegraph weakened the advantage of morning papers in the news but the power of the Republican party was evident in the difficulties attending attempts of the Democratic party to establish morning papers in northern cities during election years, for instance as in Cleveland in 1852, 1872, and 1880.[75] Morning papers largely dependent on subscriptions were essentially aristocratic. During the Civil War Sunday papers became important and began to compete for advertising[76] and to destroy the old weeklies. The Sunday paper and the evening paper

[71]O. Carlson and E. S. Bates, *Hearst, Lord of San Simeon* (New York, 1937), p. 229.

[72]*Editor in Politics* (Chapel Hill, N.C., 1941), p. 567.

[73]Johnson *et al., The Sunpapers of Baltimore,* 311.

[74]Emile Gauvreau, *My Last Million Readers* (New York, 1941), p. 121.

[75]A. H. Shaw, *The Plain Dealer: One Hundred Years in Cleveland* (New York, 1942).

[76]G. P. Rowell, *Forty Years an Advertising Agent, 1865-1905* (New York, 1926), p. 434.

were sold through news dealers and efficiency was enhanced by the amalgamation of competitors in the American News Company in 1867. In the evening papers news and politics were adapted to the increasing demands of labour. While Horace Greeley had attracted the interest of labour to the Republican party and contributed to the embarrassment of competing papers by his support of unions, the development of machinery and particularly the linotype had alienated it. The remark of Victor Lawson that "no man is smart enough to run more than one newspaper although he might own a dozen"[77] applied to evening and morning papers. This was evident in the comment, "I don't want the *Evening World* to have an editorial policy. If you want good editorials rewrite those in the *Morning World*."[78]

The development of afternoon and evening papers in relation to the demands of labour enabled the Scripps family[79] to start numerous papers and in 1897 to organize the Scripps-McRae press association. Supported from this, the Scripps News Association developed on the Pacific coast, and the Publishers Press, which included papers excluded by the Associated Press, led to the formation of a new United Press. The Associated Press was regarded as conservative, capitalistic, and guilty of holding back news for the morning papers. The United Press built up its own news-collecting organization in European countries and elsewhere. Arrangements were made with South American papers opposed to Allied propaganda during the First World War for the purchase of news at Buenos Aires. In 1918 a small cable service was started to Japan. Difference in time between Europe and America during the First World War gave afternoon papers a great advantage in securing war news and contributed to the expansion of the United Press, but its limitations were evident in the report of the false armistice in 1918. With an expanding service new papers were acquired. Roy Howard, whose influence was recognized in the formation of the Scripps-Howard press in 1921, stated at Detroit: "We come here simply as news merchants. We are here to sell advertising and sell it

[77]Gene Fowler, *Timber Line: A Story of Bonfils and Tammen* (New York, 1933), p. 129.
[78]Oliver Carlson, *Brisbane: A Candid Biography* (New York, 1937), p. 102.
[79]N. D. Cochran, *E. W. Scripps* (New York, 1933).

at a rate profitable to those who buy it. But first we must produce a newspaper with news appeal that will result in a circulation and make that advertising effective."[80] The effectiveness of the United Press policies in the presentation of news compelled the Associated Press to replace its stilted writing and wooden reporting by low salaried reporters with work of a more effective character.[81] In time the acquisition of a large number of papers had a moderating influence on the Scripps-Howard press in its sympathies toward labour.

In the struggle against the Associated Press, the Hearst and Scripps interests were compelled to develop large-scale chain enterprises covering a vast area as a means of increasing outlets and news coverage and reducing the costs of an extensive news service, with disastrous results to independent newspapers. After the death of C. A. Dana, the New York *Sun* found the Laffan Bureau inadequate. In 1908 Munsey wrote, "there is no business that cries so loud for organization and combination as that of newspaper publishing."[82] He acquired the *Sun* and amalgamated it with the *Herald,* cancelling advertising contracts and introducing higher schedules applicable to a larger circulation.[83] The *Herald* was sold to the *Tribune* and the *Sun* continued until its recent demise. The New York *World* waged effective battles in an editorial page which was said to owe its power in part to Pulitzer's blindness since it was necessary to have all editorials read to him.[84] A libel suit by President Roosevelt in reply to its attacks regarding the Panama Canal brought a Supreme Court decision on January 3, 1911, which vindicated the *World* and was regarded as "the most sweeping victory won for freedom of speech and of the press."[85] The *World* and the St. Louis *Post-Dispatch* carried on an effective attack against the Ku Klux Klan. But in spite of its independence the *World* was acquired by Scripps-Howard interests.

[80]George Seldes, *Lords of the Press* (New York, 1939), p. 78.

[81]C. B. Driscoll, *The Life of O. O. McIntyre* (New York, 1938), p. 193; also Ernest Gruening, *The Public Pays: A Study of Power Propaganda* (New York, 1931), p. 174.

[82]F. M. O'Brien, *The Story of the Sun, New York: 1833-1928* (New York, 1928), p. 206.

[83]George Britt, *Forty Years—Forty Millions: The Career of Frank A. Munsey* (New York, 1935).

[84]Ford, *Forty-Odd Years in the Literary Shop,* p. 218.

[85]W. G. Bleyer, *Main Currents in the History of American Journalism* (Boston, 1927), p. 348.

The disappearance of independent newspapers was accompanied by a change in character of content.[86] Weeklies, monthlies, and quarterlies, the pulpit, platform, and bar, literate intellectuals, social settlements, and universities provided an outlet for muck-raking activities, non-partisan interests, and radical writing.[87] Successful muck-raking was taken up by newspapers. There was a "crusading time with uplifters harrying every major American city and every newspaper of any pretensions took a hand in the dismal game."[88] Crusading activities were supplanted by features. Personal journalism was replaced by the grand entry of the clown-comedy and buffoonery. The wit's cap and bells determined circulation.[89] The trend toward uniformity was accompanied by periodic outbursts of protest in other media. "One must never write on controversial subjects, the first of which was religion, and . . . one must never report even the truth in any case in which the Catholic hierarchy might be offended."[90] As a result the *Menace* had a phenomenal increase in circulation during the First World War. The decline in political activity was registered in the emergence of large-scale political advertising in 1921.[91]

The decline of the political influence of the newspaper was offset by the increasing importance of other media, particularly the book,

[86]"A large body of persons has arisen, under the influence of the common schools, magazines, newspapers, and the rapid acquisition of wealth, who are not only engaged in enjoying themselves after their fashion, but who firmly believe that they have reached, in the matter of social, mental, and moral culture, all that is attainable or desirable by anybody, and who, therefore, tackle all the problems of the day—men's, women's, and children's rights and duties, marriage, education, suffrage, life, death, and immortality—with supreme indifference to what anybody else thinks or has ever thought, and have their own trumpery prophets, prophetesses, heroes and heroines, poets, orators, scholars, and philosophers, whom they worship with a kind of barbaric fervor. The result is a kind of mental and moral chaos, in which many of the fundamental rules of living, which have been worked out painfully by thousands of years of bitter human experience, seem in imminent risk of disappearing totally." E. L. Godkin, *Reflections and Comments, 1865-1895* (New York, 1895), pp. 203-4.

[87]See E. A. Ross, *Changing America: Studies in Contemporary Society* (New York, 1919).

[88]H. L. Mencken, *Newspaper Days, 1899-1906* (New York, 1945), p. 37; see also Silas Bent, *Newspaper Crusaders: A Neglected Story* (New York, 1939).

[89]G. L. Edson, *The Gentle Art of Columning—a Treatise on Comic Journalism* (New York, 1920).

[90]Seldes, *Lords of the Press*, p. 171. "Catholics must be treated like bank presidents" (Brisbane). Gauvreau, *My Last Million Readers*, p. 240. See Paul Blanchard, *American Freedom and Catholic Power* (Boston, 1949), chap. ix and Reuben Maury, *The Wars of the Godly* (New York, 1928).

[91]Daniels, *Editor in Politics.*

after the establishment of international copyright in 1891. Before that date the influence of the newspaper on the book was pronounced. Political or military figures who had been widely advertised in the news became the subjects of biographies.[92] W. D. Howells wrote a campaign life of Lincoln in 1860 and was rewarded with a consulship at Venice.[93] Raymond of the *Times* wrote a life of Lincoln after his assassination and Greeley became the author of a work on the Civil War which had an enormous sale until he signed a bond for the release of Jefferson Davis. Publishers exploited the subjects of news interest with effective advertising, especially in the period in which newspapers neglected advertising. George Jones became part owner of the New York *Times* and G. W. Childs,[94] from the profits of a book by Kane on the Franklin tragedy of the Arctic, became the owner of the Philadelphia *Public Ledger* in 1864. American authors unable to withstand competition from pirated editions of English publications were compelled to write for newspapers, magazines, or various societies.[95] The increasing dominance of New York as a publishing centre, because of its accessibility to England, attracted writers such as W. D. Howells from other centres. "Commercial influences prevailed over purer influences of literature. The publisher took command."[96]

After 1891, Harper and other New York firms found themselves with large printing plants adapted to the rapid printing of books from England, limited contacts with American writers, and a heavy overhead cost, which brought them into financial difficulty and exposed them to control from newspaper and financial interests. George Harvey,[97] with experience acquired on the *World*, assumed control of Harper and the firm was reorganized by J. P. Morgan and Company in 1902. Harper were publishers of Woodrow Wilson's *History of the American People* and Harvey was said to have thought of Wilson as a

[92]See W. L. Mackenzie, *The Life and Times of Martin Van Buren* (Boston, 1846).
[93]L. F. Tooker, *The Joys and Tribulations of an Editor* (New York, 1924), p. 237.
[94]G. W. Childs, *Recollections* (Philadelphia, 1890).
[95]Antonia Gallenga, *Episodes of My Second Life* (London, 1884).
[96]G. W. Smalley, *Anglo-American Memories* (London, 1910), p. 188.
[97]W. F. Johnson, *George Harvey* (Boston, 1929).

possible president in 1902 and put his name forward in 1906.[98] The monopoly control of Republican papers was broken in the election of Wilson as president by the influence of media other than newspapers[99] and by a revival of the South as a regional political force.[100]

Political activity declined as a direct and effective device for advertising newspapers and increasing circulation. Greeley wrote on April 3, 1860, "Remember that . . . the tax-payers take many more papers than the tax-consumers," and advised a policy in opposition to taxes.[101] Attacks on the corruption of cities were designed to weaken other media including rival newspapers. Campaigns against certain types of advertising such as bill-boards in the interest of the country-side had more immediate explanations. Attacks on the trust movement were not unrelated to its threat to advertising since the baking-powder trust was said to have dealt a shattering blow to advertising.[102] In the struggle over food and drug bills on the one hand newspapers favoured an increase in revenue from better pro-

[98]E. P. Mitchell, *Memoirs of an Editor: Fifty Years of American Journalism* (New York, 1924), p. 387.

[99]The influence of the book was limited, particularly as prices increased after 1900 while the prices of magazines declined. Books were handicapped further by postage charges from which they were not relieved until the administration of F. D. Roosevelt. Moreover, in the words of Mr. Dooley, "Books is for them that can't enjoy themselves in any other way." The influence of the magazine was suggested in the following comment on *Collier's*: "Nevertheless, although the fundamental aspect of the problem was not completely worked out, there was every sign that while we could hold the intellectual level and have a circulation approaching half a million, at thirty-five cents a copy, we could not double the circulation at that price, and keep the standard; and for my part I remain unconvinced that at any price a magazine can have a circulation of a million while keeping a quality that is stimulating to the most intelligent readers. . . ." Norman Hapgood, *The Changing Years: Reminiscences* (New York, 1930), pp. 282-3. In the period after 1918 the influence of books and magazines was greatly affected by technological advances. The rise of photography on the one hand destroyed illustrations in magazines and compelled them to be literary and on the other hand became the basis of special publications. The verbosity of books and magazines was exploited by digests. In the Second World War the pocket-book industry expanded rapidly and threatened the position of writers. See J. T. Farrell, *The Fate of Writing in America* (New York, 1946); also W. T. Miller, *The Book Industry: A Report of the Public Library Inquiry* (New York, 1949).

[100]See T. D. Clarke, *The Southern Country Editor* (Indianapolis, Ind., 1948).

[101]J. M. Lee, *History of American Journalism* (Boston, 1917), p. 406.

[102]See *Printers' Ink, Fifty Years, 1888-1938* (New York, 1938).

ducts and on the other hand Brisbane prepared advertisements of patent medicine groups as news or editorials and collected on the basis of current advertising rates.[103] In the words of Chesterton, a journalist became one who wrote on the backs of advertisements. Weakening of the regional press in relation to a political machine dominated by railways, following the abolition of railway passes by the Interstate Commerce Commission, enabled larger metropolitan papers such as those controlled by Hearst[104] to urge the election of senators by direct vote. The front porch campaign disappeared with the railway pass. The spread of dailies and weeklies destroyed the system of joint discussion.[105] The Senate became less a deliberative body and more exposed to the influence of newspapers. Primaries in populous states were followed by a debauching contest of pocket books of wealthy contestants.[106] "Since the executive has control of patronage there has been a tendency for newspapers and magazines to write down the legislative branch."[107]

The full power of the press was illustrated in the demand for cheaper raw material by which the demands of advertisers for circulation could be more effectively met. Newspapers opposed attempts of the International Paper Company to maintain and to increase prices of newsprint. President Taft was attacked because of an inadequate tariff reduction from $6.00 to $3.75 a ton on newsprint in the Payne-Aldrich schedules and for the proposal in his message in 1909 to increase second-class mailing rates. He regarded his remarks on the "hogs of magazine publishers" particularly on Albert Shaw as one of his fatal errors[108] since they alienated magazines and newspapers. The tariff was reduced in the reciprocity negotiations but it was left to President Wilson to exploit the low tariff policy of the Democratic party. Paper mills were built on a large scale in Canada following the effectiveness of newspaper pressure on public opinion in the United States and the encouragement of Canadian authorities.

[103]Carlson, Brisbane: A Candid Biography, p. 189.
[104]Mrs. Fremont Older, William Randolph Hearst, American (New York, 1936), p. 348.
[105]Champ Clark, My Quarter Century of American Politics (New York, 1920), II, 355.
[106]H. L. Stoddard, As I Knew Them: Presidents and Politics from Grant to Coolidge (New York, 1927), p. 187.
[107]Clark, My Quarter Century of American Politics, I, 427.
[108]Pollard, The Presidents and the Press, pp. 610, 613, 625.

In actively supporting a policy of holding down the price of news-print and of increasing production, newspapers favoured a marked extension of advertising. The economy became biased toward the mass production of goods which had a rapid turnover and an efficient distributing system. The advertiser was concerned with constant emphasis on prosperity. Disappearance of muck-raking in the finan-cial field was accompanied by a decline of restrictions on speculative activity. It was significant that in the post-war decade two publishers, J. M. Cox ("a genial, sophisticated newspaper publisher") and Warren Harding, were nominated for the first time for the presidency and that a publisher was elected for the first time as president. Presi-dent Coolidge issued an ill-advised statement designed to strengthen the stock market and President Hoover talked of the new era. News-paper civilization had entered the concluding phase of its intensive development in the speculative activity of the twenties. Its bias cul-minated in an obsession with the immediate. Journalism, in the words of Henry James, became a criticism of the moment at the moment. Clarence Darrow has described "the most profound irony . . . our independent American press, with its untrammeled freedom to twist and misrepresent the news, is one of the barriers in the way of the American people achieving their freedom."[109] The monopoly of communication built up over a long period in the newspaper invited competition from other media. Freedom of the press had been an essential ingredient of the monopoly for it obscured monopolistic characteristics. Technological inventions[110] were developed and adapted to the conservative traditions of monopolies of communica-tion with consequent disturbances to public opinion and to political organization. The printing press and the inventions associated with it, including the development of illustrations, were directed to com-munication through the eye. It involved an emphasis on regionalism

[109]Irving Stone, *Clarence Darrow for the Defence* (New York, 1941), p. 48.
[110]Schumpeter in his *Business Cycles* has emphasized the importance of the Kondratieff cycle but has neglected the problem of organization of communication by which innovations are transmitted. As monopoly of communication with rela-tion to the printing press, built up over a long period under the protection of freedom of the press, accentuated discontinuity and the destruction of time, it eventually destroyed itself and compelled a recognition of a medium emphasizing time and continuity. Veblen's emphasis on the pecuniary and industrial dichotomy overlooks the implications of technology, for example in the printing industry, and its significance to the dissemination of information in a pecuniary society. A monopoly which accentuates more rapid dissemination brings about a profound disruption of society.

and decentralization and was adapted to control over vast areas. It was concerned with the destruction of time and continuity.

Competition from the new medium, the radio, involved an appeal to the ear rather than to the eye and consequently an emphasis on centralization. The disastrous culmination of a monopoly over space ending in the First World War and the depression was followed by a monopoly over time. Political organization responded to the possibilities of the new medium. Political leaders in representative assemblies could appeal directly to the public. In 1924 A. E. Smith exercised control over opposition in the assembly of New York State by an appeal to public opinion. Radio advertising became immensely profitable after 1928. With the depression F. D. Roosevelt developed the radio as a major approach. The traditions of decentralization of the press were replaced by new traditions of centralization and continuity reflected in a fourth term for the President. The postmaster-general no longer maintained control over patronage.[111] The Democratic party became obsessed with the theory that government was an agency of broad welfare.[112] Influential elements of the party machine such as Tammany Hall were destroyed by the new medium.

Shifts to new media of communication have been characterized by profound disturbances and the shift to radio[113] has been no exception.

[111]For an illuminating account of the change see J. A. Farley, *Jim Farley's Story: The Roosevelt Years* (New York, 1948).

[112]*We Saw It Happen,* by thirteen correspondents of the New York *Times* (New York, 1938), p. 25.

[113]"The telephone, the teleprinter and the wireless made it possible for orders from the highest levels to be given direct to the lowest levels, where, on account of the absolute authority behind them, they were carried out uncritically; or brought it about that numerous offices and command centres were directly connected with the supreme leadership from which they received their sinister orders without any intermediary; or resulted in a widespread surveillance of the citizen, or in a high degree of secrecy surrounding criminal happenings. To the outside observer this governmental apparatus may have resembled the apparently chaotic confusion of lines at a telephone exchange, but like the latter it could be controlled and operated from one central source. Former dictatorships needed collaborators of high quality even in the lower levels of leadership, men who could think and act independently. In the era of modern technique an authoritarian system can do without this. The means of communication alone permit it to mechanise the work of subordinate leadership. As a consequence a new type develops: the uncritical recipient of orders." Albert Speer, German Armaments Minister in 1942, in a speech at the Nuremberg trials, quoted in Hjalmar Schacht, *Account Settled* (London, 1949), p. 240.

An emphasis on continuity and time in contrast with an emphasis on space demands a concern with bureaucracy, planning, and collectivism. Without experience in meeting these demands an appeal is made to organized force as an instrument of continuity. The Democratic party[114] with its limited strength appealed to force in the Venezuelan dispute under Cleveland, in the First World War under Wilson, and in the Second World War under F. D. Roosevelt. Dependence on organized power and a traditional antipathy to coloured peoples[115] weakens political sensitivity, and lack of experience with problems of continuity and empire threatens the Western world with uncertainty and war.

[114]"Mr. Secretary, you are a Republican. My party has the responsibility of this war. I know your record and I can't use you anywhere." Secretary of Navy Daniels to H. L. Satterlee, former Assistant Secretary of the Navy; Arthur Train, *My Day in Court* (New York, 1939), p. 350. The general attitude is reflected in the remark of a speaker at a political convention following a long debate on civil service reform, "What are we here for?"

[115]"What in God's name would the world think of us if we undertook to bully the Russian government into changing its policy toward the Russian Jews while we are constantly lynching coloured citizens down south." Theodore Roosevelt to Representative Granger; Clark, *My Quarter Century of American Politics*, I, 439. See H. C. Brearley, *Homicide in the United States* (Chapel Hill, N.C., 1932).

# "A CRITICAL REVIEW"[1]

MECHANIZATION has emphasized complexity and confusion; it has been responsible for monopolies in the field of knowledge; and it becomes extremely important to any civilization, if it is not to succumb to the influence of this monopoly of knowledge, to make some critical survey and report. The conditions of freedom of thought are in danger of being destroyed by science, technology, and the mechanization of knowledge, and with them, Western civilization.

My bias is with the oral tradition, particularly as reflected in Greek civilization,[2] and with the necessity of recapturing something of its spirit. For that purpose we should try to understand something of the importance of life or of the living tradition, which is peculiar to the oral as against the mechanized tradition, and of the contributions of Greek civilization. Much of this will smack of Marxian interpretation but I have tried to use the Marxian interpretation to interpret Marx. There has been no systematic pushing of the Marxian conclusion to its ultimate limit, and in pushing it to its limit, showing its limitations.

I propose to adhere rather closely to the terms of the subject of this discussion, namely, "a critical review, from the points of view of an historian, a philosopher and a sociologist, of the structural and moral changes produced in modern society by scientific and technological advance." I ask you to try to understand what that means. In the first place, the phrasing of the subject reflects the limitations of Western civilization. An interest in economics implies neglect of the work of professional historians, philosophers, and sociologists. Knowledge has been divided to the extent that it is apparently hopeless to expect a common point of view. In following the directions

[1]Extracts from a paper presented to the Conference of Commonwealth Universities at Oxford, July 23, 1948.
[2]See S. H. Butcher, "The Written and the Spoken Word" in *Some Aspects of the Greek Genius* (London, 1891), also V. H. Galbraith, *Studies in the Public Records* (London, 1949).

of those responsible for the wording of the title, I propose to ask why Western civilization has reached the point that a conference largely composed of university administrators should unconsciously assume division in points of view in the field of learning and why this conference, representing the universities of the British Commonwealth, should have been so far concerned with political representation as to forget the problem of unity in Western civilization, or, to put it in a general way, why all of us here together seem to be what is wrong with Western civilization. Some of you may remember James Thurber's story of the university professor pointing to a student and saying to him: "You are what is wrong with this institution."

In the remainder of this paper, I shall be concerned with an interest in the economic history of knowledge in which dependence on the work of Graham Wallas will be evident. He pointed to the danger that knowledge was growing too vast for successful use in social judgment, since life is short and sympathies and intellects are limited.[3] To him the idol of the pulpit and the idol of the laboratory were hindrances to effective social judgment, arising, as they do, from the traditions of organized Christianity and the metaphysical assumptions of professional scientists.[4] He assumed that creative thought was dependent on the oral tradition and that the conditions favourable to it were gradually disappearing with the increasing mechanization of knowledge. Reading is quicker than listening and concentrated individual thought than verbal exposition and counter-exposition of arguments. The printing press and the radio address the world instead of the individual. The oral dialectic is overwhelmingly significant where the subject-matter is human action and feeling, and it is important in the discovery of new truth but of very little value in disseminating it. The oral discussion inherently involves personal contact and a consideration for the feelings of others, and it is in sharp contrast with the cruelty of mechanized communication and the tendencies which we have come to note in the modern world. The quantitative pressure of modern knowledge has been responsible for the decay of oral dialectic and conversation. The passive reading of newspapers and newspaper placards and the small number of signi-

[3]Graham Wallas, *Social Judgment* (London, 1934), p. 29.
[4]*Ibid.*, p. 161.

ficant magazines and books point to the dominance of conversation by the newspaper and to the pervasive influence of discontinuity, which is, of course, the characteristic of the newspaper, as it is of the dictionary. Familiarity of association, which is essential to effective conversation, is present but is not accompanied by the stimulus which comes from contacts of one mind in free association with another mind in following up trains of ideas. As Graham Wallas pointed out, very few men who have been writing in a daily newspaper have produced important original work. We may conclude with the words of Schopenhauer, "To put away one's thoughts in order to take up a book is the sin against the Holy Ghost."

The impact of science on cultural development has been evident in its contribution to technological advance, notably in communication and in the dissemination of knowledge. In turn it has been evident in the types of knowledge disseminated; that is to say, science lives its own life not only in the mechanism which is provided to distribute knowledge but also in the sort of knowledge which will be distributed. As information has been disseminated the demand for the miraculous, which has been one of the great contributions of science, has increased. To supply this demand for the miraculous has been a highly remunerative task, as is evidenced by the publications of firms concerned with scientific works. Bury described the rapidly growing demand in England for books and lectures, making the results of science accessible and interesting to the lay public, as a remarkable feature of the second half of the nineteenth century. Popular literature explained the wonders of the physical world and at the same time flushed the imaginations of men with the consciousness that they were living in the era "which, in itself vastly superior to any age of the past, need be burdened by no fear of decline or catastrophe but, trusting in the boundless resources of science, might surely defy fate."[5] "Progress itself suggests that its value as a doctrine is only relative, corresponding to a certain not very advanced stage of civilization, just as Providence in its day was an idea of relative value corresponding to a stage somewhat less advanced."[6] The average reader has been impressed by the miraculous, and the high priests of science, or perhaps it would be fair to say the psuedo-priests of

[5] J. B. Bury, *The Idea of Progress, an Inquiry into Its Origin and Growth* (London, 1920), pp. 345-6.
[6] *Ibid.*, p. 352.

science, have been extremely effective in developing all sorts of fantastic things, with great emphasis, of course, on the atomic bomb. I hoped to get through this paper without mentioning the atomic bomb, but found it impossible.

Geoffrey Scott has stated that the romantic movement gave nature a democratic tinge. The cult of nature became a political creed with the theory of natural rights. The worship of nature supplanted a more definite and metaphysical belief. The creed of nature meant emphasis on representation, a fidelity to natural fact, and a prejudice against the Renaissance, order and proportion.[7] We may well heed his words: "It is thus the last sign of an artificial civilisation when Nature takes the place of art."[8]

The effects of obsession with science have become serious for the position of science itself. It has been held that the scientific mind can adapt itself more easily to tyranny than the literary mind, since "art is individualism and science seeks the subjection of the individual to absolute laws,"[9] but Casaubon was probably right in saying that "the encouragement of science and letters is almost always a personal influence." The concept of the state in the Anglo-Saxon world has been favourable to the suppression or distortion of culture, particularly through its influence on science. Under the influence of the state, communication among themselves has become more difficult for scientists with the same political background and practically impossible for those with a different political background, because of the importance attached to war. Mathematics and music have been regarded as universal languages, particularly with the decline of Latin, but even mathematics is a tool and has become ineffective for purposes of communication in a highly technical civilization concerned with war.

I can refer only briefly to the significance of mechanized knowledge, as affected by science, to the universities. Reliance on mechanized knowledge has increased with the demands of large numbers of students in the post-war period. Henry Adams wrote: "Any large body of students stifles the student. No one can instruct more than half a dozen students at once. The whole problem of education is one

[7]*The Architecture of Humanism: A Study in the History of Taste* (London, 1924), pp. 75-80.
[8]*Ibid.*, p. 92.
[9]Albert Guérard, *Literature and Society* (Boston, 1935), p. 80.

of its cost in money."[10] We have been compelled in the post-war period, with the larger number of students, to depend on text-books, visual aids, administration, and conferences of university administrators such as we have here. They imply increasing concern with the written mechanized tradition and the examination system, of which Mark Pattison remarked that "the beneficial stimulus which examination can give to study is in an inverse ratio to the quality of intellectual exertion required."[11] We can subscribe to his reference to "the examination screw, which has been turned several times since, till it has become an instrument of mere torture which has made education impossible and crushed the very desire of learning."[12]

Finally we must keep in mind the limited role of universities and recall the comment that "the whole external history of science is a history of the resistance of academies and universities to the progress of knowledge." Leslie Stephen, referring to the period in the late eighteenth and early nineteenth centuries in England, when there was no system of education, said: "There is probably no period in English history at which a greater number of poor men have risen to distinction." "Receptivity of information which is cultivated and rewarded in schools and also in universities is a totally different thing from the education, sometimes conferred even by adverse circumstances, which trains a man to seize opportunities either of learning or of advancement." One need mention only the names of Burns, Paine, Cobbett, William Gifford, John Dalton, Porson, Joseph White, Robert Owen, and Joseph Lancaster.[13] Compulsory education increases the numbers able to read but does not contribute to understanding. Some of you may remember the comment in a discussion on literature by university graduates: "Literature? Sure; we took it in the senior year. It had a green cover."[14] Education is apt to become "merely the art of reading and writing, without training minds to principle of any kind, and destitute of regard for virtue and even decency."[15]

[10]*The Education of Henry Adams* (Boston, 1918), p. 302.
[11]*Essays by the late Mark Pattison* (Oxford, 1889), I, 491.
[12]Mark Pattison, *Memoirs* (London, 1885), p. 303.
[13]A. V. Dicey, *Lectures on the Relations between Law and Public Opinion in England during the Nineteenth Century* (London, 1930), pp. 113, 114.
[14]H. W. Boynton, *Journalism and Literature and Other Essays* (Boston, 1904).
[15]Cyrus Redding, *Fifty Years' Recollections* (London, 1858), III, 316.

We are compelled to recognize the significance of mechanized knowledge as a source of power and its subjection to the demands of force through the instrument of the state. The universities are in danger of becoming a branch of the military arm. Universities in the British Commonwealth must appreciate the implications of mechanized knowledge and attack in a determined fashion the problems created by a neglect of the position of culture in Western civilization. Centralization in education in the interests of political organization has disastrous implications. This becomes one of the dangers of a conference of British Commonwealth universities, since, as Sir Hector Hetherington pointed out, the search for truth is much broader than that which can be undertaken by any political organization. Referring to the dangers of centralization, Scott wrote over a century ago: "London licks the butter off our bread, by opening a better market for ambition. Were it not for the difference of the religion and laws, poor Scotland could hardly keep a man that is worth having."[16] The problem is perhaps even more acute for the broader English-speaking world, with its common law tradition. The overwhelming influence of the United States as the chief centre of power points to the serious limitations of common law in making politics part of law and of emphasizing the position of the state, particularly in those nations with written constitutions. In Roman law countries, notably France, culture has had an opportunity to expand, politics have become less of an obsession, and leadership has been given to Western civilization. Culture survives ideologies and political institutions, or rather it subordinates them to the influence of constant criticism. Constant whining about the importance of our way of life is foreign to its temper.

The universities should subject their views about their role in civilization to systematic overhauling and revise the machinery by which they can take a leading part in the problems of Western culture. For example, we should extend our scholarships to universities on the Continent. Lecturers should be encouraged to write books as a means of compelling them to give new lectures. The universities must concern themselves with the living rather than with the dead.

[16]*The Journal of Sir Walter Scott* (Edinburgh, 1890), II, 256.

# APPENDIXES

# APPENDIX I

## A Note on Communication and Electromagnetic Resources in North America

### D. Q. INNIS

ELECTROMAGNETIC waves travel at the speed of light—186,000 miles a second. Visible light waves are electromagnetic waves with frequencies, i.e. the number of wave-lengths which pass a given point in a second, between 15 and 100 trillion cycles per second. Electromagnetic waves used for ordinary radio short wave and television have much longer wave-lengths and greater frequencies. Radio is one of the most recent and most important uses to which the electromagnetic spectrum has been put. The frequencies of sound waves in air vary between 30 cycles per second (the deepest audible sound) and 16,000 cycles per second, but individual notes cannot usually be distinguished above 4,500 cycles per second. To reproduce speech or music with all the overtones, the radio wave must oscillate between 30 and 16,000 times a second on each side of a basic frequency of say 550,000 cycles. A radio wave will therefore have a frequency which varies between 534,000 cycles per second and 566,000 cycles per second, that is, a variation of 32,000 cycles for all audible sounds. In practice the electromagnetic spectrum is so crowded that only 10,000 cycles can be allowed to each station—5,000 on each side of the basic frequency. High frequency sounds and overtones are not transmitted.

A radio receiver picks up the signal by a device which tunes the length of the aerial to the wave-length of the desired transmitting station. When the aerial is the same length as some submultiple of the wave-length of the radio station, the signal from that station will be strongest and it can be amplified and turned into sound. A receiver which can tune into a great many different wave-lengths is more complicated than one which picks up only a few, consequently short-wave receiving sets cost more than sets which receive ordinary radio stations only. At one end of the broadcast band stations are quite far apart and the result is increased cost of detection. The unique length of waves is the most important limiting factor in this part of the spectrum since interference of waves reflected from the sky with waves which go along the ground causes fading. This also limits the use of short wave radio. At the other end of the broadcast band, stations are much closer together and it becomes difficult to separate them. Limitations on the number and variety of programmes available to a listener are therefore a result of the nature of the electromagnetic spectrum. Most big cities have five or six radio stations and there are a few places where ten or fifteen radio stations are easily available to a listener. If any large part of the population listens, each station must have thousands of listeners. The number of points of view which can be presented is limited by the number of stations available. The fact that each programme must appeal to thousands of listeners limits still more the range of ideas which can be presented. Radio programmes can only deal in lowest common intellectual denominators since only a few people have the necessary background of knowledge for understanding any one complex idea or any single piece of information. Radio cannot become involved in prolonged disquisitions on any subject nor introduce any fact or class of fact not very widely known. Repetitive advertising indicates the kind of message which has been found suitable for radio. The emphasis which radio places on fear, death, love, religion, human interest stories, music, the public, money, material things, and war is well known. The physical characteristics of the electromagnetic spectrum are such that while two amateur or industrial radio operators may talk to each other, an exchange of ideas between any large number of individuals cannot be carried out. Since the economical and technological range of frequencies is small and since each radio station uses a band of frequencies 10,000 cycles wide, the use which can be made of the electromagnetic spectrum is limited.

Television is similarly limited by the electromagnetic spectrum. Since the upper half of an electromagnetic wave is the same shape as the lower half only the upper half is used in transmitting the signal in television and more stations can be crowded into less spectrum space. The picture is reproduced by an electromagnetic wave modified so that a light spot of varying brightness travelling across a phosphorescent screen makes one line below the other until the whole picture of five hundred lines is complete. Five hundred variations of light and shade are allowed from top to bottom of the picture and 700 variations from side to side since the picture is wider than it is tall. Thirty pictures composed of $500 \times 700$ possible variations are reproduced each second and the total number of possible variations per second is $500 \times 700 \times 30 = 10,500,000$ cycles per second. A television station must have a band of frequencies millions of cycles wide. In practice 5 megacycles (million cycles) are allowed to each television station. Thirteen television channels (bands of frequencies) are at present available in North America. The resulting short waves for television signals usually do not follow the curvature of the earth and are not usually reflected by the sky but stations on the same frequency must be hundreds of miles apart to avoid even occasional conflicts. New York City has seven television channels, Chicago has four. Cities which are close together have few channels. If a large part of the population looks at television, each station must broadcast to thousands, and sometimes, millions of people. A lowest common denominator programme such as dominates radio must also dominate television. Picture clarity and intellectual clarity are limited by electromagnetic resources.

Competition for space among electromagnetic waves is already acute. Police calls interfere with radio broadcasts, radio-telephone with television. Diathermy machines, street cars, and powerful gasoline engines all produce radiations which interrupt neighbouring radios. Clear channel radio stations and television channels are extremely valuable. Government control of wave-lengths is strict and limitations on development of the electromagnetic spectrum are definite.

Most of the spectrum is unsuitable for communication. Radio-size waves are large enough to get around buildings and topographical obstructions but television-size waves meet difficulties. Radar-size waves are smaller than hills, buildings, aeroplanes, and ships; they are reflected by them and can be used for detecting such objects. X-rays are so small that they can travel between the atoms which compose the human body while cosmic and gamma rays are short and powerful and some of them harmful. Thus the electromagnetic spectrum is made up of many kinds of waves and there is little space for new mass communication media.[1] Radio and television must remain confined to wave-lengths assigned to them.

With only a few radio and television stations thousands must listen to each station and progress must be based on the few simple ideas which large groups of people have in common. The immediacy of radio has been used effectively in politics for uncomplicated nationalistic appeals. That national leaders have remained in power for unusual lengths of time is a fact not unrelated to the use of radio. Personal magnetism reflected over national networks has produced tendencies toward centralized control, the importance of which cannot be fully assessed. Television has an even more direct impact on its audience. Magazines, books, the cinema, and other media adapt themselves to a milieu influenced by the radio and television with consequent disadvantage to small units of enterprise. Education, reading, entertainment, politics, religion, and philosophy have been profoundly affected by radio and television.

[1]The uses of the electromagnetic spectrum are as follows:
   domestic current, 60 cycles per second (waves not used)
   ordinary radio, 550,000—1,600,000
   amateur, police, industrial, radio-telephone, navigation, military and short wave, 2,000,000—100,000,000
   television, 54,000,000—88,000,000; 174,000,000—216,000,000; 480,000,000—1,000,000,000 (waves assigned but not yet in use)
   radar, 3,000,000,000—10,000,000,000
   cooking and diathermy, 8,000,000,000—10,000,000,000
   infra-red, 100,000,000,000—15,000,000,000,000
   visible light, 15,000,000,000,000—100,000,000,000,000

# APPENDIX II

## ADULT EDUCATION AND UNIVERSITIES[1]

THE Manitoba Royal Commission on Adult Education has been concerned with the problem of adult education in relation to government and the dangers of propaganda. Propaganda has been described as "that branch of the art of lying which consists in very nearly deceiving your friends without quite deceiving your enemies";[2] unfortunately in a bureaucracy it effectively deceives the vast majority of people who are neither friends nor enemies. We have assumed that government in democratic countries is based on the will of the governed, that people can make up their minds, and that every encouragement should be given to enable them to do so. This implies that the state is concerned with strengthening intellectual capacity, and not with the weakening of that capacity by the expenditure of subsidies for the multiplication of facts. It also implies that adults have been so trained in the educational system that they can choose the facts and reach their own decisions. We should, then, be concerned like the Greeks with making men, not with overwhelming them by facts disseminated with paper and ink, film, radio and television. Education is the basis of the state and its ultimate aim and essence is the training of character. "One of the aims of education is to break the strong hold of the present on the mind."[3] "To build up in every man and woman a solid core of spiritual life which will resist the attrition of everyday existence in our mechanized world— that is the most difficult and important task of school and university" (Sir Richard Livingstone).

In the oft quoted remark of Lord Elgin, education "fits one for nothing and trains him for everything." Again, it is "the purpose of

[1]Revised extracts from *Report of the Manitoba Royal Commission on Adult Education* (Winnipeg, 1947), pp. 141-8.
[2]F. M. Cornford, *Microcosmographia Academica: Being a Guide for the Young Academic Politician* (Cambridge, 1933), preface to 2nd ed.
[3]*General Education in a Free Society: Report of the Harvard Committee* (Cambridge, Mass.).

204 THE BIAS OF COMMUNICATION

education not to prepare children for their occupations but to prepare them against their occupations" (C. G. Sampson).[4] It is not easy to focus on this broad objective. "The history of education is indeed a somewhat melancholy record of misdirected energy, stupid routine, and narrow one-sidedness. It seems to be only at rare moments in the history of the human mind that an enthusiasm for knowledge and a many-sided interest in the things of the intellect stirs the dull waters of educational commonplace."[5]

A major problem of society emerges in the development of institutions which enlarge the capacities of individuals and enable them to use such enlarged capacities to the greatest advantage of the individual and the institutions. In this the state occupies a crucial position. Education has been largely concerned with conservation of knowledge, and in turn becomes extremely conservative. This con- servatism is evident in the lack of interest in educational philosophy and in the tendency of educational institutions, particularly those concerned with the teaching of Education as a subject, to avoid the major philosophical problems of Western civilization. Institutions thus concerned with the teaching of Education and their expanding activities are in themselves a comment on the poverty of education and may become obstacles to the attainment of broad objectives. "Educative discipline tends to preserve what has been acquired and presents very real obstacles to further advance."

The tendency towards conservatism has been accentuated by the mechanization of communication in print, radio, and film. They have tended not only to eliminate the personal factor but also to emphasize the factual and the concrete. Abstract ideas are less sus- ceptible to treatment by mechanical devices.[6] Moreover, ideas must

---

[4]Cited by E. B. Osborn, *Our Debt to Greece and Rome* (London, 1924), p. 16. "Perfect good breeding consists in having no particular mark of any profession" (Samuel Johnson). "The outstanding mark of an education is the ability of a person to hold his judgement in suspense in unsettled questions" (Newton D. Baker).

[5]Hastings Rashdall, *The Universities of Europe in the Middle Ages* (Oxford, 1895), II, Pt. ii, 705.

[6]"It is difficult to find a common ground for exact science and the public. The public craves immortality, and other miracles, and the Sunday papers murder science to meet the prevailing appetite. On the other hand, real science refuses to talk English, but instead writes a dialect of its own, and seems to believe that scientific ideas cannot be expressed accurately in English." Norman Hapgood, *The Changing Years: Reminiscences* (New York, 1930), p. 285.

be ground down to a convenient size to meet the demands of large numbers. "Any purpose, any idea of training the mind itself, has gone out of the world. . . . Those studies which produce no fruits obvious to the sense are fallen into neglect" (John Stuart Mill). Mechanical devices become concerned with useless knowledge of useful facts. Complaints of duplication and confusion are inevitable.

But I do see all the injury to the higher literature inflicted by the torrential multiplication of printed stuff coinciding with the legal enforcement of mechanical reading—absurdly misnamed *Education*. To teach boys and girls to read print, whilst leaving them sunk in the materialised state of mind and morals typical of modern anarchy, without beliefs, or ideals, or principles, or duties—this is to inaugurate a millennium of vapid commonplace and vulgar realism."[7]

. . . in spite of the vast increase of general education and of all forms of literary product . . . literature is on the down grade. I hazard the paradox in good faith that the decline is not merely in spite of all this instruction, but is a result of the universal schooling. The incessant education drill, the deluge of printed matter, asphyxiate the brain, dull beauty of thought, and chill genius into lethargic sleep. . . .
. . . I seriously maintain that a direct result of our mechanical schooling . . . and that whether primary, middle, or highest; Board schools, high schools, academies, or universities—is the gradual deterioration of literature into dry specialism and monotonous commonplace. . . .
The double effect of making life a race or a scramble, working with the ceaseless cataract of commonplace print, just good enough to occupy the average mind having a superficial school training, debases the general intellectual currency, and lowers the standard. Scientific and historical research piles up its huge record of facts with a sort of scholiast's attention to minute scholarship and inattention to impressive form. It would seem as if the higher order of literature were produced in inverse ratio to the number of the reading public and the volume of literary product. . . . The printed book was the death of the cathedral. To-day we may say—the school has been the death of literature.[8]

The modern community of the Western world has been disciplined by the spread of machine industry. The vacuum created by the Industrial Revolution must be assiduously filled. Large-scale capital

[7]Frederic Harrison, *Autobiographic Memoirs* (London, 1911), I, 23-4.
[8]*Ibid.*, II, 324-7.

equipment has dominated the paper industry and the newspaper, the radio, the movie, and television, and each in turn has become monopolistic in character and concerned with reaching the largest number of people. The advertiser upon whom they have come largely to rely wishes to appeal to the largest possible number. He assumes an average age of twelve, and information in all media, to achieve the greatest possible results, is directed to that level.[9] The Anglo-Saxon world has become "distinguished for its lack of intellectual strenuousness."

This mania for special research in place of philosophic principle, for tabulated facts in lieu of demonstrable theorems and creative generalisations, attenuates the intelligence and installs pedantic information about details, where what man wants are working principles for social life. The grand conceptions of Darwin and of Spencer are too often used by their followers and successors as a text on which to dilate on microscopic or local trivialities which mean nothing. . . . The enormous accumulation of recorded facts in the last century goes on as blindly in this, quite indifferent to the truth that infinite myriads of facts are as worthless as infinite grains of sand on the sea-shore, until we have found out how to apply them to the amelioration of human life.

It was obvious that the literature of the first half of the nineteenth century greatly surpassed that of the second half. And it is sadly evident that literature in the twentieth century is far inferior even to that of the second half century.[10]

Any community has only a limited number capable of sustained mental effort. According to biologists they may be found in all

<hr/>

[9]"Psychologists have estimated that when the brain is receiving visual and aural impressions of a scene simultaneously about seventy per cent of the intelligence comes through the eyes and about thirty through the ears." John Swift, *Adventure in Vision* (London, 1950), p. vi.

[10]Harrison, *Autobiographic Memoirs*, II, 322-3. See also W. R. Inge, *Diary of a Dean, St. Paul's 1911-1934* (London, 1950), pp. 222-3. ". . . I cannot doubt that the main cause of the decay is the pernicious habit of writing hastily for money. If we take the trouble to consult Mudie's catalogue of fiction, we shall learn to our amazement that there are several writers, whose names we have never heard, who have to their discredit over a hundred works of fiction apiece. They obviously turn out several books a year, just as a shoemaker manufactures so many pairs of boots. The great novelists have generally written rapidly, rather too rapidly; but such a cataract of ink as these heroes of the circulating library spill is absolutely inconsistent with even second-rate work. Literature flourishes best when it is half a trade and half an art; and here again the Victorian Age occupies the most favourable part of the curve."

regions and in all strata. A democratic society can thrive only by the persistent search for its greatest asset and by constant efforts to conserve, to encourage, to train, and to extend it. Throughout the community assiduous interest must be taken in the discovery, conservation, and improvement of limited intellectual resources. In concentrating on the training of the best brains, it will be necessary to make certain that every device has been exhausted in the primary schools of rural and urban areas, the high schools, the colleges and the universities to detect and to encourage every sign of intellectual capacity. Every obstacle should be removed from the path of the brightest student particularly if he is found in the least advantageous circumstances. Scholarships on an extensive scale contribute to this end—the abolition of fees would contribute more—but even these would not be adequate.

The examination system by which students are selected from the schools for admission to universities reflects the worst evils of the mechanization of education. The results are evident in the success of students in large cities and of middle-class parents. Uniformity of examination systems over wide areas involves wholesale discrimination against districts which cannot attract the best teachers or command the best equipment. In large urban centres state schools are supplemented by private "cram" schools. An emphasis on uniformity of examinations is accompanied by an emphasis on uniformity of subjects. The matriculation system as an intelligence test has become a gigantic maze and the resources for training students to thread the maze have been built up in the large centres. A glance at the failure rate of small rural centres suggests the results. Similarly a careful study of the failure rate and of the success rate in the first year of university work brings out sharply the contrast between university teaching and high-school teaching. A large failure rate is accompanied by tremendous public pressure on the universities to adopt the standards of teaching of the high schools. The blight of mechanization spreads from the high schools to the universities. It has been said that "equality of educational opportunity is more essential to social justice than equality of fortune—and more easy of attainment"[11] but the difficulties can scarcely be exaggerated.

[11]A. M. Thompson, *Here I Lie* (London, 1937), p. 39.

The universities must attempt to select the ablest students and must concentrate on the most efficient method of training them. They must be encouraged to achieve the objectives of an educational system in the most effective fashion. But universities are influenced by the mechanization of education, and hampered by tradition. "The academical establishments of some parts of Europe are not without their use to the historian of the human mind. Immovably moored to the same station by the strength of their cables and the weight of their anchors, they enable him to measure the rapidity of the current by which the rest of mankind is borne along."[12] The breaking down of ideas and the emphasis on factual information have been evident in the narrowing of professional education and of arts courses. Textbooks of systematized knowledge have been altogether too much in evidence. Courses have been carefully calculated with a view to the inclusion of all the relevant information during the three or four years of undergraduate work. The results have been a systematic closing of students' minds. Initiative and independence have been weakened. Factual material, information, classification, reflect the narrowing tendencies of the mechanization of knowledge in the minds of staffs and students. Professions become narrow and sterile. The teaching profession suffers perhaps most of all. A broad interest in the complex problems of society becomes almost impossible. The university graduate is illiterate as a result of the systematic poisoning of the educational system. Student and teacher are loaded down with information and prejudice. The capacity to break down prejudice and to maintain an open mind has been seriously weakened.

[12]Sir Richard Jebb, *Essays and Addresses* (Cambridge, 1907), p. 601. See also Rashdall, *The Universities of Europe in the Middle Ages*, II, Pt. II, 710-11. "The very idea of the institution is essentially medieval, and it is curious to observe how largely that idea still dominates our modern schemes of education. . . . However much the modern mind may in certain directions be reverting to the ideas and spirit of the old world, education, like so much else in the modern world, will always exhibit a vast and incalculable difference from the education of ancient Greece or ancient Rome just because the Middle Ages have intervened. . . . Something of the life and spontaneity of old-world culture certainly seems to be gone for ever. Universities have often had the effect of prolonging and stereotyping ideas and modes of thought for a century or more after the rest of the world has given them up. It is surprising how slowly an intellectual revolution affects the course of ordinary education. But educational traditions are marvellously tenacious, quite apart from institutional machinery such as that of the Universities: and education itself must always be, from the necessities of the case, a tradition. . . ."

APPENDIXES 209

The difference between the principles of this ancient education and our modern principles of education is rightly found in this, that to it the development of the aptitude and the possession of it counted for more than the work for which it was used and the fruitfulness of that work in result. Every individual was to be made a model example of his species: the species itself had nothing else to do but to exist and to enjoy the use of its powers. . . . To this many-sided development, finding an end in itself, the spirit of modern education is no doubt less kind; it sets a higher value than it justly should on range of concrete knowledge in comparison with a general aptitude for knowing—on productive specialized labour in comparison with the free exercise of all the powers —on professional effort working in a groove in comparison with an interest in human relations generally. [R. H. Lotze]

The traditions of the university in the Western world have centred around the direct oral method of instruction but these have been weakened by the impact of mechanization. "All originality is screened out of whatever is produced. Teaching, that noblest of all vocations, degenerates into pedantry. . . . University lectures become infected with . . . true moral cowardice, until the lecture-room style can be recognized and readily distinguished from the independent exposition of the original investigator. . . . Along with the dwarfing effect of this state of things, there goes the further demoralizing influence of egotism and conceit."[13]

Universities must strive to enlist most active energetic minds to train most active energetic minds. "Education properly understood ıs little more, at best, than the creation of an artificial environment calculated to call into exercise all the latent talents of those who receive it. The number manifesting this kind of genius may, therefore, be greatly increased through a form of education which should be really adapted to calling it forth."[14] Students and staff should concentrate on the development of capacities to resist the influence of mechanization and to make fresh contributions to the solution of the age-old problems of Western civilization. The university should be concerned with the release of mental energy and with its training for an effective attack on these complex problems rather than with systematic destruction. It should produce a philosophical approach

[13]L. F. Ward, *The Psychic Factors of Civilization* (Boston, 1906), pp. 106-7.
[14]*Ibid.,* p. 205.

which will constantly question assumptions,[15] constantly weaken the overwhelming tendency, reinforced by mechanization, to build up and accept dogma, and constantly attempt to destroy fanaticism. Once the university, and in particular the arts faculty, becomes thoroughly seized of the vital significance of its role in Western society and staff and students realize the necessity of constant emphasis on training to produce the open mind, the whole educational system will begin to show signs of vitality. The university, in training the best intellectual resources and in developing a philosophical approach which assumes an open mind on the part of staff and student, can contribute powerfully to a solution of the problems of adult education. Society must regard the university as a community of scholars concerned with its vital problems.

The university tradition as developed in Europe and in Great Britain cannot find effective expression under the constitutional devices characteristic of North America. The institution of the board of governors in Canada is contrary to the European tradition which assumes the self-government of the university, which recognizes the capacity of scholars to govern themselves and thereby enhances their self-respect, their prestige, and their effectiveness. In the words of Lord Baldwin:

The University is an epitome of true democracy. Merit alone is the hall-mark and freedom—ordered freedom—its birthright. Never must that freedom be bartered away. Universities need money; much of modern scientific research and teachings works through expensive tools; money has come to them generously from wealthy men or from the State. But let us never forget that the wealthy men and the State are honoured by being allowed to take part in the sacred work of education and, while their contributions are received with sincere gratitude, nothing gives a right either to the wealthy man or the State to interfere in any way with the freedom of the University itself. It must always be its

[15]"It is difficult to see how . . . a country can . . . survive . . . under the continual necessity of so controlling education that the people may not become aware of the meaninglessness of the whole elaborate superstructure. It constitutes a problem of probably superhuman difficulty to promote enough intelligence to enable the country to maintain its position in the race of material progress, without leaving open the possibility that that intelligence may sometime begin asking questions about the foundations of its own society." P. W. Bridgman, *The Intelligent Individual and Society* (New York, 1938), p. 136.

own master, responsible to its conscience and sound tradition for what it teaches and how it teaches.[16]

In Canada there have been cases of harrying of individual members of staff by the community and by boards of governors. University professors are exposed to a continual sense of frustration. University presidents and administrative officers have been placed in intolerable positions by those who have no conception of the character of the university tradition. As a first step in adult education university statutes should be carefully studied and revised in the light of broad principles strengthening the university in the community.

It is probable that the university cannot bridge the gap between its level of intellectual training and that which characterizes the modern community under the influence of machine industry. It cannot yield to the obsession for information and instruction without neglecting education. The staffs of universities may be loaded down with abortive attempts to solve the problem by a direct attack. "New opinions, founded on a legitimate process of observation and inference, are generally worked out in solitude by persons of studious and reflective habits; and they are, when once accredited and established among men of science, expounded, illustrated, and diffused, by popular writers. The two provinces of discovery and diffusion are usually divided; for the power of original thought, and the power of perspicuous elementary exposition, are often not combined in the same mind."[17] "Discovery of the great principles of nature demands a mind almost exclusively devoted to such investigations."[18] Large ideas can only be conceived after intensive study over a long period and through the direct and powerful device of the spoken word in small groups. It can be extended by small numbers of highly trained students of exceptional mental capacity.

. . . the name [university] has got to be associated with education of the highest type: to degrade the name of a University is therefore to degrade our highest educational ideal. . . . It is natural and desirable . . . that efforts should be made to diffuse knowledge and intellectual interests

[16]Baldwin of Bewdley, *The Falconer Lectures, 1939* (Toronto, 1939), p. 27.
[17]G. C. Lewis, *An Essay on the Influence of Authority in Matters of Opinion* (London, 1849), p. 286.
[18]Charles Babbage, *On the Economy of Machinery and Manufactures* (London, 1841), p. 380.

among all classes by means of evening lectures. The English Universities may well be proud of having taken the initiative in a movement of the most far-reaching social and political significance. But it would be a delusion, and a mischievous delusion, to suppose that evening lectures, however excellent and however much supplemented by self-education, can be the same thing as the student-leisure of many years, duly pre-pared for by a still longer period of regular school training. Examinations, too, and private preparation for them, are an excellent thing in their proper place: but it is a mistake to suppose that an Examining Board can discharge any but the very lowest of a University's real functions. The two most essential functions which a true University has to perform, and which all Universities have more or less discharged amid the widest possible variety of system and method and organization, hardly excepting even the periods of their lowest degradation, are to make possible the life of study, whether for a few years or during a whole career, and to bring together during that period, face to face in living intercourse, teacher and teacher, teacher and student, student and student. . . . it behoves us not to lose or lower the ideal of the University as the place *par excellence* for professed and properly trained students, not for amateurs or dilettantes or even for the most serious of leisure-hour students; for the highest intellectual cultivation, and not merely for elementary in-struction or useful knowledge; for the advancement of Science, and not merely for its conservation or diffusion; as the place moreover where different branches of knowledge are brought into contact and har-monious combination with one another, and where education and research advance side by side.[19]

Administrators may be attracted to the advantages of publicity from adult education as a means of influencing the public and the legislators and of securing funds, and may fail to appreciate the signi-ficance of advanced work in research. University aims are then obscured, a belief in stereotypes is developed, and it becomes im-possible to maintain the freedom of the open mind. University administrators become exposed to new burdens and encroachments are made on the work of scholars. It is necessary to set up a buffer to avoid the misuse of funds for propaganda purposes. In the main, adult education has tended to fall into the hands of those who do not command the respect of scholars and are looked upon with suspicion

[19]Rashdall, *The Universities of Europe in the Middle Ages,* II, Pt. II, 714-15.

by them. Both scholars and the public look upon them as concerned
with vested interests including parties, governments, or their own
positions. Bringing the university to the people may become a pick-
pocket device which the public ought to suspect. As a part of the
university machinery designed to impress legislators with the necessity
of supporting the university, adult education may become a device to
fool the public and the university administration. University extension
courses may serve to relieve the pressure on other courses, but the
cost must be carefully considered. Adult education is apt to involve
the standardization of information and propaganda; the university
has a special function to offset these tendencies.

Adult education, appealing to large numbers with limited training, can be disentangled with difficulty from the advertising of large
organizations concerned with the development of goodwill. An agitation for the clearance of slums may be sponsored by organizations
concerned with the sale of their products. Universities may engage
in adult education programmes on a large scale to build up their
goodwill and to create new interest. The advertiser has created distrust[20] through his power of penetration in the field of education
and in turn education has been the object of mistrust. To reach lower
levels of intelligence and to concentrate on territory held by newspapers, radio, and films, adult education follows the pattern of
advertising. "No adult education which we have at present seems
to me much more than a puerile gesture. Nothing that I have seen
does much more than continue the sort of instruction that was given
in elementary schools, modified a little perhaps by the recognition
that discipline becomes irksome and cannot be enforced when the
enterprise on the part of the pupil is a voluntary one. Where is the
scheme of adult education that recognizes that maturity has problems
of its own and capacities of its own? . . . The adult, then, has
problems and capacities to solve them peculiar to himself, and adult
education should be built around them."[21] The growing incompati-
bility between those who like to think, and those who do not has
been described as characteristic of the Western world. "People who

    [20]See H. M. McLuhan, *The Mechanical Bride: Folklore of Industrial Man*
(New York, 1951).
    [21]Bridgman, *The Intelligent Individual and Society*, pp. 202-3.

want to preserve to themselves the opportunity to think have got to do something about it as a matter of sheer self-interest."

On the other hand the increase in numbers of books and the growth of a book civilization contribute to the difficulties of the universities. There has developed a more extensive hierarchy of those who know more about books than others, and institutions to foster book knowledge and create hierarchies. It is difficult for adult education to make an impression on these and to develop new points of view. Freshness and vitality are lost. An indirect attack on the problem of adult education is essential. The graduates of the university in medicine, dentistry, law, theology, and teaching can play an important role in keeping the university closer to the public and preventing it from drifting beyond its range. The teacher can link books to conversation and oral education. He should be given refresher courses and courses in summer schools to enable him to serve as an effective link between the university and the community, between research and the public. He can provide the link between a written and an oral tradition. The graduate can fill a basic role in making the university available to the largest possible number.

# INDEX

# INDEX

ABBASIDS, 51, 120 f.
Acacius, Patriarch of Constantinople, 118
Achaean League, 45
Acton, Lord, 170
Adams, G. M., 178
Adams, Henry, 54, 84, 175, 193
Adams, John, 157
Adams, John Quincy, 163 f., 166
Addison, Joseph, 26, 56, 143 ff., 154
Adrianople, 15
advertising, 27, 30, 57, 74, 77, 149, 153, 158, 160 ff., 168, 172, 185
Aeschylus, 43
Ahmose I, King of Egypt, 95
Ahura-Mazda, 105
Akhetaton, 95
Akkadians, 97 f., 134
Albany, N.Y., 162, 164 f., 167
*Albany Evening Journal,* 167
Albertus Magnus, 19
Albigensians, 52
Alcuin, 17, 49
Alexander the Great, 10, 13, 31, 40, 45, 50, 69, 105, 112, 136, 141
Alexander, Samuel, 89
Alexandria, 5, 10, 31, 45, 47 f., 69, 112, 114 ff., 135 ff.
algebra, 63, 98
almanacs, 71
alphabet, 3, 6-9, 14 f., 17, 23, 31, 38 ff., 43, 50, 51, 101 f., 126, 136
Ambrose, St., 126
Amenhotep IV, King of Egypt, 95
American News Co., 181
Amon-Ra, 94 ff.
Amsterdam, 26, 54, 133
Anastasius I, Roman Emperor, 121
Anaximander, 110 f.
Anaximenes, 111
Anne, Queen of England, 144 f., 148 f., 154
Anno Domini, 61, 65
antiquarianism, 61-2
Antwerp, 26, 54, 138
Anu, 98
Apollo, 108
Aquinas, St. Thomas, 19 f., 52, 88

Arabic numerals, 19 f., 72, 125
Aramaeans, 38, 67, 135
Aramaic, 14, 39, 101
archaeologists, 33, 63
architecture, 66, 92 f., 127, 131, 133 ff.
Areopagus, 107 f.
*Argus* (Albany), 164-5
Arianism, 73, 117 ff.
Aristides, 133
Aristophanes, 9
Aristotle, 10 f., 13, 19-21, 29, 44, 52
arithmetic, 42 f., 63, 68, 98, 111
Arminius, 113
Artaxerxes I, King of Persia, 104
Artaxerxes II, King of Persia, 105
artillery, 25, 72, 137
Ashur, 38, 99
Ashur-bani-pal, King of Assyria, 100
Associated Press, 78, 168, 175-82
Assyria, 6, 36, 38-40, 66-7, 96, 99 f., 104, 108, 134-5
astronomy, 6, 63, 65, 69, 72, 128
Athanasius, St., 122
Athens, 4, 8, 9, 16, 42-4, 51, 106, 109-10, 113, 116, 136
Attalids, 46, 136
Attis, 70
August, 69-70, 114
Augustine, St., 48, 132
Augustus, Roman Emperor, 69-70, 113
Aurelian, Roman Emperor, 47
Austria, 59
Avesta, 104, 114
Avignon, 20, 52

BABYLONIA, 6, 14, 18, 36-40, 47, 64, 66-7, 98-101, 104, 108 f., 112, 134-6
Baghdad, 19, 31, 51 f., 72, 120 f., 124, 137
Baltimore, 168
Bank of England, 25, 56; of United States, 161, 165, 167
bards, 123
Barnum, P. T., 172
Barrie, J. M., 28
Barry (Postmaster-General), 165
Bartholomew, St., Massacre of, 26
Basil of Caesarea, 118